The Trinity and Creation in Augustine

SUNY series on Religion and the Environment

Harold Coward, editor

The Trinity and Creation in Augustine

An Ecological Analysis

Scott A. Dunham

State University of New York Press

Published by
State University of New York Press, Albany

Printed in the United States of America

For information, contact State University of New York Press, Albany, NY
www.sunypress.edu

Production by Diane Ganeles
Marketing by Michael Campochiaro

Library of Congress Cataloging-in-Publication Data

Dunham, Scott A., 1968–
The Trinity and creation in Augustine : an ecological analysis / Scott A. Dunham.
p. cm. — (SUNY series on religion and the environment ; 10020)
Includes bibliographical references and index.
ISBN 978-0-7914-7523-2 (hardcover : alk. paper)
ISBN 978-0-7914-7524-9 (pbk. : alk. paper)
1. Augustine, Saint, Bishop of Hippo. 2. Trinity—History of doctrines. 3. Creation—History of doctrines. I. Title.

BR65.A9D86 2008
231.092—dc22 2007038539

10 9 8 7 6 5 4 3 2 1

To Mount Hamilton Baptist Church

Contents

Acknowledgments

This book began as my doctoral dissertation in Religious Studies at McMaster University. I am grateful for the dedication and patient assistance of my supervisor, Peter Widdicombe, and the members of my dissertation committee, Travis Kroeker and Stephen Westerholm. I also would like to thank my examination committee, and especially Brian Daley, who made helpful suggestions about how the thesis might be revised. My thanks to the Philosophy Department at the University of New Brunswick, who granted me research resources to complete this project. I also acknowledge the assistance of the Social Sciences and Humanities Research Council of Canada.

Introduction

From whence does our help come? More and more, people agree that environmental devastation is a serious matter and that steps must be taken to slow such devastation down and, one hopes reverse the frightening trend. And yet, it seems, the help offered in many solutions do not seem readily achievable. In fact, even the choice of solutions is open to much disagreement. Disputes over the economic and technological impacts of solutions easily derail plans and proposals to address the problem. There is no doubt that technological knowledge and economic considerations will be key in the actual solutions. However, the disputes related to competing environmental solutions are rooted in more fundamental issues such as how we understand our lifestyles as a determinative basis for making choices and why we even should care about long-term solutions for the environment. In other words, economic and other technological solutions are not the starting point for help in addressing our environmental problems. There are more basic points of departure that pertain to our view of the value of reality and how we relate to it.

Behind the competing solutions put forward for solving our environmental problems are sets of assumptions and beliefs about reality that are often referred to as worldviews. Many worldviews are embodied through religious perspectives. We can safely assume that religious views of the world will affect at least some significant percentage of a population's evaluation of the varieties of technological solutions, as well as providing a moral basis for how they ought to act because of their perspective on reality. Not surprisingly, then, we find that discussions of ecology and environmental ethics are happening within religious communities, and that scholars also have taken an interest in studying religious views of the world—offering analyses of how religion and the environment are related.

This book is concerned with how a significant Christian thinker in the later patristic period understood the relationship between God and the creation. Augustine of Hippo exercised an enormous influence on the Christian tradition in the Western world. However, modern assessments have been mixed concerning the ways in which his influence ought to be evaluated. It would seem that a large contingent of modern scholars have tended to see that influence in a negative light, owing to both Augustine's conception of God and his view of the world. To many scholars, Augustine's conception of God is one that became detached from the spirit of the Nicene discussion about God's triunity and moved to a more Platonic and monistic conception of a God who rules over a world that—because of its material composition—is bad. Such a God, of pure will and power, has nothing positive to do with a fallen, material world. As Colin Gunton puts it, "[I]n Augustine's theology of creation . . . the Christological element plays little substantive role, and the pneumatological even less. The result is that the way is laid open for a conception of creation as the outcome of arbitrary will [of the Father]. . . ."[1]

Not surprisingly, such a view of God and the world can lead to a worldview in which one finds creation to be unworthy of too much attention, and where God's greatness is to be emulated so that human vocation is oriented to using the world as merely a tool. One need not worry about the world anyway, since humans ought to seek the God who is outside of it. It would make sense that such a view of God and the world, if put forward by an influential historical figure, could form part of the foundation for subsequent developments that eventually have led to modern worldviews and to modern environmental problems. And so, current portrayals of Augustine often are dismal, especially when viewed with an eye to how Christianity in the modern West developed its views of nature.

Does such a reading of Augustine's conception of God and the world do justice to what he actually thought and wrote? I would contend that such a reading is severely deficient. If one undertakes a close reading of several of Augustine's key writings about the Trinity and his commentaries on Genesis 1–2, one finds instead a rich vision of God and how God is related to the world. Augustine's defense of the goodness of all creation is undertaken precisely because of his understanding of God as Trinity. In fact, even if one takes up Augustine with very specific questions in mind arising from modern, scientific knowledge rooted in ecology, there are positive ideas and attitudes to be discovered and perhaps used in modern discussions.

The obvious problem that faces the attempt to find a bridge between contemporary questions about the environment and Augustine is that he did not think in ecological categories, nor do we think as people in fifth-century North Africa thought. How can one attempt to find ecological significance from a theologian so far removed from the ecological knowledge and problems that must be confronted today? This is a serious question, but one that can be answered. It must be acknowledged that if ecological and religious critiques of classical theology can attribute, at least in indirect ways, the undesirable effects of doctrines that subsequently influenced social, political, technological, and scientific developments, then there also should be the possibility of learning positive lessons from classical thought. By uncovering or questioning influential worldviews and beliefs, one makes a case for the possibility of the retrieval and use of classical sources in modern thought, not only their dismissal.

In any case, the problem of anachronism must be avoided. Modern ecological interests in ideas such as interrelationality (which we shall take up in a few pages) arise from scientific knowledge as well as from modern religious and philosophical thought. Whatever might be meant by ecological interrelationality and its ethical implications, one does not simply turn to the Bible or the creeds for ready-made definitions and applications, since interrelationality was not a term that was in use in those periods. Similarly, religious thinkers who turn to historical theological developments to find terminological guidance must adapt traditional terms to the nuances of contemporary religious dialogue. For example, "perichoresis" is used quite often as a theological equivalent for interrelationality, though the term has no natural connection to modern social, political, or ecological ideas about interrelationality. It has to be filtered, typically through social Trinitarianism, in order to be freighted with its new meaning.[2]

Likewise, in this book, we cannot merely "lift" Augustine's understanding of the world and dominion from his time and put it into ours. There is no one-to-one correlation of ideas. We will examine how Augustine understood certain key themes that are of importance in the modern theological dialogue with ecology. However, we will consider these themes through a close, detailed analysis of his major writings about the Trinity and creation. Our first aim will be to read him and understand what he has to say about God and creation. Similarly, while we will use the resources of Augustine scholars to aid our reading of Augustine, we will not engage the debates within Augustine scholarship in detail. Our first priority is to let him speak for himself. Only after we have sorted through his own words will we be in a position to offer some concluding remarks on how the main themes of his understanding of God and creation relate to modern religious thinking about God, the world, and ecology.

The book is divided into two parts; the first is concerned with Augustine's doctrine of the Trinity, and the second with his trinitarian understanding of creation. The conclusion will discuss the themes that arise from the analysis of Augustine in terms of the modern interest in interrelatedness, hierarchy, and stewardship (these concepts will be discussed more fully at the end of this introduction as a way of setting the context for our reading of Augustine).

In chapter 1 we will examine in more detail the form of the modern theological critique of Augustine's conceptions of Trinity and creation. Chapter 1 will provide not only a critique of Augustine, but also offer a preliminary evaluation of how Augustine approached the questions of God and creation. We will be concerned with his articulation of the basic doctrine of the Trinity in chapters 2–3. We will focus on how he explained the doctrine, including how he developed his explanation using the themes of love and equality to talk about the divine persons in their substance and relations. We also will show how he developed his doctrine in light of God's economy of salvation, and the importance of the Christian's experience of salvation as a basis for knowledge of God.

Having set out a detailed explanation of Augustine's doctrine of the Trinity, we will then turn to his doctrine of creation in part 2. He wrote much about creation, and we will be concerned chiefly with his interpretation of the first two chapters of Genesis. In chapter 4, we will seek to understand precisely how he understood the structure of God's creative work, and the significance that the doctrine of the Trinity played in his explanation. In chapter 5 we will turn to his description of the relationship that exists between God and creatures in his understanding of providence and the moral implications that he identified in his description of divine providence—again we will do so by drawing out the centrality of the Trinity for his explanation. This will lead to the key analysis of how Augustine conceived of dominion in chapter 6. As we have noted, Augustine, like his contemporaries, did not think of dominion in the ecological sense that guides contemporary theological reflection. We will try to understand what human dominion means to him, its relationship to a hierarchical view of the world, and also how Augustine's definition of dominion fits within the context of divine providence.

The discussion of how these various themes in Augustine's trinitarian doctrine of creation may be related to ecological discussion will be undertaken in the concluding chapter. There we will consider how his discussion of the divine, triune nature of love relates to God's concern for the goodness of creatures. As well, we also will consider the importance of nonhuman creatures in Augustine's doctrine of creation, and how this can be related to modern discussions of interrelatedness. Our goal will not be to come up with ethical prescriptions ready-made for today. Rather, we will seek to describe the religious worldview Augustine employed to account for the goodness of creation, and the moral language that he employed. We will do so as a means of showing the practical significance of the doctrines of the Trinity and creation in providing Christian belief with a moral framework. We will offer some basic suggestions on how these relate to modern ecological concerns, focusing on the moral significance of a classical Christian worldview.

Prior to entering this presentation about Augustine's doctrine of God and creation, it will be helpful for us to set out some of the ways in which the relationship of religion and ecology has developed in recent scholarship, especially how the moral language of religion has been linked to ecological knowledge. The following sections will spell out, briefly, how concerns about the biblical use of dominion have arisen, and the role the concepts of interrelationality and hierarchy have had in conditioning the modern reading of historical sources. We will reference these ideas throughout the book, but especially when we arrive at our concluding chapter.

The Ecological Problem of Dominion and the Doctrine of God

A substantial amount of attention has been given to whether the biblical doctrine of human dominion over the world can be ecologically sound. This ecological question, focused on the divine command for humans who are created in the divine image to have dominion in Genesis 1:26–28, has been a significant thread in biblical and theological thinking for several decades now. Lynn White's epochal 1967 article "The Historical Roots of Our Ecologic Crisis" tried to address how the West's religious roots had contributed to the environmental destruction that faces the world, and indirectly took up the problem of dominion and stewardship.[3] Since his article, many theologians have made claims for how to understand human dominion over the earth.[4] At issue for environmental thinkers is how the claim that humanity is to exercise dominion over creation can be ethically positive (divinely mandated or not), since it would seem to imply a sense of superiority that can only undermine a positive relationship of human beings with the rest of creation.

Now, to be sure, an ecological reading of Genesis 1:26–28 has not dominated the interpretation of this text in the history of Jewish or Christian thought until recently.[5] Nevertheless, ecofeminist theologians such as Rosemary Radford Ruether[6] and Anne Primavesi[7] have attempted to draw out a correspondence between dominion (and more generally the place of the human being in a theology of creation) and the anthropocentric, androcentric, and patriarchal structures that they argue contribute to a negative understanding of nature.[8] In their estimation, to attempt to form an environmentally sensitive ethic founded upon traditional concepts such as dominion faces the problem of also having to overcome such negative structures. Because understandings of God often are tied to these oppressive structures of thought and practice, it is argued that revision of traditional understandings of God is required in order to find a way in which Christianity can contribute to the removal of these destructive structures in contemporary society. In this way, it is argued, the Christian doctrine of God is tied to the anthropocentric ideas that have contributed to the ecological crisis about which White wrote. The alternative to this problematic legacy is a theological ethic founded upon ecologically positive ideas.

Augustine's conception of dominion is presented in ways that require a careful discernment of how humanity is related to God and also to other creatures. Central to these relationships will be his emphasis on goodness. By paying attention to his description of the trinitarian structure of creation as well as how divine providence is articulated, we will be in a better position to evaluate his interpretation of dominion in Genesis 1:26–28.

Ecologically Informed Theological Ethics: Interrelatedness in Ecology

The most important ecological idea that has been advocated as a solution to the problematic idea of dominion as anthropocentric is the concept of the interrelationality of all of nature, including humans, within and through overlapping ecosystems.[9] One feature of the interrelatedness of ecosystem components is self-perpetuating development. When something happens within an ecosystem, its effects reverberate throughout the system and condition the whole (and vice versa). For example, just as an organism can respond to the stimuli around it as part of its survival mechanism by developing attributes to protect itself against other organisms, so ecosystem components develop characteristics as they encounter new stimuli. This self-perpetuating development of ecosystem components affects the whole ecosystem. A similar relationship exists between ecosystems, which themselves are nestled within wider systems. This idea of smaller systems nestled within larger ones extends to the description of the planet as an ecosystem made up of numerous smaller ecosystems. In other words, each component of an ecosystem has an effect on other components, the ecosystem itself, and other ecosystems. Obviously, then, human activity has an enormous impact on the world, extending well beyond perceived local boundaries.

The concept of the interrelatedness of ecosystems and their components has come to form part of the basis for normative explanations favoring the development of ethically sound human activities in response to current ecological crises.[10] To this end, some ecological ethicists will describe ecosystems as communities. By doing so, it also is possible to introduce the discussion of justice with respect to ecosystems in ways that are similar to how human communities and individuals are described in law and by social ethicists.[11] In particular, theologians tend to favor this mode of speech for describing ecosystems. The conception of the interrelatedness of ecosystems, which they see not only as a modern scientific description but also as a basic building block for a Christian understanding of the world, entails certain duties to be performed by humankind in relation to the planetary ecosystems. By using the results of scientific research on ecological interrelatedness and linking it to analogous religious perspectives on individual and social interrelatedness, religious thinkers such as Ruether, Leonardo Boff, and James Nash[12] hope to promote a religiously sensitive understanding of nature and ecological virtues.

James Nash puts forward an ecologically informed theological ethic that finds the concept of interrelatedness within and between ecosystems germane to ethical practice. In order to maintain a healthy ecosystem in the face of ecological crises, he describes the moral imperative of ecological integrity:

> Ecological integrity is the "holistic health" of the ecosphere and biosphere, in which biophysical support systems maximally sustain the lives of species and individuals, and, reciprocally, in which the interactions of interdependent life-forms with one another in their ecosystems preserve the life-sustaining qualities of the support systems. The concept is relative and dynamic, since not only do all human actions have ecosystemic effects but "natural" change is also a normal part of the process. The concept also implies moral constraints on human behavior to maintain the dignity of all life to the fullest possible extent.[13]

While others may want to extend or limit what Nash says here, he nonetheless is an example of how a theologian moves from describing the integrity of ecosystems (emphasizing interrelatedness) to a corresponding moral responsibility. He relates this to theology by arguing that creation is unified: "Since God is the source of all in the Christian doctrine of creation, all creatures share in a common relationship."[14] In other words, the coming into existence of the universe from a single source, God's creativity, is the basis for its ecological unity—namely, the common relationship all creatures share as being from God's creativity.

From a religious perspective, this theocentric understanding of creation in Christian doctrine has moral implications, since the Bible affirms the goodness of all that God creates. The intrinsic goodness of all creation requires action that promotes that goodness which God has bestowed and continues to intend for the whole creation. Thus, for Nash, upholding the health and integrity of ecosystems is simply a modern, scientific way of describing such moral activity. Nash's method moves from modern, scientific "facts" to moral imperatives (developed as a list of ecological virtues)[15] and then finally to a study of whether "Christian theology and ethics support and nurture these ecological virtues."[16] He appeals to the contextual nature of ecological ethics as a contemporary phenomenon rooted in ecological science, but also relates the implications of traditional Christian theology and ethics to this context. He presents the contribution of theology to ecological ethics by locating implicit ideas and background assumptions about the intrinsic goodness of creation and the interrelatedness of people and nature found within traditional doctrines,[17] in order that those implicit assumptions may be applied to ecological concerns.[18] The adoption of ideas from ecology, especially about interrelatedness, is a key part of the foundation for such theological reflections in recent thought.

Augustine likewise saw creation as consisting of a unity of creatures whose unifying source is the triune God of scripture. We will see how the moral basis of his religious worldview springs from the fact that creation is the product of a good God creating good creatures. Such an emphasis on goodness in Augustine's thought provides a means for him to see how the diversity of creatures are interrelated in the creative activity of God. As well, such interrelatedness is underscored by the fact that creation is drawn to move toward God—a dynamic relationship between God and creation that is manifest also in creaturely interrelationships, which are possible through divine providence.

The Problem of Hierarchy in Modern Theology

While the theme of interrelatedness found in ecological science aids in certain types of Christian responses to ecological problems, it also can be used to justify the negative assessment of an ecological moral theory that is founded upon Christian stewardship (dominion) as a unique and positive human activity. One may cite as an example the criticism leveled against Douglas John Hall's retrieval of a theology of stewardship that has strong environmental overtones.[19] By advocating a biblical model of stewardship over against the domination approach to the world that Lynn White criticized, Hall has met with the criticism that he simply has watered down what is still a domination theology because he sees the human being as having a special place in the care of nonhuman creation. For example, Catherine Roach asks how humanity, which is clearly part of the world and dependent upon it, can be stewards over it, especially in light of the negative impact of human activity in recent centuries.[20] She argues that the stewardship model advocated by Hall gives human beings a special status as caretakers, which implies an unhealthy hierarchy of humanity over the rest of creation. Such a hierarchy, she says, contradicts an ecosystem approach to ethics that recognizes the interrelatedness of all creatures.

From a theological perspective, Jürgen Moltmann suggests that Augustine understood dominion and the image of God to be precisely about the rule of dominating power.[21] This is based on Moltmann's reading of Augustine's discussion of the superiority of the male, who is created in the image of God, over the female: "The soul . . . which dominates the body, and the man who dominates the woman, correspond, and in actual fact constitute the human being's likeness to God. *Imago Dei* is then on the one hand a pure analogy of domination, and on the other . . . a patriarchal analogy to God the Father."[22] This judgment of Augustine is meant to show that in the end Augustine has developed a doctrine of the Trinity that is not so much trinitarian as it is monotheistic, giving pride of place to the Father, and interpreting the Father in terms of patriarchal and dominating power. Such a hierarchy, where God the Father is at the top of a pyramid of power relations that are essentially about the domination of those below him in the hierarchy, is about exercising one's superiority through control.[23] Furthermore, Augustine's treatment of the image of God is one where the body is rejected as not having any value, and instead a psychological explanation is given of the image of God. This low view of the body, of course, corresponds to a low view of nature.[24]

In contradistinction to this hierarchical, anthropocentric view of reality and the human claim to power attributed to classical theology, ecological science is interpreted by many to support a different view of relations between humans and the rest of the world/universe that gives priority to interdependence and egalitarian relations. We shall see that while Augustine does view the world hierarchically, there is also room given for the equality of creatures under God. Moreover, the Augustinian understanding of love is important for correctly interpreting hierarchy. The basis of creation's goodness and equality in divine love, for example, is spelled out in terms of how humanity may use and enjoy the world. It also creates a basis for understanding dominion as stewardship.

The problem that has been raised in modern ecological and religious discussions is whether the gulf between traditional theological doctrines and modern ecological knowledge is ultimately incommensurable, because traditional thought did not appreciate the interrelationality of ecosystems and, in particular, human well-being as integral to ecosystems. However, to answer this question requires us to pay close attention to the context in which such ideas were developed. Traditional theological categories of the Trinity and creation, in the ways that Augustine developed and employed them, can be of benefit to modern theological discussions of ecology. God's relationship to the creation as creator and redeemer is central to Augustine's view of the goodness of all creatures, and also to his understanding of dominion. As well, he brings to his reading of Genesis a creativity that values the integration of doctrines, so that he looks beyond the mere appearance of the world to seek an understanding of the spiritual unity that binds creation to God and creatures to one another. When we develop a careful reading of Augustine, we will see how his trinitarian understanding of God and creation can be related to contemporary moral questions about environmental problems and their solutions. Such doctrinal building blocks can have significant value in the articulation of an ecologically positive worldview.

Part I

Augustine's doctrine of the Trinity is foundational to understanding how he conceived of God and how he understood God in other doctrines, such as creation. The reception of Augustine's doctrine of the Trinity has largely been negative, though. In the opening chapter, we will look at the contemporary critique of Augustine's doctrine of the Trinity by focusing on Colin Gunton's assessment of Augustine. We will show how his critique finds its justification within a broader understanding of the history of theology that identifies Augustine with a Western method that is unduly abstract and philosophical in thinking about the Trinity, and negative in its attitude toward the body in its theology of creation. Then, after setting out the critique, we will consider Augustine's own understanding of his method for understanding the doctrine of the Trinity.

In chapters 2 and 3 we turn to Augustine's argument for the doctrine of the Trinity, and whether the contemporary critiques of his approach do justice to his model of trinitarian relations. The primary text we will consult will be *The Trinity*, as well as some of his later anti-Arian writings, particularly the *Debate with Maximus the Arian*, *Answer to Maximus the Arian*, and *Answer to the Arian Sermon*. We will deal with how Augustine explains the doctrine of the Trinity according to the economic work of God as revealed in scripture and also according to his understanding of the simplicity of divine being. We will focus on Augustine's explanation of the doctrine with an emphasis on how the Son and the Holy Spirit are from the Father, who is the beginning of the Godhead, which is typically associated with the Nicene tradition but not with Augustine's doctrine. We will also consider the nature of the Son's and Holy Spirit's relations of origin from the Father, and how they relate to Augustine's discussion of divine substance and love. This understanding of the Son and Holy Spirit as originating from the Father is often rejected by social trinitarian thinkers, who argue that relations of origin lead to a hierarchical conception of the Father over the Son and Holy Spirit, and of oneness over plurality. We will argue that, for Augustine, relations of origin indicate the logical ordering of the persons based on the revelation of that order in the divine economy described in scripture. Furthermore, their origin from the Father confirms the eternal equality of substance of the persons, without denying their individual identity.

By analyzing Augustine's doctrine of the Trinity in light of modern critiques of the classical tradition, we are setting out the context from which we can then explore the question of the general ecological implications that arise from Augustine's theology of creation in part 2. In the introduction to part 2, we will be able to assess the nature and importance of the relations between the Father, Son, and Holy Spirit in his doctrine of the Trinity, which relate to modern concerns about taking seriously interrelationality. The implications will only be indirect at this point, since we are taking account of his foundational conception of God, in order that we may more fully appreciate the importance that the Trinity plays in his explanation of the doctrine of creation.

Chapter One

The Contemporary Critique of Augustine

In the introduction we described in a general way how aspects of classical Christian theology are suspected of cultivating tendencies that have led to a less than adequate understanding of creation and the human place in it. Often, it is argued, this traditional way of understanding creation was justified because of the way that the church understood the biblical portrayal of the immaterial, omnipotent God in relation to the creation and, more specifically, to human beings who bear God's image of power and dominion. Furthermore, the idea of God has a crucial effect upon the idea of creation for Christians, since the ascription of the image of God to human beings suggests that human beings are able to act within and toward the creation in a manner proportional to how God acts toward the creation. The conception of God as omnipotent and outside of the physical creation is one of power over the creation, and human beings share in that type of power by being able to exercise dominion over the creation. The several problems listed in the introduction, such as anthropocentrism and androcentrism, a sense of human detachment from and superiority over a passive creation because human beings occupy a higher place on the created hierarchy, and domineering conceptions of power—all can be traced back to conceptions of God as separate from and disinterested in the creation that is now under the control of humanity. The basis for projecting this relationship between belief and human attitudes toward nature lies in the actual experience of the human exercise of power against the creation.

Many ecological and theological critiques of the Christian doctrines of God and creation are based on stories of the history of Christian thought that employ a schema dividing Eastern from Western forms of Christianity based on their reliance upon scriptural or philosophical foundations. Augustine especially has been targeted for criticism because of his trinitarian understanding of God and the corresponding deficit that it creates in his understanding of creation. This scrutiny is due, in part, to his authoritative stature in the history of Christian thought. In this chapter, in order to set up our discussion of Augustine in subsequent chapters, we will trace in more detail the modern schema that divides Eastern and Western thought, noting how this would imply a certain interpretation of Augustine according to his place in Western Christianity and the trinitarian problem of a modalist conception of God. Then we will turn to more specific critiques of Augustine's doctrine of the Trinity and the way in which his understanding of the Trinity apparently affected his understanding of creation. We will closely trace Colin Gunton's critique of Augustine in particular. Gunton understands the important relationship between conceptions of God and how one understands God's creation. His critique of Augustine's doctrine of the Trinity has led him to note the ways that he thinks Augustine's doctrine of creation is lacking. Among them, he says, is the way Augustine fails to appreciate how God's involvement in creation through the trinitarian economy promotes a positive understanding of material being. According to Gunton, Augustine favored, instead, a distant God of overpowering will who wants nothing to do with materiality.

The Forms of Eastern and Western Trinitarian Thought

The idea that a distinction between an Eastern and Western form of Christianity can be used to trace the development of two forms of the doctrine of the Trinity is a widely held assumption today.[1] To get at an understanding of how this distinction typically is described, we shall concentrate our attention upon Leonardo Boff's interpretation of the way that the doctrine of the Trinity developed in its Eastern and Western forms, and some of the pitfalls that each distinction could lead to. We also will explore some of Boff's concerns about the classical understanding of God that he believes led to the overall problems that he sees in both Eastern and Western models of the Trinity—namely, the incorporation of ideas that are not consonant with the strands of biblical material with which he does agree.

Boff suggests that the form of trinitarian doctrine found primarily in the Eastern churches begins with an emphasis on the Father as the fount of divinity. Patristic references to the Father's place in the Trinity as fount of the Son and the Holy Spirit are rooted in scripture, such as when God is named as "Father, Son, and Holy Spirit" in Matthew 28:19. The idea that the Son and the Spirit proceed from the Father is known as relations of origin, since the Son and the Spirit are understood in terms of their relationship to the Father who is their origin. Thus, one could speak of the Father's monarchy, because the Father was the first (*monas*) principle (*archē*) of the Son and Holy Spirit.[2] Monarchy was a key concept that lay behind the Nicene tradition.[3] The term *monarchia* was first employed by early patristic writers, particularly the economic trinitarians, who detected in the dispensations of the divine economy a relational pattern (*taxis*) between the divine persons in which the Father was the origin of the Son and the Holy Spirit.[4] The phrase continues to be used in modern theology as a means of expressing the conception of the Father as the source of divine unity.[5]

However, in describing the logic of scriptural statements about the Son and Holy Spirit in their relationship to the Father, other problems arise for the Eastern form of the doctrine of the Trinity. Below the surface of the language of monarchy and relations of origin, Boff contends, lingers the problem of subordinationism. The reason is that when one conceives of the Son and the Spirit existing from a common origin (the Father), it is like calling the Son or the Spirit an effect of the Father's will, whereby they are reduced to the status of creatures, rather than being coequals of God.[6] This diminishes the Son's and Holy Spirit's status, because they are under the Father in terms of priority of being.[7]

If an ontological hierarchy of the Father over the Son and Holy Spirit remained a constant and potential threat in the trinitarian ruminations of the Eastern churches, Boff points out that it was despite the scriptural example of an egalitarian Trinity. In fact, in the scriptural presentation, the divine persons are an example for the church, which is to "live the ideal of union proposed by Christ himself: 'that they may all be one. As you, Father, are in me and I am in you, may they also be in us' (John 17:21)."[8] Boff's concern is that an emphasis on relations of origin does not adequately account for the equal emphasis that scripture teaches concerning the oneness of Father and Son in their economic activity together, which also brings the church into the same divine fellowship.[9] Instead, relations of origin focus upon the numerical oneness of the three as a single substance, where priority is given to the Father. If the scriptural understanding of unity as equality is lost, then the potential for a hierarchy that stresses the one over the many can arise, through an appeal to the Father's basic priority in the Godhead. This ordering also could easily reinforce the tendency toward patriarchalism in the church, where one person who acts as the earthly head (just as the Father is the first in the Trinity) dominates the many members of the body of believers.[10] An explanation of divine unity that is based on the ordering of the persons of the Godhead from one person is clearly not egalitarian and leads to subordinationism of the Son and Holy Spirit, even though the conceptual model of relations of origin was not intended to lead in that direction.[11]

For Boff, the second form of trinitarian doctrine, found primarily in the Western tradition, especially from the time of Augustine, started from an emphasis on the one "divine, spiritual nature." This nature was conceived of in two ways: God either as absolute Spirit[12] or as the highest good.[13] From this one nature (or substance), Western theologians then reasoned their way to an explanation of the three persons.[14] Unity is basic to God's nature, and the relations of the persons are the triune logic of that unity. Such a starting point for the doctrine of the Trinity has a tendency to favor a static metaphysics inherited from Greek thought, where truths about God are derived from deductive reasoning that conceives of God as unchanging, indivisible, and without direct relationship to an ever-changing created reality.[15] In other words, God is necessarily conceived as an immutable first principle whose threeness (derived from scripture) must be reconciled and explained to maintain the divine unity.

This approach of locating threeness within the logic of the immutable oneness of God falters by removing the dynamism of the economic Trinity in history, effectively shutting out the biblical experience of God for understanding the doctrine of the Trinity.[16] The danger of this is modalism, whereby the persons simply become manifestations of the One.[17] Boff recognizes that this problem may be overcome through an explanation of real and distinct relations between the persons, which both Augustine and Thomas tried to explain.[18] However, subsequent Western tradition still emphasized the One over against the three, and continued to favor a tendency toward reducing the one God to one mind, which then led to the Barthian and Rahnerian mistakes of reading modern theories of subjectivity into the unity rather than into each of the three persons.[19] Furthermore, the same problem arises with the Western model as with the Eastern model: in both oneness becomes such a strong focus that it pervades the social and political aspects of life. The threat of totalitarianism by one (or a few) over the many finds justification in an understanding of the immutable, all-powerful, one God whose plurality is more of a logical problem than a reality.[20]

Boff, then, while setting up this historical distinction between the Eastern and Western forms of the doctrine of the Trinity, based on their starting points of scripture or Greek philosophy, nevertheless is critical of both traditions. The primary emphasis that guided both the Eastern and Western traditions when developing the doctrine of the Trinity was that of monotheism. Maintaining God's unity (oneness) was necessary in order to keep to the monotheistic teaching of scripture. For Boff, monotheism is an aspect of ancient thinking that posed significant difficulties for truly grasping an egalitarian understanding of the trinitarian persons as they were manifested in Jesus Christ and the Holy Spirit.[21] He argues that monotheism "maintained that God is absolutely whole, without division or multiplication" and was "the matrix from which the doctrine of the Trinity was struck."[22] This monotheistic understanding of God influenced the way people acted by producing a religion of the Father:[23]

> God is presented as Great Father because he created heaven and earth. As such he is the supreme authority of the universe, from whom all other religious and civil authorities derive, in descending orders of hierarchy. As there is only one eternal authority, so the tendency to have only one authority in each sphere of the world is confirmed: a single political leader, a single military chief, a single social leader, a single religious head, a single guardian of truth, and so on. God is presented as the great universal Superego, alone and unique. Much of the atheism of developed societies today is no more than a denial of this sort of authoritarian God and of the patriarchal sort of religion that follows from it and obstructs the development of human freedoms.[24]

The problem is that a monotheistic doctrine of God can be used to justify an oppressive political agenda, because one then has an argument as to why such authoritarianism is justified: it is the way that God wants people to be "God's image" in the world.[25] In history, this has led to totalitarian rule, rooted in unhealthy hierarchies. Boff cites both the rule of the pope over the church and monarchs over states as examples of totalitarianism that have been justified using a monotheistic belief in the "great patriarch, supreme Father and absolute Lord."[26]

In Boff's view, it would have been wiser for the church to reinterpret monotheism to fit the revelation of God's name, "Father, Son, and Holy Spirit,"[27] because the unity of God is understood better by recognizing it as the eternal communion of Father, Son, and Holy Spirit. The unity of God as one Lord is attested in even the earliest biblical writings (e.g., Deuteronomy 6:4), but is not the sole description of God in scripture. One also must keep in mind that the revelation of God as three began in the New Testament period.[28] In fact, according to Boff, the Trinity became a doctrine of the church because of the church's attempt to understand how the biblical witness to Jesus and his Spirit affected the unity of the Godhead. Boff wishes to maintain the biblical description of the economy as central to the doctrine of the Trinity, since it is the Trinity's relationship to humanity that can help advance the liberation of the poor, whom the Trinity has created and to whom they direct their eternal love.[29] The doctrinal challenge was, and is, to have an integrated understanding of the three while also avoiding an emphasis on any one person. To have an integrated understanding of three persons, the best conception of unity is one founded on communion rather than on the idea of God as an unchanging, absolute, indivisible whole.[30] Thus, the classical definitions of the Trinity, by holding to monotheism and a metaphysical emphasis on unity, could not "postulate a society that can be the image and likeness of the Trinity."[31] However, a modern understanding of society, where the whole is greater than the sum of its parts,[32] can yield a better basis upon which to conceive of the integrated unity of the three.

Boff's description of trinitarian doctrine in two forms, Eastern and Western, is typical of how modern systematic theologians have come to characterize the matter of the development doctrine of the Trinity. Behind this delineation of two different trinitarian models lurks a deeper problematic in Boff's mind. He sees the contrasting appeals to scripture or philosophy in the early church not simply as the attempt to find reasonable explanations of how the divine persons are related to divine oneness, but also as perpetuating a commitment to ideologies that could use those flawed explanations for their own ends. For Boff, the doctrine of the Trinity developed in such a way that it could be used for perpetuating totalitarianism, not only within the church hierarchy or the broader political sphere, but also later in the Enlightenment triumph of society over nature through modern technological science.[33] Boff, then, uses his analysis of the historical development of the doctrine of the Trinity to explain problems in theological anthropology and the doctrine of creation. If the doctrine of the Trinity is not well formed, then the other theological topics are affected by its deficiencies. In other words, doctrines not only exist to state formally accepted teachings, but also to orient the way in which one relates to the world.

Augustine's Western Form of the Trinity: Modalism

Colin Gunton also has recognized the relationship between a well-formed doctrine of creation and the conception of God as Trinity. He develops his understanding of trinitarian creation based on the division of East and West in the historical development of doctrine, and he does so with the aim of redressing the lack of a strong doctrine of creation in modern times.[34] For Gunton, one of the challenges that faces a theology of creation in the modern West is to overcome the influence of Augustine, who not only deprived the doctrine of the Trinity of its economic roots and vitality, but also developed a doctrine of creation that was founded on a dislike of the material order of things in favor of the immaterial mind that is derived from the Platonic forms. The impoverished Trinity that was most fully expressed in Augustine could not help but be cut loose from his doctrine of creation, where he showed a concern less for the particular goodness of creatures than for the abstract notion of God's omnipotent will to create.

Gunton is noted for his critique of Augustine, especially in relation to the doctrine of the Trinity.[35] Gunton concludes that two problems that arose in the Western church, "the problem about the knowledge of God and [the problem] of the relegation to secondary status of the doctrine of the Trinity," can be answered "by enquiring how far responsibility for the state of affairs is to be laid at the door of St. Augustine."[36] The conclusion of his analysis is that Augustine completely misunderstood and misused the doctrine that had been skilfully developed by early theologians such as Irenaeus, and later by the Cappadocians, who explained the doctrine through reflection on the scriptural revelation of God's activity through the Son and the Spirit rather than through reflection on Greek philosophical theology.

In particular, Gunton claims that modalism is the result of Augustine's work on the doctrine of the Trinity: "The only conclusion can be that, in some sense or another, it is divine substance and not the Father that is the basis of the being of God, and therefore, *a fortiori*, of everything else."[37] However, going further than the charge of modalism, Gunton suggests that Augustine simply does not have the "conceptual equipment" to deal with the problems that face the doctrine of the Trinity—namely, the problems of Arianism, Eunomianism, and modalism, all of which his position finally collapses into at one point or another in *The Trinity*.[38] What is the case that Gunton makes?

He argues that the key to understanding Augustine's failure lies in his doubts concerning the goodness of materiality and his belief that true knowledge cannot be found in creation. These make it impossible for him to take seriously the Incarnation as a basis for knowledge about the Son and the Son's relationship to God.[39] His attempts to explain the doctrine of the Trinity are not grounded in the humanity of Jesus, but rather in the divine Son. This means that the perspective of God as related to the incarnate Jesus, which protects the doctrine of the Trinity from becoming merely an abstract, rational triad, fails in Augustine.[40] The reason for this is Augustine's Neoplatonist philosophical position, which also leads him to embarrassment over the tradition that the Old Testament theophanies were associated with God. Augustine instead opts to associate the theophanies with angels.[41] If he can dismiss God's direct involvement through theophanies, then it only stands to reason that he also can cut loose the importance of the mediatorship of the Word of God. When the Word is no longer uniquely identified as the mediator, the relationship of the Word to the Father and the Holy Spirit becomes abstract and "flattened out," so that the trinitarian relations become meaningless over against the oneness of God's substance.

In other words, Augustine no longer follows the tradition of Irenaeus and Tertullian, whereby the Father relates to the world through his Word and Spirit.[42] This is why Augustine will not look in the material world for analogies of the Trinity, but instead turns to the rational nature of the immaterial soul. Rather than develop the doctrine out of God's redemptive work in Jesus's life, death, and resurrection and the Holy Spirit's outpouring on the first Christians, Augustine looks to the Platonic doctrine of knowledge as recollection, assuming that God is some sort of "supermind."[43] Not surprisingly, given this concern to promote a Greek emphasis on the importance of the rational over the physical, the Trinity becomes reduced to a process of the mind, and those analogies of the Trinity are favored that investigate the human mind. Of course, this also means that Augustine falls into a real trap of reducing the three divine persons to the overarching mind of which they are merely processes.[44]

Augustine's decision to minimize the place given to the economic activity of God through the Son and Holy Spirit shows his commitment to Platonist philosophy over against the scriptural portrayal of God at work in the world. Gunton then goes on to contrast him with the Cappadocians, whose Eastern Trinitarianism represents the best tradition of post-Nicene thought about the Trinity. According to the Cappadocians, the three persons (hypostases) did not refer to three individuals, but rather to how the three are "concrete particulars in relation to one another."[45] The three together constitute one substance or nature (*ousia*). Following Zizioulas, Gunton describes *ousia* as "being in communion."[46] Though the hypostases are conceptually distinct from the divine *ousia*, the two also are mutually related in trinitarian thought, so that the communal nature of the Godhead is reflected in the idea that *ousia* is the relationship of the hypostases to one another.[47] Augustine simply could not grasp this conceptual understanding of the hypostases and *ousia* as both distinct and mutually integrative.[48] According to Gunton, Augustine viewed this move as merely a "linguistic usage" without grounding in reality.[49] From this point of view, the root of Augustine's thinking is that persons cannot be easily integrated into an *ousia* in the way that the Cappadocians argue (by appealing to a dynamic understanding of *ousia* as three hypostases in communion), because to do so would contradict basic "Aristotelian subject-predicate logic."[50] What Augustine is doing, in Gunton's view, is placing Greek philosophy, which favors a static (i.e., unchanging) conception of *ousia*, ahead of the Cappadocians' conception of God's *ousia* (which they derived from their attention to the dynamic relationships of the three persons described in scripture). Augustine's reliance on this "dualistic ontology," whereby divine *ousia* is more basic than hypostasis because changelessness is a more fundamental category than dynamism, does not allow him to use hypostasis as an ontological predicate but only as a logical predicate. The mutual exclusion of these two ideas exists because *ousia* must remain without any accidents, which hypostasis represents in Augustine's subject-predicate logic. Thus, the three hypostases "disappear into the all-embracing oneness of God."[51] A conception of substance, then, is that from which the Son and Holy Spirit are derived, not the Father.[52] Gunton's conclusion is that Augustine is a modalist.[53]

Gunton's critique of Augustine follows the standard modern theological method of dividing classical theology into Eastern and Western forms, and correspondingly, it locates Augustine within the Western and modalist tradition of understanding the Trinity. Gunton's approach is thus consonant with Boff's reading of the history of doctrine. Where they depart is that Gunton favors Eastern Trinitarianism and argues that the Cappadocians represent the high-water mark of the doctrine. Boff's skepticism concerning both traditions, based on the inadequacy of the scriptural accounts for giving an accurate reflection of God as an egalitarian Trinity, is largely ignored by Gunton, who resolves the historical trinitarian drama by favoring the East over the West. Gunton's account of the rise of the doctrine is not limited to the specific questions of the development of trinitarian logic, nor is his criticism of Augustine merely that he was a modalist who severely crippled the doctrine's place in the Western church. He recognizes that the ramifications of the development of the doctrine of the Trinity were far-reaching. Indeed, Gunton sees the question of how Christian views of creation (as good, evil, or neutral) hinge in large part on how one conceives of God, because God's creative work either will lead to the praise of God for the goodness of creation in its plurality and particularity, or to a lower view of creation in favor of the omnipotent, invisible, immaterial divine will that creates by command. Thus, as we will now see, Gunton also criticizes Augustine in his examination of the history of Christian thinking about God's creative work, drawing out the consequences of his Western, Greek, Neoplatonic understanding of the Trinity.

The Trinity and the Doctrine of Creation: Cause and Effect

For Gunton, Christian views of the world as God's creation largely can be divided into two major camps. On the one hand, there is the "straightforwardly trinitarian construction of the act of divine creation"[54] that was developed by such early Christian thinkers as Irenaeus, who famously described God's economy as accomplished by his two hands in the world—namely, the Son and the Holy Spirit. The will of God in Irenaeus's theology is a "particularizing will" that gives rise to the existence of creatures and guides their "directedness to [their] perfection" through the Son and the Holy Spirit. Such an understanding of divine will is open to, and supportive of, the particularity of embodied creatures within the world.[55] On the other hand, there are the "more sophisticated but also more Platonizing approaches" of thinkers such as Origen and Augustine, who take God's creation of forms as they received it through Greek philosophy and thus find the importance of God's work in the conceptual forms that God employs rather than in the actual world of particular beings. The particularity of creatures is disdained as leading the mind away from contemplation of the immaterial and immutable One.[56]

In Gunton's reading of Augustine, the creation is not one creation by God, but rather a twofold creation. There is a creation of the Platonic "intellectual" world of forms and then the physical world "in imitation of the (created) eternal forms."[57] This goes against the grain of scriptural teaching about the goodness of creation by setting up a hierarchical understanding of creation, where the immaterial is higher than, and to be favored over, the material creation, which is less good than the immaterial creation. This Platonic approach also had the undesirable effect of linking material creatures to timeless and unchanging forms, thus making subsequent Western theology unable to deal with theories of evolution, which are based on the observation of change.[58] Resistance to evolutionary theory was the result of devaluing things that are subject to change.

The philosophical assumption that the Platonic understanding of the world is intellectually most viable corresponds to Augustine's lack of a robust Christological element (and even less of a pneumatological element) in his doctrine of creation. Augustine favors the description of the creator as the one God who creates by arbitrary will. God, in essence, is a divine will abstractly conceived and unknowable.[59] Such a God is absolutely separated from the material creation, while among creatures a higher value is placed upon spiritual and intellectual creatures that are, by definition, closer to God. While God's role as creator is related to will, the actual creative activity takes place through angels, who are intermediaries.[60] The idea of divine providence as a trinitarian work by the Father's Son and Holy Spirit is lost by Augustine, who takes up a Neoplatonic conception of angels as the first created forms, through which all other creatures are made. This is also reflected in Augustine's desire to reconcile the idea of a timeless God with the Genesis account of God's creative work happening within the constraints of time. To reconcile the two, he ends up demythologizing the text by arguing that all the days of creation are actually made instantaneously, by the eternal Son through the forms.[61]

In fact, creaturely particularity is only a result of the "function" of the divine will, while human will is described, in parallel fashion to Augustine's understanding of God, as "arbitrary self-assertion."[62] Just as the Christological element is less determinative for Augustine's understanding of creation because the Incarnation is less important than the eternal will of God, so the human will is most important in Augustine's understanding of the shape of the creation, while the plurality of other creatures are manifestly less interesting to him. "Material beauty, which the Augustinian tradition regards as of importance only as the route to a higher, immaterial beauty . . . is necessarily linked with plurality, with the manyness of created reality."[63] Similarly, for Augustine temporality itself is falleness and disorder, instead of human sinfulness "whose redemption is the hope of the Christian Gospel."[64]

The relationship of God's redemptive economy is not related to creation as such, but only to those creatures who have minds that can transcend the finite material realm and live in an intellectual world of forms. One sees this play out in Augustine's writings about Genesis in terms of the allegorizing and spiritualizing of the text, rather than taking it as referring to the actual creation of material things that are good in themselves.[65]

For Gunton, this diminished view of creation is seen in the way that Augustine affirms the "only-begotten Son" to be distinct from the creation.[66] In itself, Gunton accepts such a view of the eternal Son as a positive enough step, allowing the Son to be considered creator with the Father. In its most positive sense, Augustine understands creation to be "Christological" in the limited sense that the eternal Son creates with the Father. Nevertheless, this limited sense stands in contrast to that of Irenaeus, who conceived of the Christological nature of creation not in terms of the eternal Son, but in terms of the incarnate Son, because he related the proper understanding of creation to the "Son's becoming material."[67] He insists that Augustine uses the idea of the eternal Son's distinctness from creation to undermine any positive relationship in the distinction between the creation and eternity, because it only refers to the eternal Son rather than the incarnate Son.[68] Theological reflection on the eternal Son always takes precedence over that on the incarnate Son, because the eternal, immaterial God is higher and better than a material and finite creature.

This lack of concern for God's economic work as the basis for theological reflection about the creation corresponds with Augustine's trinitarian theology. We already have seen how Gunton criticized Augustine's trinitarian theology as minimally noting the importance of the divine economy for understanding who God is as Trinity. Since the redemption of creatures through the work of the incarnate Son and the Holy Spirit is the best means to construct a doctrine of the Trinity, one would expect that the doctrine of creation also should reflect such trinitarian belief, by being concerned with the creation as an object not only of God's will, but also of his personal involvement through the work of the Son and Holy Spirit.[69] In Augustine, however, the link between creation and redemption is "weakened to the point of disappearing."[70] Not surprisingly, given this lack of trinitarian involvement in the creation, the oneness of God is "manifestly elevated over the plurality of the Trinity" through conceiving of the creator as "arbitrary will." And, in logical fashion, the intellectual order also is superior to the sensible world, because the will is the supermind of God. In the end, Gunton sees in Augustine's doctrine of creation the assertion that "unity, but not plurality, is transcendental."[71]

The trajectory of Western theology owes its course to the path chosen by Augustine: "The Western tendency to divorce creation and redemption took its direction from Augustine, whose discussion of creation is, with one exception, virtually abstracted from christology."[72] What is most striking to Gunton is how the doctrine of creation in the West seems to be concerned only with knowing a creator that is sheer will, because Augustine chose to develop his understanding of creation without the trinitarian insights of the church that were grounded in the economy of salvation. Gunton describes the Western emphasis on God's unitary will over the goodness of the creation by linking it to the philosophical speculation of Augustine: "Augustine's interpretation of Genesis 1 in terms of a creation of forms, eternal archetypes, turns that celebration of particularity and variety into something dangerously like its subversion, because the replacing of christology by Platonic universals generates a very different conception of the relation of universal and particular. Not the particularizing will of God, but general conceptual forms come into the centre."[73] In the end, Augustine is not trinitarian in his conception of the doctrine of creation, but monistic.[74]

In subsequent chapters we will consider whether such a portrayal of Augustine as having a severely deficient trinitarian understanding of creation is representative of what he actually wrote about the creation and the doctrine of the Trinity. We will devote a significant amount of attention to a close reading of Augustine, and in doing so, show how his writings are not susceptible to the criticisms we have found Gunton, Boff, and Moltmann. As well, we will also seek to delineate some of the aspects of his doctrine of creation as they relate to modern concerns about interrelationality.

The Scriptural Basis of Augustine's Trinitarian Doctrine

The question of Augustine's modalistic tendencies with regard to the doctrine of the Trinity, and their effect on his understanding of creation, arises out of the modern assessment of the historical development of the doctrine. The ascription of Augustine's theological indebtedness to a Western reliance on Greek philosophy as central to how to understand God, in contrast to the Eastern reliance upon the biblical presentation of the divine economy, will color how one reads Augustine's arguments. It is important, then, before turning to our actual analysis of his argument in *The Trinity*, that we make clear the basis on which we will proceed with our analysis of Augustine's writings over the next few chapters. In opposition to many modern theological pictures of Augustine, we will take seriously his own stated concern to maintain the biblical and Nicene traditions. What follows is an explanation of why Augustine makes the divine economy revealed in Scripture the central theme on which he then develops his doctrine of the Trinity. Thomas Marsh states a similar position to that we have seen in Gunton when Marsh writes, "But where that [Eastern] tradition would have maintained a strong sense of the divine monarchy . . . Augustine abandons this position and understands the one God to mean the one divine substance or nature which *then* is verified in the Father, Son, and Holy Spirit."[75] Thus, the *taxis* (order) described in scripture of the Father, Son, and Holy Spirit is treated as of secondary importance in Augustine's understanding of the Trinity, which orders the divine persons according to an immutable substance. Marsh takes Augustine's statement in the opening book of *The Trinity* as the basic evidence for this: "In this way let us set out along Charity Street together, making for him of whom it is said, *seek his face always* (Ps 105:4). This covenant, both prudent and pious, I would wish to enter into in the sight of the Lord our God with all who read what I write, and with respect to all my writings, especially such as these where we are seeking the unity of the three, of Father and Son and Holy Spirit."[76]

In this passage, according to Marsh, Augustine makes clear that unity is the primary focus of trinitarian doctrine, in distinction from the Eastern approach that stresses the *taxis* of the three persons. He claims that Augustine describes this as a unity of substance a few lines later: "The purpose of all Catholic commentators . . . has been to teach that according to the scriptures Father and Son and Holy Spirit in the inseparable equality of one substance present a divine unity."[77] The net result of Augustine's Western approach to the Trinity is that the three persons are lost in speculation about substance and unity that will pave the way for the later separation of the economic Trinity and the immanent Trinities, a separation that will render the doctrine irrelevant to Christian piety.[78]

It should be noted, though, that in terms of Augustine's method for understanding the doctrine in *The Trinity*, one also sees in 1.7 a commitment to exploring trinitarian faith using the received tradition of Nicaea, as well as the necessity of grounding such an exploration in the biblical revelation of God's identity. This method is stated succinctly when he describes *The Trinity* as an answer to those who doubt the Catholic doctrine of the Trinity: "[W]e shall undertake . . . to give them the reasons they clamour for. . . . But first we must establish by the authority of the holy scriptures whether the faith is in fact like that [God being a Trinity]. Only then shall we go on, if God so wills and gives his help. . . ."[79] Here he indicates that the understanding of the triune nature of God, known specifically from scripture, is his starting point, as part of the task of establishing a basis on which to give the "reason-mongers" the answer they seek. Rather than making oneness or unity the overarching focus for his work, it is the scriptural basis for threeness.[80] Moreover, Augustine does not appeal *either* to scripture and tradition as his starting point, *or* to the triune nature of God as his primary focus, but rather to *both*—that is, to the scriptural evidence for the triune nature. The foundations provided by biblical faith are at the heart of the answer that Augustine uses in response to those who would seek other rational models and theories to explain God's threeness.

The emphasis that Augustine places upon the scriptural basis for the doctrine of the Trinity is not at the expense of a rational explanation of doctrine, to which he also adhered. The two were inseparable for Augustine. The classical philosopher was committed to living the rational life, but this did not necessitate opposition to theological explanation. Similarly, the explanation of the faith did not preclude reference to philosophical ideas when they could clarify the meaning of biblical faith.[81] Augustine's own background included training in skepticism and Neoplatonism, and his generally Platonic philosophical approach had a profound effect upon his theology, though after his conversion, no philosophical school (such as that of Plotinus or Porphyry) can be said to have pride of place, but all were subjected to the critique of scriptural faith.[82]

In contradistinction to the schema that makes a division between the East and the West in patristic thinking about the Trinity, then, Augustine states a method that will follow the Nicene path of starting with scripture and recognizing the need to protect the plurality of the Godhead in trinitarian doctrine. Who are the "reason-mongers" that have compromised the correct reading of biblical revelation, and developed misleading, alternative doctrines of the Trinity? According to Michel R. Barnes, Augustine directed *The Trinity* against, in part, Latin, anti-Nicene, "homoean" (subordinationist) theologies. These subordinationist interpretations of the Son's and Holy Spirit's relationship to the Father were based on interpretations of scripture that were developed in ongoing debates in the post-Nicene church.[83] Not only does Augustine place himself within the historical tradition of Nicaea, but he also writes with a polemical edge, in order to defend the orthodoxy he claims to uphold.

Therefore, while Marsh is correct in noting that unity of substance is a concern for Augustine, it is not because he has accepted the primacy of the concept of divine substance over the biblical presentation of God's economy in three persons, or that he wishes to subsume questions of trinitarian relations to a theory of substance.[84] Rather, the plurality of the divine persons is the basis for Augustine's attempt to come to an understanding of the idea of unity of substance that does not dissolve the reality of the three into a prior substance, or reduce the Son and the Holy Spirit to creatures of the Father. Augustine conceives the unity of substance as an issue with regard to two questions: firstly, how the unity of divine substance is related to the Father's begetting the Son and spiration of the Holy Spirit;[85] and secondly, how one can talk of the unity of substance in terms of the three persons' common activity.[86] Rather than conceiving of unity in terms analogous to human nature, where the begetter and begotten can be greater and lesser in relation to each other, Augustine will show how talking about divine unity as eternal, simple Being can shed light on how God could be three and one. He will do this by exploring the scriptural basis for speaking about the Trinity (following the Nicene tradition of the Father as origin of the Son and Holy Spirit), without subordinating the other persons to the Father[87] or making the Father (or some other underlying divine substance) the true God of which the other persons are simply manifestations.[88] In short, Augustine's focus on unity of substance begins and ends with the monarchy of the Father rather than precluding the relations of origin.

In *The Trinity* 1.7, one can detect the methodological premise on which Augustine proceeds. After the quotation we noted above ("The purpose of all Catholic commentators . . . has been to teach that according to the scriptures Father and Son and Holy Spirit in the inseparable equality of one substance present a divine unity"),[89] Augustine continues his explanation of what he understands the "purpose of all the Catholic commentators" to be:

> It was not however this same three . . . that was born of the virgin Mary, crucified and buried under Pontius Pilate, rose again on the third day and ascended into heaven, but the Son alone. Nor was it this same three that came down upon Jesus in the form of a dove at his baptism, or came down on the day of Pentecost after the Lord's ascension, with a roaring sound from heaven as though a violent gust were rushing down, and in divided tongues as of fire, but the Holy Spirit alone. Nor was it this same three that spoke from heaven, *You are my Son*, either at his baptism by John (Mk 1:11), or on the mountain when the three disciples were with him (Mt 17:5), nor when the resounding voice was heard, *I have both glorified it* (my name) *and will glorify it again* (Jn 12:28), but it was the Father's voice alone addressing the Son; although just as Father and Son and Holy Spirit are inseparable, so do they work inseparably. This is also my faith inasmuch as it is the Catholic faith.[90]

Augustine places his understanding of the trinitarian faith within the Nicene tradition by giving direct reference to the creed in the first lines of this quotation ("born of the virgin Mary, crucified and buried under Pontius Pilate, rose again on the third day and ascended into heaven"), with his own explanation of its trinitarian significance.[91] He also cites scriptural events where each of the three divine persons are explicitly associated with the particular action. His use of both scripture and the creed reveal that for Augustine the problem of triune being is not simply about defending the unity of the divine substance, but more specifically about understanding how the threeness of the persons is both particular (i.e., the works of each in the economy) and inseparable. He sees the explanation of the trinitarian nature of God as including the belief that all three persons are indeed the one God of scripture, but not in such a way that the three became incarnate in Jesus. As well, the three were not all manifest in the dove at Jesus's baptism or in the tongues of fire at Pentecost, which belonged to the work of the Holy Spirit; and it was not the three who addressed the Son at his baptism and at the transfiguration, but the Father alone. Nevertheless, the Catholic faith that Augustine also claims as his own faith also understands the three to work inseparably.[92]

Augustine's immersion in the scriptural foundations of the doctrine of the Trinity informs his whole attempt to defend the doctrine against subordinationism in his day. Building on that foundation he will develop a sophisticated account of the trinitarian logic that helps to explain how the relationship of the Father, Son, and Holy Spirit does not undermine the church's conception of the unity of the divine substance. The challenge for Augustine is to explain how the three are one substance in a way that also affirms the Father, Son, and Holy Spirit's work as it is portrayed in scripture and summarized in the Nicene Creed. In other words, how can one affirm the unity of God and recognize the threeness of the Godhead, without dividing unity from plurality and plurality from unity? We now are ready to turn to an analysis of his defense of trinitarian doctrine, keeping in mind his method, which begins in the careful explanation of the meaning of scripture and the Nicene tradition.

Chapter Two

Augustine's Doctrine of the Trinity

In this chapter, we will concentrate on how Augustine explained the foundations required for the doctrine of the Trinity. We will note that for him the threat of subordinationism shapes the question of how to conceive of the doctrine of the Trinity in the first four books of *The Trinity*. After this, we then will take up the question of how the concept of the Father's monarchy and the simplicity of the divine being formed the foundation for Augustine's understanding of the unity of the Trinity. In doing so, we also will address the charge of modalism that has been made against Augustine. Then, in the next chapter, we will consider how Augustine understood the order of persons in the Godhead, and how it resembles the hierarchy of rule (i.e., lordship) that writers like Boff and Gunton have criticized. This analysis of his doctrine of the Trinity will provide a basis on which to then interpret his trinitarian conception of God's creative work as it is described in Genesis.

Subordinationism and the Divine Missions

In the first four books of *The Trinity* Augustine focuses his argument on defending the scriptural basis for maintaining the equality of the persons, given their distinctiveness as scripture reveals it, when formulating the doctrine of the Trinity. He argues that Paul, in Philippians 2:6, distinguishes between the human and divine forms of the Son, thus giving a basis for interpreting seemingly subordinationist passages without requiring the Son to be less than the Father: "In the form of a servant which he [the Son] took he is the Father's inferior; in the form of God in which he existed even before he took this other he is the Father's equal."[1] The human form of the Son is a creature, finite and limited, and therefore to be considered less than the eternal Father. However, the Son in his eternal nature (substance) is equal to the Father. When interpreting biblical passages that refer to the Son's inferiority, says Augustine, one will find that they are to be ascribed to his human form rather than his eternal form.

This rule—to interpret Scripture either according to the Son's divinity or to his humanity—is not meant to be employed alone, as if that were all that is needed to interpret correctly the Son's relationship to the Father in isolated texts.[2] Instead, by "keeping in view the whole range of scriptures" (i.e., remaining attentive to the general shape and message of the scriptures, whose shape and message are discovered when one reads them within the traditions of the Catholic faith), the rule will help to guide one to a proper understanding of the relationship between the Father and Son and Holy Spirit. As an example of how the form of the eternal Son is described, he immediately cites John 1:3, "the Word *through whom all things were made.*" As an example of interpreting scripture according to the Son's humanity, he refers to Paul's mention of the incarnate Son in Galatians 4:4, who appeared according to the form of a servant. Paul, he says, wrote of "one *made of woman, made under the law, to redeem those who were under the law.*"[3] So whereas in the John 1:3 passage the eternal maker of creatures is being referred to, and therefore the passage is to be interpreted according to the Son's divine form, in the Galatians passage the Son's incarnation as a servant is being referred to and thus ought to be interpreted according to the Son's human form. Indeed, Augustine understands this rule to be part of his inheritance from the faith of the church, and thus he can refer to it as a *canonica regula*.[4]

Even this rule, which helps to clarify problematic passages that appear to subordinate Jesus Christ to the Father, does not address many other passages, including the Old Testament theophanies. The theophanies were often interpreted as manifestations of the Son, and so constituted a powerful body of evidence that the Son always is portrayed as the sent one.[5] If all of the instances of the Son being sent by the invisible Father are taken together, then the picture painted from the beginning to the end of the scriptures would be that the invisible Father is true God, while the visible Son is subordinate to the Father, because it is the Father who remains invisible and sends his Son as the servant or messenger.[6] According to Augustine, the potential for ambiguity and confusion about the status of one who sends and one who is sent gives rise to the subordinationist reading of scripture, which the Arians use as a basis from which to perpetuate their heresy.[7] The Son being sent from the Father does not seem to support the equality of the Father and Son, because the one who sends (and is not sent)[8] seems to be the superior who gives orders, while the one sent is an obedient servant to the superior.[9] Augustine's conclusion about the Old Testament theophanies is that unless the context provides sufficient grounds to associate a theophany with a particular person,[10] then the theophany is to be understood as the inseparable work of the whole Trinity acting through physical symbols or signs that convey the significance of the received message.[11] The theophanies potentially reveal a message from any of the three, or the three together, to the intended recipients. In claiming this ambiguity, Augustine intends to make the Incarnation the primary instance of the Son being sent.[12] Then, in book 4 he will argue that the idea of being sent in the Incarnation is not subordinationist.

Furthermore, to make clear that the theophanies are not to be understood in the same way as the Incarnation, or as the Holy Spirit appearing in the form of a dove or as fire (even though these latter events were temporary, like the theophanies),[13] he develops an argument in book 3 that the common work of the three persons is better understood as mediated by angels.[14] In other words, there are strategies for understanding the Old Testament theophanies that do not require a single interpretation of all the passages as the sending of the Son into the creation. Moreover, any divine "appearance," whether through the work of angels or in the proper missions, is the work of the whole Trinity, thus undermining the subordinationist reading of Scripture, which fails to see that the Son, even in his mission, remains equal to God, uncreated and invisible.[15]

For Augustine the New Testament missions of the Son and the Spirit are unique and therefore to be understood as distinct in kind from the theophanies of the Old Testament. The missions reveal something of the particularity of the persons themselves and their relationship to the Father,[16] while the theophanies cannot always be clearly associated with particular persons. In books 2–3 he has only shown that the theophanies need not be interpreted as the physical manifestation of the Son in creation, and that arguments can be made for sometimes identifying one of the three, or even the whole Trinity, with different theophanies. The question still remains as to why the missions of the Son and the Holy Spirit in the New Testament do not entail their subordination to the Father. In particular, while the mission of the incarnate Son is at once the work of all three, since the three act inseparably,[17] why is it proper to the Son to be the mediator?[18] The essence of his argument for the Son's and Father's equality in book 4 is rooted in soteriology: "So God became a just man to intercede with God for sinful man. . . . So he applied to us the similarity of his humanity to take away the dissimilarity of our iniquity, and becoming a partaker of our mortality he made us partakers of his divinity."[19]

Humanity's salvation requires lifting humanity up to God by God. Christ's work of salvation thus reveals his divinity. Likewise, "the Lord

Jesus gave the Holy Spirit twice, once on earth for the love of neighbour, and again from heaven for the love of God."[20] Here the Holy Spirit is explained as being the one who perfects Christians in loving their neighbors and loving God.[21] Like Christ, then, the work of the Holy Spirit unites the believer to God, because saving belief is "in Christ by the gift of the Holy Spirit."[22] The importance of the Spirit's work in the salvation of humanity is reiterated in book 5, where he describes the Spirit as "of the Father and Son," who gave the Spirit so that humanity could receive holiness. The Spirit's giftedness for perfecting human holiness makes it appropriate for the church to speak of the Holy Spirit as "our Spirit," because the Spirit is given to humanity for the sake of grace.[23] This does not mean, though, that the Spirit originates in the Father and Son in the manner of creaturely origination in the Trinity. The Spirit is not a creature.[24]

The mission of the Spirit, like the mission of the Son, is related to creaturely salvation. The saving missions of the Son and the Holy Spirit are the means by which humanity can understand the divine relations. Books 1–4 lead to the conclusion in 4.27–32 that the New Testament missions reveal the eternal processions of the Son and the Holy Spirit in the Trinity. In short, the Son and the Holy Spirit (who proceeds from both the Father and the Son, though principally from the Father) were sent from the Father who is never sent. These missions are parallel, with the Son being Son because he is eternally begotten from the Father who is unbegotten, and the Holy Spirit eternally being Gift because he proceeds from the Father and also is given by the Son.[25]

It should be noted that Augustine does not mention the Holy Spirit being from the Father and the Son until he has first described the Spirit as proceeding and being sent from the Father. Thus, just as the Son is begotten by the Father, so the Spirit proceeds from the Father, because the Father is the origin of deity.[26] However, after establishing that the origin of the Son and Holy Spirit is from the unique source—namely, the Father—Augustine then distinguishes between the origin of the Holy Spirit and the origin of the Son, so that they are not conceived as brothers (which would raise the question of how exactly the Son and Holy Spirit really are different from each other).[27] Augustine recognizes that the Holy Spirit proceeds principally from the Father, because of the Father's monarchy, but also that the mission of the Holy Spirit is described in scripture as proceeding from the Son, who gives the Spirit to the disciples.[28] In terms of the eternal relations of the three persons, the Holy Spirit is given by the Father and the Son, as Augustine deduces from the missions described in scripture. (In assuming that the missions reveal something about the prior reality of the eternal relations, one then has a basis on which to interpret the missions correctly.) The Holy Spirit is not subordinate to the Son, but is equal by being from the Father just as the Son is from the Father. In establishing the Holy Spirit's origin in the Father, Augustine maintains the received orthodoxy that the Father is the eternal source of divinity of the Son and Holy Spirit, and thus the basis of unity of the three persons in one Godhead, because they originate in him.[29]

In *Answer to Maximus the Arian* 2.14.1, Augustine describes the double procession this way: "The Father begot a Son and, by begetting him, gave it to him that the Holy Spirit proceeds from him as well." In this way, he is able to maintain the monarchy of the Father and explain Jesus's sending of the Holy Spirit to the disciples (John 20:22). The eternal origination of the Holy Spirit in the Son has its beginning in the Father, who, in his eternal begetting of the Son, gives or hands over (*dedit*) to the Son what the Father has—namely, that the Spirit proceeds from the Son, just as the Spirit proceeds from the eternal Father (John 15:26). Logically speaking, the Holy Spirit is first from the Father, and then from the Son, to whom it is given that the Spirit would proceed from him. However, as will be shown later, the simplicity of the Godhead, such that there is no division in it, means that a logical distinction between the origination of the Spirit in the Father first and in the Son second is only true conceptually. The unity of the Father and the Son in eternity, revealed in the divine missions, is the basis for Augustine's understanding of the double procession.

The equality of the persons in the Godhead is revealed by the missions of the Son and the Holy Spirit from the Father. But Augustine does not understand the missions to be the Father's begetting of the Son and procession of the Holy Spirit. Rather, on the one hand, when scripture speaks of the Son and the Holy Spirit being sent, he takes it to indicate that those to whom the Son and Holy Spirit have been sent have perceived from whence they have been sent—namely, from the Father for the salvation of humanity; on the other hand, being begotten or proceeding from the Father also refers to their eternal origin in the Father.[30] The correspondence between the begetting and the sending of the Son is predicated on an understanding of the scriptural description of the Son as the Word of the Father, rather than on an understanding that collapses their eternal relations into the economic activity of the Godhead. As the Word of God, the Son must be sent from the Father, because a word does not precede the one who speaks it. However, the divine Word can be eternally one with the divine Father who speaks it, because of the divine simplicity.[31] As further evidence for this, Augustine also argues that when the Father is known in time by a creature, scripture never refers to the Father as having been sent, since there is no one for him to be from.[32] The correlation of eternal begetting and sending into the creation reflects Augustine's recognition that in the ordering of the missions is seen the eternal order of divinity, but that the missions do not constitute the eternal ordering.

The mission of the Son and Holy Spirit is to impart a saving knowledge of the Father to humanity. Such saving knowledge leads creatures to be able to know and contemplate the divine being—which the divine persons share equally.[33] Thus in 4.29 Augustine explains that "just as being born means for the Son his being from the Father, so his being sent means his being known to be from him. And just as for the Holy Spirit his being the gift of God means his proceeding from the Father, so his being sent means his being known to proceed from him."

"Being from the Father" refers to the Son's and Holy Spirit's eternal generation from the monarchy of the Father. Augustine understands their economic activity as the basis for thinking about the eternal Trinity, and specifically an eternal Trinity in which the Son and the Holy Spirit have their relations of origin in the Father (who sends them but is never sent). The key word, though, is "being known," which shows how Augustine's approach in books 1–4 has been to focus on the Son's and Holy Spirit's work as revealed in scripture, so that humanity's reconciliation to God takes them from ignorance of God to true knowledge of God. Recognizing the Son and Holy Spirit to be eternally from the Father is a direct implication of their missions.[34] Directly related to this correspondence between the missions and the immanent Trinity is Augustine's understanding of the equality of the three, since the missions disclose the relationship of the Son and the Holy Spirit to the eternal Father. He reiterates this point later when he writes, "We should understand that these sendings are not mentioned in scripture because of any inequality or disparity or dissimilarity of substance between the divine persons, but because of the created visible manifestation of the Son and the Holy Spirit; or better still, in order to bring home to us that the Father is the source and origin of all deity."[35]

The basis on which the Son and Holy Spirit are known to be from the eternal Father are through their missions as described in scripture; in effect, their identities are described according to their relations of origin in the Father. The Father's monarchy is true not merely with regard to the Son's and Holy Spirit's visible manifestations (which is also true of all created beings), but because their visible manifestations as presented in scripture point beyond their mission to their direct origin in the Father. Their relations of origin in the Father, which Augustine affirms with his Nicene forebears, are discovered through their economic activity.

It makes no sense, then, to assert that Augustine's conception of the Trinity is based firstly on anything like a metaphysical conception of unity at the expense of plurality, since his understanding of the Trinity is founded on the economic activity of the Son and Holy Spirit, who are sent by the eternal Father. His so-called Western orientation to conceive of God as the one, supreme good does not take priority over the so-called Eastern understanding of the Father's monarchy. Moreover, to argue that Augustine conceives of some type of abstractly conceived divine substance apart from the Father, Son, or Holy Spirit is to ignore that for Augustine knowledge of God is precisely knowledge gained from the biblical presentation of the Father in the work of the Son and the Holy Spirit.

Monarchy, Simplicity, and Relations of Origin: Augustine's Trinitarian Logic

The thoroughgoing defense of the equality of the Son and Holy Spirit with the Father, gained through knowledge of the economic activity of the Son and the Holy Spirit, based on Augustine's interpretation of scripture in books 1–4, is followed in books 5–7 by an analysis of how one can explain three equal, eternal, divine persons as one substance without necessarily implying subordinationism or modalism. As we saw in the previous chapter, despite Augustine's careful examination of the biblical texts, the criticisms leveled against him, and his so-called abandonment of the Eastern understanding of relations of origin from the Father, tend to focus on his argument in books 5–7 of *The Trinity*, where he considers how one can speak of divine substance without losing the threeness (and specifically the equality of the three persons) of the Godhead that he has defended in books 1–4. Remembering Augustine's method in the first four books of *The Trinity* and how his commitment to a pro-Nicene doctrine points to an affirmation of the Father's monarchy, we turn now to his detailed explanation of the logic of relations of origin based on a *taxis* that begins with the Father's monarchy.

It should be noted that Augustine does not use the Latin *monarchia* to describe the Father's monarchy, preferring instead the Latin terms *principium* and *principaliter*, which mean "origin."[36] To get at a clear understanding of monarchy, we must first take into account Augustine's explanation of divine simplicity, which refers to the Father as having his being fully and undividedly in himself. The Son's being also will have this attribute of simplicity by virtue of his being eternally begotten from the Father, since begetting a Son whose being is not simple would mean that the undivided being of the Father can be divided, thus destroying the divine simplicity. Therefore, the Son's being must be simple like the Father's. If the Son did not have the fullness of being undivided, then he could not be from the Father whose being is undivided.[37] In *City of God*, Augustine writes concerning the divine persons, "In respect to Himself, however, and not to the other, each is what he has: thus, in respect to himself He is said to be alive, for He has life, and He is Himself the life which He has."[38] Each of the three persons has life that is not separable from his being. The indivisibility of the being of the Son and the Holy Spirit is because they are eternally from the Father. This is a foundational point in Augustine's conception of the Father's monarchy.[39]

The reason that divine simplicity has an important place in Augustine's theology is that it helps to guard against basic mistakes in how one conceives of God. For example, he recognizes that human thinking about God can become confused when the mutable, divisible, and temporal structure of human reasoning distorts the invisibility and immateriality of God's perfection by applying spatial limits to God.[40] That is why, in Letter 120, he writes concerning the misleading language of spatial limits: "Let us not believe . . . that . . . the mass of these three great Persons, which are limited on however large a scale from above and below and round about, have a single godhead as if it were a fourth person, not like any of them, whereas it is common to all as the divinity of all in all, and wholly in each one; through which sole Godhead the same Trinity is said to be God."[41] In this passage, Augustine denies that the Godhead (that is, the divine substance) is something distinct from the three, functioning as the basis by which they are identified as divine. Divine simplicity, which does not divide the Godhead into parts, functions as a guard against the imposition of the material and temporal limits (such as spatial imagery) that human language naturally works within.

Later in Letter 120, he again notes how human language, which expresses its ideas according to the corporeal context of human existence, can lead to a distorted conception of the three divine persons. He argues that that thinking "is to be unhesitatingly rejected by which it is held that the substance of the Father, whereby the Father is one Person of the Trinity, is in Heaven, but the divinity is everywhere and not in heaven only—as if the Father were one thing and his divinity something else, something which He shares with the Son and the Holy Spirit. Thus, the Trinity itself would be somehow corporeal and subject to corporeal space."[42] The context of this quotation is Augustine's explanation of Jesus's words to Mary in John 20:17, "Do not hold on to me, because I have not yet ascended to the Father." He argues that Jesus's words do not indicate that the Father lives in the heavens, while divinity as such exists apart from the Father, Son, and Holy Spirit, as well as within each divine person as something of which each shares a part. Such an idea fails to account for the simplicity of divine being by locating the three persons in places ("heaven," "everywhere") as if they were divided from each other. In other words, Augustine is pointing out that John 20:17 does not speak of God according to creaturely conceptions, so that divinity is divisible like a corporeal object into constituent parts. Each person's divinity is not separate from his being. Augustine goes on to make this very point by writing, "For, if their nature existed—and God forbid that in the Father or the Son or the Holy Spirit the nature should be different from the substance—if their nature could exist, doubtless it could not exist more largely for anyone of Them than it does in their substance, but if the substance is different from Themselves, it is another substance, and this plainly is a completely false belief."[43]

The Latin word *qualitas* is translated here as "nature." This is confusing in this context, where Augustine is explaining how the divine *qualitas* is not different from the divine substance. A better translation would be simply "quality,"[44] since the English word "nature" also can suggest the divine substance/being. What Augustine is arguing in the quotation is that the way one speaks of divine qualities is also the way that one speaks of divine substance. For example, while human beings can have a quality attributed to their being, such as wisdom, they can also lose that quality and become foolish (i.e., be without wisdom). Qualities are not inseparable from created being. However, in God, whose being is simple, all qualities are inseparably part of God's substance, because quality and substance are not two different things.[45] Augustine recognizes that speaking of the unity of quality and substance in a perfect, indivisible, simple substance protects against this idea that substance is distinct from the three persons and their qualities. To separate quality from substance would destroy the very idea of a Trinity, because there would be three persons plus one substance, rather than three who are one substance. To use the corporeal language of created being—which is divisible—without the safeguard of a concept such as divine simplicity brings confusion into theological language.

Keeping in mind this discussion of divine simplicity, and how divine substance is not different from divine qualities, we can begin to see how Augustine's conception of the Father's monarchy works. At *The Trinity* 7.4, in discussing how the Son is the wisdom of God, he describes the unity of divine being in terms of the Father as the fount of life: "Thus *Christ* is *the power and wisdom of God* (1 Cor 1:24), because he is power and wisdom from the Father who is power and wisdom, just as he is light from the Father who is light, and the fountain of life with God the Father who is of course the fountain of life. . . . Because *just as the Father has life in himself, so he has given the Son to have life in himself* (John 5:26)." Augustine is attempting to explain how Christ can be called the wisdom of God, without meaning that divine wisdom is only Christ's (so that the Father's wisdom is Christ, but that the Father cannot be said to have wisdom in himself; or that wisdom is an attribute common to the divinity of the two as if there were a common divinity apart from the two) instead of properly belonging to each.[46] By speaking of the Son's being from the Father ("the fountain of life," which is a reference to the Father's monarchy), one can also speak of wisdom predicated of the Son himself, just as the Father has it in himself. For wisdom, which is identical with the simple, divine substance,[47] exists in the Father, who is the origin of the Son.[48] The Son's wisdom is the Father's wisdom, because it originates in the Father, just as the life of the Son originates in the Father (that is, in the Father's monarchy)—thus Augustine's use of the quotation from John 5:26, where Christ declares that the Son only has life in himself because the Father has given him to have life in himself. Since wisdom is identical with God's being because of the divine simplicity (nothing exists in the Father separate from who he is), the Son must also have that wisdom as his being, since he is eternally begotten of the Father.

The argument from the divine simplicity, based on the Father's monarchy in *The Trinity*, finds a parallel in Augustine's *Answer to Maximus the Arian*: "The Father did not lose the life he gave to the Son. . . . The one's life is identical with the other's. Because he is the true Son, because he is the perfect Son, because God the only Son is not inferior to God the Father, he is equal to the Father."[49] The life of the Father and Son is identical only if the Father does not lose life in communicating it to the Son. Otherwise, the divine life would be divisible, which contradicts the simplicity of divine being. As a result, if the Son is begotten from the Father, then he must have what the Father has perfectly in himself, because the eternally begotten Son is equal to the Father. Having identically what the Father has in himself requires that the Son has the same simple, divine nature (substance) and life in himself. If it were otherwise, the Son would not be identical in being with the Father, but would be either merely the same as the Father (which would be tantamount to modalism)[50] or radically different from the Father (i.e., a creature, which would be subordinationism). In both *The Trinity*[51] and *Answer to Maximus the Arian*, he develops his argument for their equality of substance by emphasizing that the wisdom and life of the Father is not different from the wisdom and life in the Son, because the Son is identical in being with the Father, from whom he is begotten.

Modalism

Modalism is a conception of the three persons of the Trinity not as distinctly subsisting persons, but as manifestations of the one God, whether the Father or a divine substance. For example, Sabellius apparently held that the one God of scripture is God the Father, the creator of the world and lawgiver, while the Son is the mode of God's redemption, and the Holy Spirit is God's mode of imparting life and grace.[52] The Son and Holy Spirit are not different from the Father, but are displays of his work, since monotheism requires one person in the Godhead, not three eternally subsisting persons.[53]

If one has a tendency toward modalistic thinking about the Trinity, then even though one affirms the three persons, it may be in such a manner that their distinctness appears to be of secondary importance to the preservation of divine unity. Thus, Augustine's so-called prioritizing of the unity of the divine substance over the three persons favors a modalistic tendency, where the three are experienced in the divine activity in the creation but are not of fundamental priority when speaking of the Godhead, where substance is given the priority for talking about God. The result of such a methodological starting point is that one's trinitarian theology appears to treat the description of the three persons as a linguistic problem to be solved in order to preserve the unity of the immanent Trinity. Robert Jenson detects such a modalistic tendency in Augustine, describing his trinitarian logic in this way: "[T]he three persons are not only equally related to the one substance, but *identically* related, so that the difference between them, that is, the relations, are irrelevant to their being God. . . . When the Nicenes called the Trinity as such God, they so named him *because* of the triune relations and differences; when Augustine calls the Trinity as such God, it is *in spite of* them."[54]

According to this reading of Augustine, the divine substance, which is called God, is understood not only as the basis for talking about who the three persons are, but as a means of insuring that their relations do not undermine the divine substance as the true basis on which one can understand divinity. Therefore, to Jenson's dismay, as he perceives Augustine's trinitarian thought, the three persons, singly and together, are equally God, because the divine substance is identically present in each singly and in the three together (this is the principle of divine simplicity, where the divine substance is not divisible into parts).[55] According to Jenson, because of the idea of a simple divine substance, Augustine sees in the threeness of God simply a logical problem, but does not consider the persons to be ontologically distinct in the Godhead.

Augustine, however, wants to avoid exactly this kind of misunderstanding whereby there is thought to be an underlying substance, either distinct from the three persons or ontologically more real than the divine relations of the persons. He understands the three persons to be equal with each other in substance,[56] and each alone to be equal with all three together: "Since therefore the Father alone or the Son alone or the Holy Spirit alone is as great as Father and Son and Holy Spirit together, in no way can they be called triple, or three by multiplication."[57]

This thoroughgoing understanding of equality provides a basis for understanding how he avoids a modalistic conception of the Trinity, since the equality of the persons is such that neither the idea of a difference in substance between any of the three, nor the idea that the divine substance exists apart from the three, can be thought of (keeping in mind his understanding of the Father's monarchy): "In God, therefore, when the equal Son cleaves to the equal Father, or the equal Holy Spirit to the Father and the Son, God is not made bigger than each of them singly, because there is no possibility of his perfection growing. Whether you take Father or Son or Holy Spirit, each is perfect, and God the Father and the Son and the Holy Spirit is perfect, and so they are a three, a triad or a Trinity rather than triple or three by multiplication."[58] Here, when Augustine speaks of "God" he means the Trinity, rather than specifically the Father. He claims that the perfection of God the Trinity—the fullness of simple, divine being—is not affected by the action of the Son cleaving to the Father, nor of the Holy Spirit cleaving to the Son and Father, because these three are perfect (i.e., simple and indivisible) God, just as they are each perfect in themselves. The image of cleaving is taken from 1 Corinthians 6:17,[59] where Paul uses the example of the Christian clinging to Christ and thereby becoming one spirit in him to argue against sexual relations with prostitutes. What is of interest to Augustine is how being made "one spirit" describes the result of a Christian cleaving to Christ. Augustine notes that the Christian grows in his or her spirit by being united with Christ, but that Christ does not grow bigger because the Christian unites with him.[60] Augustine's main point is not that the Christian's spirit is made larger, but rather that the soteriological activity of Christ in the believer's life also has implications for how to conceive of the substance of God. The reason that the Christian grows in his or her spirit, but that Christ does not, is that Christ is divine and therefore perfect in being. His salvific work perfects the creature.[61] However, there is nothing in the human-Christ relationship that would effect growth in Christ, because he is already perfect in his divinity. Likewise, therefore, the Father-Son relationship does not make Christ (or the Father, for that matter) bigger, because Christ is the divine Son begotten of the divine

Father. Theirs is already a relationship of eternal, divine perfection, where both are perfect, including perfectly equal.[62]

In the second half of the quotation from *The Trinity* 6.9, reproduced here again, Augustine draws his conclusion about what the meaning of the three persons' relations of perfect equality is for speaking about the Godhead: "Whether you take Father or Son or Holy Spirit, each is perfect, and God the Father and the Son and the Holy Spirit is perfect, and so they are a three, a triad or a Trinity rather than triple or three by multiplication." What they are in common is unchanging perfection, because each is unchanging perfection in himself (i.e., singly or properly). The Son and the Holy Spirit have this simple being in themselves because they have it from the Father (i.e., according to his monarchy) who has perfect being in himself.[63] Augustine speaks this way about the equality of each person with the others and with the whole not because he understands the Trinity to be a substance without distinctions between the persons (so that the three are the whole but do not subsist distinctly), but because the idea of divine simplicity enables him to conceive of the three as each having being in himself perfectly and equally. Put another way, the three persons are the divine substance—it is not something that underlies them—and the divine substance is a perfect, simple unity of three persons. Likewise, he denies that the three persons are a Trinity "by multiplication," since their substance is not divisible. One cannot add them together to get the Trinity, as if divinity were a corporeal object that could be explained according to mathematical formulas.[64] Rather, the three persons are a Trinity because each properly and equally is divine.

Augustine's conception of the Father's monarchy and the related idea of divine simplicity are signposts of his attempt to explicate trinitarian doctrine according to the received Catholic faith and scripture. He did not depart from his forebears, but instead sought to uphold their faith. The criticisms outlined in the previous chapter—criticisms of Augustine's so-called Western approach to the Trinity, with a starting point in an abstract conception of divine substance—do not adequately take account of his own stated method. We have already seen how he set out to explain the doctrine in light of the scriptural presentation of the divine missions of the Son and Holy Spirit. As well, the criticisms about how his substance language was based upon a modalistic conception of God do not account for how his substance-language was shaped relative to his understanding of the Father's monarchy and divine simplicity. The equality of the persons with each other and with the Trinity as a whole does not mean that the persons are flattened out into an indistinct substance, since the persons' equality is such that the three persons are each divine in themselves, and together are one God. The one substance is the Father, Son, and Holy Spirit who are each in themselves what the others are, without being the others. How does this understanding of the doctrine of the Trinity relate to the more general criticism we saw raised in the introduction and first chapter about the hierarchical nature of classical theological thought? We now turn from the concept of the Trinity and substance to the broader question of whether there are hierarchical problems in Augustine's trinitarian thought—a problem we have answered here based on his understanding of the economic activity of the Trinity, but which can also be approached on the basis of his understanding of the divine substance as love.

Chapter Three

Augustine and Hierarchy in the Trinity

We have seen how scholars have identified hierarchical conceptions of reality and God as problematic on different levels. Gunton argues that the Western form of the Trinity proposed by Augustine cannot adequately deal with the threeness of the persons, and ultimately falls into a modalistic trap in which the Father as ultimate will triumphs. Boff argues that beneath the attempts to reject subordinationism and modalism in the classical debates about the Trinity was still an adherence to hierarchical and patriarchal conceptions of order. He suggests that the attempt to understand the Trinity through a rigid, unidirectional order of relations (rather than the mutual dependence of each person upon the others in no particular order) is due, in part at least, to the monotheistic view of God in the Hebrew scriptures. When God is conceived as "absolutely whole, without division or multiplication" (and only subsequently as trinitarian), the result is a totalitarian political perspective that favors unity over plurality and that produces an unhealthy hierarchy of one over many.[1] (Similarly, McFague has linked the trinitarian God of the classical church to deficient understandings of the interrelatedness of creation. Thus, the trinitarian doctrines of the classical church reflect more the idea of God as ruler and patriarch than they do community in relation to creation. This hierarchical view of God's rule of the world is part of the development of Western society, which came to view the domination of nature as a legitimate part of its calling.[2]) Even if Augustine's doctrine of the Trinity can be shown to avoid the theological pitfalls, its social and ecological implications may still be problematic.

Here we shall discuss how Augustine's understanding of the divine substance of the immanent Trinity is conceived along lines of loving relations, rather than along the lines of the modern portrayal of classical Trinitarianism as a hierarchical monarchy of the Father that implicitly precludes equality.

Hierarchy and the Trinitarian Relations

Hierarchy is the ordering of persons over other persons, or over the creation,[3] so that some enjoy the ability to exercise controlling power according to their discretion. The pervasiveness of hierarchy in human societies is a given, and so it is reasonable to expect that it has affected the way that Christians think and act, including their theological reasoning. The real question, though, is whether the presence of hierarchy in theological reasoning and beliefs lends itself necessarily to negative outcomes. While we cannot tackle that question directly, we can at least inquire as to how Augustine's conception of the Trinity reflects the hierarchical thinking that he assumed, and whether it is obviously negative.

A survey article by Basil Studer considers the relationship between Augustine's understanding of divine fatherhood, on the one hand, and patriarchal ideas and images of human fathers (biological and political) as dominant overlords in classical society, on the other.[4] Studer finds that Augustine worked carefully and simultaneously with exegetical methods, philosophical concepts such as "substance" and "lordship," and metaphorical images in describing God's fatherhood. The first person of the Trinity is both Lord (*dominus*) and Father (*pater*), corresponding to the scriptural experience of God as eternally powerful over the creation and the merciful one who loves his children (though that love can seem harsh, when the righteousness of God is challenged by the sins of his creatures). The pastoral image of God that is found throughout Augustine's sermons, that of the paterfamilias, comes from the technical term for the Roman father (which was not limited to the father of a family household, but also encompassed the political sphere of the ruler over a city or an empire). This terminological usage shows, in part, Augustine's indebtedness to his context as he worked out his ideas. The image of the paterfamilias serves Augustine's pastoral purposes by expressing his exegetical findings that the God of scripture is humble and merciful (which includes God's *disciplina paterna*), while not undermining his need for other language about God that conveys the eternal and ineffable nature of the divine that is sought out by philosophers. Studer's article presents the modern scholar with a challenge to recognize that within the limits of an individual sermon, exegetical work, or treatise, Augustine's portrayal of God worked on various levels, depending on the question he was investigating and the audience to whom he was communicating. Even when Augustine uses the Roman concept of the father, the metaphor does not overpower the rich layers of biblical and philosophical ideas that also informed his understanding and experience of God. Any attempt to reduce Augustine to merely a patriarchal thinker is to miss the complexity of Augustine's thinking.[5]

Narrowing the focus from Augustine's broader conceptions of God's fatherhood in relation to the creation to the Father's place in the doctrine of the Trinity, one is reminded of Augustine's emphasis on the Father's monarchy, whereby the Son and Holy Spirit are described in terms of their relations of origin in the Father. It has already been shown from books 1–4 of *The Trinity* that his understanding of the Father stressed the divine persons' equality rather than the Son's and Holy Spirit's subordination to the Father. Furthermore, it also was noted that the argument in books 5–7 rejected any conception of the persons' relations that undermined their equality of power or goodness. In fact, the equality of the persons is of such an order, because of their unity of substance, that the idea of the Trinity can even be said to resemble a type of mutuality, rather than a patriarchal or totalitarian ordering. To develop this further we will consider a passage from Augustine's *Answer to Maximus*, where he explains his understanding of relations of origin in the Father with specific attention to the equality and goodness of the order of the divine persons. This builds upon the reasoning of books 5–7 of *The Trinity*. We will note that Augustine's understanding of the Son as the word of God does not entail that the Son is less than the Father because he receives commands from the Father, but rather that he is the Father's Word and command and is thereby equal to him. Building on this, Augustine then explains how the Word of God is related to the expression of God's love, which the Father and Son mutually have for each other.

In the *Answer to Maximus*, which we have had occasion to look at in the previous chapter, Augustine is following up a public debate with an Arian bishop (circa 427/8). The work comprises two books in which Augustine goes through the written record of the public disputation and expands his responses, which were apparently cut short due to Maximus's lengthy speeches. As such, the work is structured as a point-by-point response to the list of topics that were debated, rather than as a single logical argument or treatise. Some topics receive repeated comment, because they arose in different forms during the debate, and other topics are passed over briefly because they received less attention in the debate than other topics.[6] In this work Augustine repeats many of the arguments concerning the equality of substance that he had developed already in *The Trinity*.

In one part of a long discussion of the equality of substance, he specifically turns to the question of hierarchy.[7] Here Augustine defends the idea of Christ's equality with the Father, using several references to Gospel passages (John 1:41–42, 6:11, 9:4; Matthew 26:26; Mark 8:6) where Christ is presented as speaking of his own submission to the Father, and as doing things that are pleasing to the Father (John 8:29).

Maximus had argued that these passages pointed to the Son being an inferior substance.[8] Against this reading, Augustine invokes the rule of "the form of a servant" as the correct way to interpret such language.[9] Then, in further explanation of this rule, he specifies that one ought to be careful not to confound the begetter-begotten relationship with the sending of the Son in the form of a servant by the Father (though the Son is sent just as the Son is begotten, while the Father is not sent, just as the Father is not begotten).[10] As an alternative, Augustine shows that the distinction between the Son as begotten by the Father and the Son in the form of a servant (i.e., in the sending) is between that of creator and creature: the Son in the form of a servant is a creature who is less than God, because he is created by the Father, Son, and Holy Spirit; but the inequality of substance between a human being and God does not hold when one talks about the relationship of the Father and Son in the form of God. Augustine explains: "What Christian does not know that the Father sent and that the Son was sent? It was not fitting that the Begetter be sent by his Son, but that the Son be sent by his Begetter. This is not inequality of substance, but the order of nature; it does not mean that one existed before the other, but that one has his origin from the other. Hence, the one who was sent had to do the works of the one who sent him, but what works does the Father have that the Son does not have as well?"[11]

According to Augustine, the reason that Jesus attributes his works to the Father (John 11:41–42; John 9:4) is that "he is mindful of him from whom he has his origin."[12] This can be said in the form of a servant, where the inequality of substance requires such submission. The order is hierarchical because the dependence of the creature upon God is a constant dependence of a mutable, created existence upon the immutable, eternal source of creaturely being.[13] Nor does the Son forget from whom he is in the form of God. The order of nature between Father and Son is not the same as the order between God and creature, because the Son is begotten of the Father in eternity, in perfect equality with the Father. Hence, in his discussion of Jesus only doing works that are pleasing to the Father, Augustine invokes the equality of the Father and Son in the rhetorical question, "What things are pleasing to the Father that are not pleasing to the Son?"[14] If one does not keep in mind the implications of the eternal equality of Father and Son, then one will misunderstand the desire of Jesus to please the Father as a subordination of the Son to the Father in their eternal relationship. The doctrine of the Trinity helps guard against this mistake by investigating the meaning of the Son being begotten by the Father. This, of course, is spelled out in detail in *The Trinity*. Augustine is not reproducing the argument here again, but is reminding Maximus that the implications of trinitarian doctrine can then clarify how to read such scripture passages correctly.

Another way to look at the question of hierarchy is by considering Augustine's description of the Son using the traditional language of *logos* Christology, which he takes up in the next part of his *Answer to Maximus*.[15] He answers a charge concerning Jesus's statement in John 10:18, "I have the power to lay down my life, and I have the power to take it up again. I have this command from my Father. No one takes it from me, but I lay it down by myself, and I take it up again."[16] In the original debate, Maximus used this scriptural passage to claim that if Christ received power from the Father by the Father's command, then he must be less than the Father.[17] For how does one receive what he did not have, unless he is lacking something—in other words, unless he is inferior? Augustine answers this challenge by describing the begetting of the Son by the Father in terms of the Father speaking the Word: "All of God's commands are contained in the only Word of God. He gave them to the Son when he begot him; he did not give them later after he had begotten him as one who needed them."[18] The Son, the Word of God, is not commanded by the Father; rather, he is the Father's command—a command being a certain type of word. Augustine concludes from this (the Son as the Father's Word, or the Father's command) that he could not be subordinate to the Father, because the Father "begot one as great as he himself is, because he begot the true Son out of himself and begot him in the perfect fullness of divinity, not as one to be made perfect by an increase of age."[19] If the Son is the fullness of God—that is, is equal to God who is complete and indivisible divine substance—then he is not one who is in need of further words or commands, because he is already eternally perfect.[20]

Hierarchy and the Divine Substance

While the ordering of the Father and Son has logical consequences for how to speak about the Trinity, it does not provide a basis to claim that order means a difference of substance, or inferiority. The Son could receive the commands of the Father and yet be one substance with the Father, because he himself is the command of the Father. The Son, then, is not inferior to the Father in the sense of being below him in a hierarchy of beings, but is the same substance as the Father. The Son is not after the Father, but is eternally from the Father. Creatures are of a different, mutable, and temporal substance than the Father. They are wholly dependent upon God for their being. But the Son is equal to the Father, having what the Father has because they are one substance, whereas creatures need what they have from the Father because they are a created substance. The relation of Father and Son is one of equality. The relation of creature and God is one of hierarchy. Having set up this basic equality of the Father and the Son/Word, Augustine now carries his argument a step further when he introduces the importance of the relationship between the Father and the Son in terms of love.

Augustine again takes up the idea of the Word as the Father's command in *Answer to Maximus* when he addresses Maximus's interpretation of the love of the Son for the Father as less than the love of the Father for the Son.[21] In the debate, Maximus had argued that Jesus's statement of his love for the Father in John 14:31, "so that this world may know that I love the Father, and I do just as he has commanded me," should be interpreted as hierarchical, because the Son's love is known through his obedience to the Father's commands.[22] Augustine counters that the Son's love for the Father is not less than the Father's love for the Son. As in the previous argument about the Son being the Word of God, here he argues that the Son as incarnate Christ obeys the commands of the Father because he has taken on the form of a servant and is therefore less than the Father because of his created substance. But in the form of the eternal Son, he is not the recipient of the commands of the Father; rather, he is "the command of the Father, because he is the Word of the Father."[23] In this case, Augustine does not repeat the argument concerning how the Son's relationship to the Father (as the Word) is not subordinationist.[24] Instead, he notes that because the Son is the Father's command, which he has already shown to mean they are of an equal substance,[25] "you should also admit that the Father's love is no greater than the Son's . . . they love each other equally."[26] One love does not overpower or control the other's love. The reason why one should accept this is that "they are equal in the nature of their divinity."[27] To refer to the Son as God's Word or Command is to refer to the Son as the Father's equal in terms of their nature (substance).[28] Even though one can specify a logical order within the Godhead—the Son is from the Father—the love of the one person for the other is equal, because they have the same divine nature (substance). The divine love is not only from the Father to the Son, but also from the Son to the Father.

Augustine's conception of the reciprocity of love between the divine persons, with regard to the hierarchical problem, is summarized by Lewis Ayres: "The Father is *principium* in the Trinity but is the originator of a truly self-giving reciprocal communion, not a hierarchy of powers."[29] Ayres refers to the divine love as "reciprocal communion," and suggests that the Father's monarchy is where this communion of love originates.[30]

Following the reasoning used to explain the Father's monarchy in *The Trinity* 7.1–6, one understands that the Father is the source of the Son, but the Son is not a different or lesser substance than the Father. Everything the Father has in himself, the Son also has in himself, because he has the indivisible simplicity of the Father's substance himself, such that when one speaks of the Son loving the Father, he loves with a perfect love from the Father.[31] The love that the Father has for the Son, the Son also has in himself to give back to the Father, because he has it from the Father. The reason why the mutual love between the Father and Son effectively conveys their complete equality rests not only in Augustine's use of the traditional idea of the Father's monarchy to explain how the Son and the Holy Spirit have the one divine being that is from the Father. In *The Trinity* 7.6, Augustine points out how the very nature of God—God's substance—is love. Working with 1 John 4:8, 4:16, "God is love," Augustine argues that what the three persons hold in common because of their one substance—which the Son and Holy Spirit have from the Father—is in fact love.[32] There is not one who loves more than another, nor do any of the three persons offer to another love that is not reciprocated. The love they have is the love that each is in his very being, and which they mutually share with one another.

The love of each for the others—what Ayres called their "self-giving reciprocal communion"—is alluded to in Augustine's use of the word "cleaving" in *The Trinity* 6.9. This may also be translated as "union," in the sense of a husband and wife who are joined in marriage. That the Son and Father cleave to each other in "absolutely inseparable and eternal mutuality,"[33] and that they do so in the Holy Spirit who is their common charity,[34] describes how the three are related in their substance. Each is turned toward the others. Mutuality refers to a union of interdependence, not only as a description of their eternal being, but also as a moral example for the believer, to be imitated, since human relationships (and the human-divine relationship) are to be founded in the unity of love.[35]

Augustine calls the Holy Spirit the common love between the Father and the Son in the Godhead.[36] This can be a confusing statement if one understands by it that the Holy Spirit is the divine substance that the Father and the Son hold in common, as if the Holy Spirit's substance had an ontological priority over the Father and Son. However, a closer look at Augustine's explanation reveals that the Holy Spirit's unique identity as the "supreme charity conjoining Father and Son to each other"[37] serves to show the Spirit's equality of being with the Father and the Son.

Two steps show that the Spirit is equally God in the same way that the Father and the Son are one God. First, Augustine cites two passages—namley, from 1 Corinthians 3:16, "Do you not know that you are God's temple and the Spirit of God dwells in you?" and 6:19, "Do you not know that the temple of the Holy Spirit in you is your bodies? You have him from God and so you are not your own. For you have been bought with a great price. So glorify God in your body."[38] In regard to the first citation, Augustine states that only God dwells in his temple and that one would be mistaken to assume that the Holy Spirit dwells there as someone other than God, like a minister in a church of God. Rather, it is better to recognize the assumption of the passage, which is pointing toward the Holy Spirit actually being God. He then cites the second passage to buttress this idea. Calling the human body God's temple in 3:16, and then the Holy Spirit's temple in 6:19, leads Augustine to the conclusion that to glorify God is to glorify the Holy Spirit, because scripture reveals them both to be divine. However, the name "Holy Spirit" does not signify the Spirit's personhood as obviously and uniquely as do the names "Father" and "Son," because both words in the Spirit's name refer to what the three have in common in their divine substance (each is holy, each is spirit).[39] Augustine uses another name to help make clear the nature of the Holy Spirit—namely, "Gift."

We have noted that Augustine's identification of the Holy Spirit with the name "Gift" appears in book 4 of *The Trinity*. The giving of the Holy Spirit by the Father and also by the Son in the economy of salvation is taken by Augustine to be indicative of the eternal ordering of the Spirit, principally from the Father and also from the Son who is given by the Father to give the Holy Spirit. Then, in book 5.12–13, Augustine again finds several scriptural passages demonstrating the association of the Spirit with gift.[40] He notes that "gift," like "Holy Spirit," poses some difficulties, because it also does not correspond with the language of fatherhood and sonship, since "[we do] not say the Father of the Holy Spirit" or "the Son of the Holy Spirit"; however, while "we cannot say Father of the gift or Son of the gift . . . [to] get a correspondence here we [can] say gift of the giver and giver of the gift."[41] From the meaning of the name of Gift (which indicates the Spirit's procession from the Father and the Son) the name of Holy Spirit also can then be seen to be the name appropriate to the third person, because the third person is given uniquely from the Father and the Son. From this affirmation of the divinity of the Holy Spirit, Augustine's second step toward affirming the Holy Spirit's equality of being with the Father and the Son is to recognize that if the Holy Spirit is God, and God is love, then the Holy Spirit also is the love that the Father and the Son are in their substance.

Given that Augustine recognizes the Holy Spirit to be equally God with the Father and the Son, and therefore to be love, just as the Godhead is love, what does he mean when he calls the Spirit the "supreme charity conjoining Father and Son to each other"?[42] Turning to *The Trinity* 6.7, one finds Augustine's answer. First, he notes that the Holy Spirit is distinguished from each of them, because it is by his love that they are joined together.[43] The point, Augustine explains, is that the unity of the Father and the Son (in the Holy Spirit) is not something they participate in as if it were some sort of substance other than they are, but rather it is "of their own very being."[44] Their unity is in their gift of their own being to each other, which is the Holy Spirit. He then goes on to write, "Call this [communion of the Holy Spirit] friendship, if it helps, but a better word for it is charity. And this [the Holy Spirit/charity] too is substance because God is substance, and *God is charity* (1 John 4:8, 16), as it is written."[45] By the friendship/charity between the Father and the Son Augustine means to refer to the divine substance, as opposed to a quality of a substance, "because with God it is not a different thing to be, and to be great or good, etc."[46] This, of course, is justified on the grounds of divine simplicity, since the divine being is indivisible: God is what he has. Therefore, the love that is between the Father and the Son—the unity of the Spirit—is of the divine substance.[47]

One must keep in mind that the name "charity" is associated with the activity of the Holy Spirit in the economy of salvation in the same manner as "gift," because the Holy Spirit unites the believer to God by the gift of love,[48] and also keep in mind that if charity is a name for the third person, it also is equally true that the divine substance is charity, so that when one speaks of the persons' mutual love for one another one is speaking of their very being. Then one can see how Augustine does not use love as a passive concept to explain what unites the Father and Son,[49] but instead uses love in its active sense: the Holy Spirit (the subject of the loving) brings about the love of the Father and the Son by uniting them in their substance, because he himself is of the same substance. The apparent synonymy of friendship and love in *The Trinity* 6.7 indicates that the love between the Father and Son refers to a mutual turning of one toward the other through the Holy Spirit's actions, since friendship is not self-centered but other-centered as two persons cleave each other.[50] The Holy Spirit brings about the love of the Father and the Son. His action is efficacious because he himself is of the same loving substance as they are.

We have seen, then, how Augustine's doctrine of the Trinity is constructed along Nicene lines, following a pattern that begins with the Father as the beginning of the Son and Holy Spirit. He attempts to come to an understanding of the unity of substance and the distinctness of the persons through a careful analysis of scriptural statements concerning the divine activity of salvation. In doing this Augustine distances himself from modalism and from the challenges posed by the Arian opponents he encountered in his African context. By addressing both of these problematic trinitarian positions, Augustine shows both an awareness of their pitfalls for a robust conception of God and an ability to work within the context of a larger dialogue that is shaped by church tradition. Within the complex discussion of how the triune God is a single, simple, and perfect substance he also maintains a firm grasp on the Trinity as three persons who are united in mutual love. He does this not by philosophical speculation divorced from the economic work of the divine persons, but through a careful analysis of the economic activity of God, who is known to be a Trinity through the missions of the Son and the Holy Spirit, who unite the believer to God.

Before moving on to the discussion of how Augustine understands the Trinity as creator in Genesis, we can step back and see how Augustine's trinitarian thought relates to the types of theological criticism raised by modern theologians about the Western classical conception of the Trinity. The theological questions relate primarily to the coherence of Augustine's theology and the degree to which patriarchal and hierarchical ways of thinking infiltrated his understanding of God, in contrast to the positive resources that are provided in the scriptural and economic Trinitarianism that preceded him, especially in the Eastern churches.

Augustine, of course, did not think about the doctrine of the Trinity from the sociological perspective that Boff wants us to rethink traditional doctrine, nor does he build his doctrine of the Trinity upon purely speculative Neoplatonist assumptions, as Gunton implies in his critiques. In fact, when looking at his exposition of the formal nature of the doctrine of the Trinity, there is little indication in Augustine's writing that he has minimized the divine persons' equality of being by emphasizing God's "oneness" in either a hierarchical sense or an ontological sense. In fact, the divine relations are formulated according to the terms of the Son's and the Holy Spirit's work of redemption, as presented in scripture. For example, in book 4 of *The Trinity* Augustine explores the mediatory role of Christ as the central point from which to explore the importance of the equality of the persons of the Trinity for the Christian understanding of salvation (the Son's mission is a divine mission from the Father). Similarly, in book 6, he links the redemptive work of the Spirit (who unites believers to one another and to God) to the mutual love of the three persons. God's economy allows the believer to see how the relations of Father, Son, and Holy Spirit are relations of one divine being of love.

Augustine's doctrine of the Trinity does show that he was working with a sense of the personal nature of the trinitarian relations. As he explains how the missions reveal the eternal relationships and attempts to trace out the trinitarian logic that enables human speech about God the Trinity, he employs scriptural examples that allow him to identify the Son's relationship to the Father in terms of love and cleaving to the Father. Likewise, the Holy Spirit is related to the Father and Son through the language of friendship and charity. These eternal relations are deduced from the redemptive mission of the Son and Holy Spirit from the Father. Only when the Christian is united to God through cleaving to the Son in love and through the work of the gift of the Holy Spirit is it possible to know the eternal relationships that make those redemptive relationships possible. Just as knowing that the Son is sent from the Father provides insight into how one can conceive of the Son as begotten of the Father, so too the mutual love of the persons is a basis for understanding God's love for creation.

These redemptive relationships with the Trinity, and their foundational importance for Augustine's doctrine of the Trinity, cannot be said to promote the social or ecological values that are being called for today. There simply is not a one-to-one connection between Augustine's doctrine of the Trinity and modern problems. What can be said, though, is that his conception of God as Trinity arose out of a keen awareness that the relationships of human creatures to God exist through the work of the Son and the Holy Spirit. The eternal trinitarian relationships are not identical with human relationships, and so Augustine makes no such claims. He does, however, argue clearly for an understanding of the nature (substance) of the Trinity as love, so that the relationships of the divine persons are in their substance loving—though far beyond the finite conceptions of love that human beings can describe through experience.

This is a key step for assessing Augustine's trinitarian theology in the modern context. The theme of the eternal relationships of the divine persons is approached not through speculation, but through divine action in the world. The divine relationships may be eternal, and therefore beyond human comprehension, yet they are not inaccessible, since divine action in the world makes it possible to know God. The unity of God does not prevail in the development of Augustine's doctrine of the Trinity as a desire to make oneness more basic to God than threeness, but serves to ground his reflections on how to understand the divine nature (substance) and the three persons. In other words, there is a theme in Augustine's trinitarian theology that resembles modern concerns about interrelationality. The unity of the persons in the divine substance is the very unity of love they are. Their threeness is inseparable from their substance, and their substance is love. This trinitarian understanding of substance is derived from God's loving action of redemption through his Son and Holy Spirit in the divine economy.

By itself, though, Augustine's trinitarian thought cannot be carried into modern discussions, as if he were simply a prototypical social trinitarian. He did not understand the Trinity to be a society like human societies. If, however, we take seriously Gunton's claim that one's conception of God will have ramifications as to how one understands the creation, then it would seem that Augustine's trinitarian thought ought to be manifest in his doctrine of creation. Gunton has described Augustine's trinitarian theology as more monistic than trinitarian, and says that correspondingly Augustine's understanding of creation tends to downplay the goodness of the manifold particularity of creatures and emphasize instead the disembodied forms that humanity will inherit. Moreover, God's involvement in the creation is apparently extremely limited and revelatory of God's oneness (primarily as an overpowering will), rather than of the triune nature. Our analysis has provided an alternative account of Augustine, and would suggest that his understanding of the triune involvement in the creation should also be perceived differently. Augustine founds his knowledge of God's triunity upon divine action in the world, which suggests that he understands God to be involved in the creation and that Augustine values creation more than Gunton may have understood. Indeed, it may be that Augustine's description of God's creative work may also tell us about how Augustine viewed the goodness of creation.

The next step in our analysis of Augustine's thought will be to look at how he sees God and creation as they are portrayed in Chapter 1 of Genesis. One can see how in his *Literal Commentary on Genesis* he understands the Trinity as involved in a dynamic relationship with the creation. The trinitarian relations explained in these next chapters will clarify how Augustine thinks about God as creator, and also how he thinks about the way in which God's love is communicated to the creation. By delineating these aspects of his thought, we will be in a better position to judge his trinitarian understanding of creation in light of modern ecological themes about interrelationality.

Part II

In order to see the relationship that holds between Augustine's conception of God as Trinity and his understanding of creation, we need to examine how he interpreted God's work of creation and providence. We will be most concerned with his commentary, *The Literal Meaning of Genesis*. We will see how his description of the Trinity's act of creation influences his conception of the goodness of creation, and what the implications are for conceiving of a moral order within the creation. In Augustine's doctrine of creation, God is over the creation as the creator of everything from nothing, and as the Lord of creation who sustains its continuing existence. A key term in Augustine's description of the sustaining activity of God is the divine "governance" (*administratio*) of creation. It also can be translated as "lordship," "rule" or "dominion." These translations are provocative terms in this book, since the issue of God's monarchy in the Trinity and the divine rule over creation are problems that many theologians have with the classical understanding of the doctrine of God. The problem lies in the conception of rule as an authorization for the exercise of arbitrary power without concern for the interrelatedness of the creation. Surely a God who creates such a complex and interrelated creation would not be one who rules in the way of an absolute monarch. Such critiques diagnose the terminology of rule as arising less from an understanding of God, and more from using classical philosophical and political ideas that infiltrated the church's theology. It is often argued that the best alternative to such ideas as monarchy, rule, and governance is egalitarianism or some other "relational" description of reality. The Trinity is thought to be a positive example of such egalitarianism, and the Augustinian approach to the doctrine is usually rejected because of its supposed conception of God as an absolute monarch from which all hierarchies are derived. However, a case can be made that the concept of divine governance, understood within the context of Augustine's *The Literal Meaning*, does not promote a theological basis for conceiving of God's or humanity's relationship to nature in a dominating or totalitarian fashion.

In chapter 4 we will trace Augustine's explanation of divine creation as a threefold creative work in his interpretation of Genesis 1–2. Augustine developed, in his explanation of the doctrine of the Trinity, a conception of divine activity as a perfect, unified operation of the three persons. God's works are not individual actions by any one person of the Godhead, though the proper missions of the Son and Holy Spirit in the New Testament show particular persons at work in the world. The emphasis Augustine places upon the unity of divine action does not minimize the importance of each of the divine persons in the divine economy.

In chapter 5, the relationship of God to creation will be considered in terms of the creation's status under God's ongoing providential work of governing the creation. Augustine understands providence, from the creaturely perspective, to be the creation's dependence on God. This dependence is explained as the participation of creation in God through a creature's place within the order of creation according to its measure, number, and weight.

In chapter 6 we will consider the providential ordering of creatures in relation to each other, and how dominion—understood as the exercise of the image of God by Augustine—enables humanity to enjoy God's love and goodness in the proper use of creation. Augustine's idea of a hierarchy of creatures is presented in terms of ordered relationships by which different created substances participate in the divine being in different ways according to the creator's design. Nevertheless, all creatures have their own goodness, perfection, and beauty relative to other creatures. The realization of creaturely goodness in God limits the ways in which a hierarchical conception of the order of creation should be understood to affect the role of dominion, as does Augustine's recognition that while individual creatures are declared good by God, the creation in its entirety is called very good, with the implication that dominion is worked out in light of the goodness of the whole of creation as well as in each creature.

After this examination of Augustine's trinitarian doctrine of creation, we will be in a position to return to the original question that was raised in the introduction: Can Augustine's classical theology provide resources for a positive, religious view of the world, and a corresponding ground for ethical behavior? We will be able to bring together the themes we have gleaned from his theological reflections on God and creation and compare them to ecological themes as those have been interpreted in contemporary theology.

Chapter Four

The Trinitarian Founding of Creation

Just as Augustine founds his doctrine of the Trinity upon the divine economy of redemption revealed in scripture, so also is his doctrine of creation founded upon the divine work of creation as revealed in scripture. The biblical record is the authoritative basis for Augustine's discussion of the nature of God's creative work of calling the creation into existence and of divine providential government.[1] Just as the biblical record of God's redemptive activity was key to Augustine's conception of the doctrine of the Trinity, so the interpretation of the biblical account of divine creation also will involve a trinitarian account of God—for it is the same God who is shown in scripture to be creator and redeemer. If he cannot show that the threeness of God makes a difference for the understanding of God's work of creating the world in a foundational scriptural text about that work, then his whole trinitarian project would seemingly fall apart.[2]

In fact, a major concern for Augustine, as he reflects upon the creation of the world, is the triune nature of God's creative activity. The one act of creation by the Trinity reflects the unity of substance of the immanent Trinity, but just as importantly, the three persons mirror in the act of creation the same pattern of (nonhierarchical) relations that Augustine discussed in his explanation of relations of origin. Augustine shows this correspondence of immanent and economic relations in the opening verses of Genesis by describing God's creativity as his speaking, by the Word of God, and seeing, by the divine goodness of his Holy Spirit. In his discussion of the ongoing providential governance of creation, he again describes it as God's work in the Word and Holy Spirit. In this chapter we shall examine the correspondence of the divine activity of creation with the eternal trinitarian relations through a close examination of Augustine's thinking about the activity of divine creation in *The Literal Meaning*. In the first several pages of this chapter, we will consider the wider context of Augustine's writings about creation, and the general structure of Augustine's argument in *The Literal Meaning* about how God is described as creating in Genesis 1. Then, an examination of the trinitarian character of God's creation of the world will be explored in the rest of the chapter.

Augustine spent considerable time reflecting on the doctrine of creation, especially in taking account of the narrative in the opening chapters of Genesis. He wrote three independent commentaries on those chapters—*On Genesis: A Refutation of the Manichees*, the *Unfinished Literal Commentary on Genesis*, and *The Literal Meaning of Genesis*—as well as giving substantial space to Genesis 1–3 within other works.[3] Unlike his first commentary, *On Genesis: A Refutation of the Manichees* (which was an answer to the Manichaean claim that matter is inherently evil), his two attempts at literal commentaries, the *Unfinished Literal Commentary On Genesis* and *The Literal Meaning*,[4] did not give preference to an allegorical reading of scripture, but rather to a literal interpretation. For Augustine, a literal interpretation tries to understand the historical events as they have been "recounted" by the author—that is, as those events actually happened. An allegorical interpretation, for Augustine, is one that tries to understand the text's meaning, "when [it is] understood as being said figuratively,"[5] by which he means as the events recorded in a text are interpreted "according to future events which they foreshadow."[6]

Augustine did not understand the literal/historical interpretation of scripture to be opposed to an allegorical/figurative interpretation. Rather, he saw them as complementary perspectives on the meaning contained in scripture. For him, the Bible is a text that requires different interpretative tools to understand the fullness of its meaning as God intends it to be understood.[7] At times, the search for a literal meaning of the text even blurs into what seems to a modern reader like a figurative interpretation. For example, when Augustine attempts to understand the meaning of the creation of "light," "evening," and "morning" (Genesis 1:3–5) as they would exist prior to the creation of the sun and moon (Genesis 1:14–15), he does not simply dismiss the "corporeal" interpretation of light that the physical eyes can see;[8] instead, he reasons that a better interpretation would take into account the fact that such terms are not actually recounting the historical process of creating physically perceivable light, since that is said to have come later.[9] Therefore, he interprets the light of verses 3–5 as indicating the angelic knowledge of creation.[10] Such a metaphysical reading of the text is not taken by Augustine to be figurative; rather, it is a literal reading of the text within a wider scope than that implied by a merely corporeal signification of the words.[11]

At other times, both a literal and a figurative interpretation seem equally well suited to a text. For example, in *The Literal Meaning* 7.1.1, he notes that the story of Adam and Eve in paradise is sometimes interpreted historically and sometimes spiritually (e.g., as an account of how Adam is a type for Christ, as explained by Paul in Romans 5:14). He advocates an approach that sees both interpretations as valid, since God can relate things that are recounted of past events to future meanings. In this case, taking the description of Adam living with Eve as if it actually occurred and taking it as a future indication of Christ are not mutually exclusive choices when interpreting Genesis 2.

When we turn to Augustine's description of the trinitarian persons' creative activity in the opening verses of Genesis, we see that he tries to understand the narrated story in its own historical context (e.g., by explaining where the water was located that was gathered together so that dry land could appear in Genesis 1:9), but also how the context of Genesis 1 contains metaphysical truths (such as the description of the trinitarian persons' work using the language of God speaking and seeing). This is not merely spiritualizing a text that was intended to recount past historical processes. He views his interpretation as literal, because the Trinity reveals itself through the work of the Son and the Holy Spirit—which is a key part of the meaning of the doctrine of the Trinity. It is therefore reasonable for Augustine to ask how scripture recounts their creative presence in their initial creative work, just as they are present in their later redemptive work. The creative work of the Trinity can be literally recounted just as the history of the corporeal world can be recounted, though because the Trinity creates time and space along with everything else, the work of the Trinity transcends creation's mutable history.[12]

The Structure of *The Literal Meaning of Genesis*

The Literal Meaning is divided into three parts. In books 1–5, Augustine considers the creation narratives up to Genesis 2:6, and includes in this treatment the trinitarian framework of creation, an explanation of the days of creation, a proposed relationship between the two creation narratives, a discussion of God's providential government and rest, and a detailed explanation of the causal reasons by which creation unfolds in its historical development. In books 6–11, among other things, he treats the creation of humanity, original sin, the origin of the soul, the relationship between men and women—especially in marriage—and the relationship between spiritual bodies and natural bodies. Book 12 is an essay on the visions of paradise, which he added after he completed the original commentary.[13]

Books 1–5 will be the primary focus for our analysis, as they provide a concentrated reflection on how God the Father creates through his Word and the divine goodness of the Holy Spirit. Augustine's explanation of this trinitarian activity also forms the basis for his understanding of the moral implications of human action in the creation: since all that the trinitarian God creates is made according to the purposes of divine goodness and love, the ends of creatures are to conform to the nature of this goodness and love. The exercise of human action, including dominion, is meant to conform to this moral nature of God's creation. In chapters 5 and 6 we will take up this question of the moral character of human activity more fully, especially the question of how the dominion exercised by human beings is related to God's trinitarian image in them.

Before considering Augustine's conception of the trinitarian creation in Genesis 1, we will look briefly at the overall structure of Augustine's argument in the first five books of *The Literal Meaning*. Augustine recognized two distinct narratives in Genesis 1–3, the first ending with the description of God's rest in Genesis 2:3 and the second beginning with the statement in 2:4a, "This is the book of the creation of heaven and earth when day was made."[14] He suggests that this introduction to the second narrative of creation in 2:4 confirms that the seven days described in Genesis 1 were seven human days that were created simultaneously in one act, signified in the phrase "when day was made," because God's work of creation is indivisible.[15] Thus, Augustine interprets God's creative work as it is described in Genesis 1, including the creation of time, from a metaphysical perspective that situates those works "before" (prior to) human historical perception—namely, during the creation of the day in which the seven days are all included.[16] Augustine's interpretation of Genesis 1 in the first four books of *The Literal Meaning* is literal in terms of the metaphysical reality being described. From Genesis 2:4ff., Augustine believes, the creation narrative is to be understood as the historical explanation of creation as it actually unfolded in humanly perceived time (history). Thus, when he takes up Genesis 2–3 in *The Literal Meaning* 6–11, he interprets the text according to the idea of literal interpretation that a modern reader might expect, because he is then dealing with the historical narrative of the first human beings as they existed in time and space.

The first four books of Augustine's commentary describe creation according to metaphysical reality. He does not doubt that there were actually seven days of creation, or that the sequence of creatures that are made by God happened in the order described in Genesis 1. So, he also discusses how these days must have unfolded in time, given the scientific knowledge he had available to him. However, from the perspective of a creation that is brought into existence by an eternal creator, the seven days were created simultaneously, which is different from humanly perceived historical reality of how seven days would progress, and so the metaphysical perspective must also be employed.

In Augustine's interpretation of Genesis 1, he develops his understanding of God's activity in relation to creation according to two phases: the founding of creation and its governance.[17] Augustine does not distinguish the two phases by means of a limited set of terms, but instead employs a variety of terms within the general framework of the two phases, some of which, as we shall see, occasionally are used in both of the phases for different purposes. The first phase is God's work of bringing creation into existence from nothing, which we will refer to throughout this book as the founding of creation,[18] and which he explains in books 1–3 of *The Literal Meaning*. The second phase is God's ongoing governance of and care for creation once it has been brought into existence, which he explains in books 4–11 of *The Literal Meaning*. His concept of divine governance, as we shall see, is based on the statement of Genesis 2.2–3., where God is said to have rested on the seventh day. Augustine asks how it is that God is said to rest there, but also is said to work again in Genesis 2:6ff., and also is said to work in John 5:17, where Jesus claims that "My Father works even until now, and I work."[19] To solve this apparent puzzle, he suggests, one must distinguish between God's work as creator (i.e., the founding) and God's ongoing work of governing the creation as it unfolds in history.[20] Augustine's discussion of God's governance allows him to affirm that God never ceases to care for the creation that he has made.

The first phase, the founding of creation, is divided into two stages by Augustine. The first stage is the establishment of all creatures from nothing (*creatio ex nihilo*) in God's Word (that is, creatures as the "eternal reasons," as he calls them at 4.24.41). This we might think of as his idea of creation from nothing proper. The second stage is the conversion (also termed perfection) of creatures from the formless void mentioned in Genesis 1:2—that is, from their state as ideas in the Word, to their being actual substantial creatures in their material and spiritual forms.[21] He thinks of the establishment and conversion of creatures in the six days of creation as simultaneous and nontemporal, inasmuch as God transcends time and creates from nothing.[22] Establishment and conversion should be treated as nontemporal, causal stages that aid Augustine as he attempts to discuss clearly God's indivisible work of creating.[23]

Augustine does not divide the second phase, the governance of creation, into stages. However, he does employ the language of conversion and perfecting in his discussion of this phase of God's activity, especially when he is considering the role of the Holy Spirit in it.[24] Before we turn to the discussion of the triune structure of God's calling of creation into existence from nothing and its conversion from the formless void, the topic of this chapter, let me briefly lay out what is entailed in Augustine's concept of divine providence. Part of the discussion of God's governance in book 4 has to do with how creatures are manifest in different times and spaces, even though God creates nothing new after the seventh day. As we have noted, Augustine thinks that the whole of creation—including time—was founded and converted simultaneously and from nothing. However, not all creatures were immediately present in their material bodies—their conversion from ideas in the Word to physical creatures is according to the timing set out by God in the beginning. Creatures were created at once in the Word of God as "eternal reasons" and were planted in the world (at its conversion from the formless void) as "causal reasons," much like seeds that are sown in the ground. It is out of these "causal reasons" that all things take their shape in time and space.[25] God's governance, then, includes the appearance of creatures at their proper times. The discussion in *The Literal Meaning* 6–11 of Genesis 2–3 is a continuation of Augustine's doctrine of creation, because it is a treatment of how God never ceases from governing the creation, even though he rests from creating—that is, from establishing and converting anything new.[26] The governance of creation is essential, since all creatures depend on God for their being. If God did not continue to govern creation, it would cease to be by descending back into the chaos of the formless void.[27] The order of creation is maintained through God's governance. The governing of creation will be considered more fully in the next chapter in terms of the creation's participation in God. In this chapter the triune structure of God's work of bringing creation into existence from nothing—that is, the establishment and conversion of creation—will be taken up.[28]

As we examine more closely in the remainder of this chapter how Augustine describes God's work as creator, we will see that his trinitarian model for creation is patterned on the same structure as his conception of the inner trinitarian relations, which he derived from the revelation of God in the divine economy. Furthermore, by maintaining a conception of God as one, expressed in terms of God's perfect simplicity and indivisible nature (substance), he understands the divine activity of bringing creation into existence to be one action rather than three actions. The three, in their threeness, are God. Yet, there is only one God who acts, not three gods. The Father speaking his Word, the Son, creates by calling the creation into being from nothing. The Father's Son carries out the Father's will to create and brings it toward its fulfillment. Likewise, the Father sees the goodness of creation, in which he delights, through his Holy Spirit. The Holy Spirit loves creatures and perfects them in accordance with the forms that the Word gives them. Just as the Spirit's charity in the Trinity unites the Father and Son in the bond of love, so in creation the Spirit is the fulfillment of the Father and Son's work.

In a particularly rich passage from book 1, Augustine lays out a summary of why he understands the establishment and conversion of creation to be triune in shape, which, as we have already argued, was a necessary part of his commitment to the authority of scripture that formed the basis for his doctrine of the Trinity. The rest of the chapter will be devoted to an analysis of this passage, drawing on other parts of *The Literal Meaning* to explicate its meaning:

> It is the Blessed Trinity that is represented as creating. For, when Scripture says, *In the beginning God created heaven and earth*, by the name of "God" we understand the Father, and by the name of "Beginning," the Son, who is the Beginning, not for the Father, but first and foremost for the spiritual beings He has created and then also for all creatures; and when Scripture says, *And the Spirit of God was stirring above the water*, we recognize a complete enumeration of the Trinity. So in the conversion and in the perfecting of creatures by which their species are separated in due order, the Blessed Trinity is likewise represented: the Word and the Father of the Word, as indicated in the statement, *God said*; and then the Divine Goodness, by which God finds pleasure in all the limited perfections of his creatures, which please Him, as indicated by the words, *God saw that it was good*.[29]

Augustine begins by noting that the trinitarian shape of creation is "represented" in the text of Genesis itself;[30] he says Genesis 1:1–4 itself represents the Trinity in the twofold establishment and conversion of creation. The first stage of God's creative activity, beginning with the phrase "For, when Scripture says" and ending with the statement "we recognize a complete enumeration of the Trinity," is the establishment of creation from nothing. The second stage of the act, presented in the text beginning with the phrase "So in the conversion and perfecting of creatures" and running to the end of the quotation, refers to the conversion of creatures from their form as eternal ideas in the Word to their own substantial existences in the universe as they are shaped out of the formless matter. These two stages of triune creativity (in the founding of the creation) explain how the Trinity brings about the creation.

We will proceed with our examination of this passage by looking at how Augustine names each of the three persons in the establishment and conversion of creation, and then turn to a fuller explanation of how Augustine understands the establishment and conversion of the creation to take place. We will see that the Father as God, the Son as beginning, and the Holy Spirit as hovering over the deep together effect the creative triune act of bringing about the creation through its two aspects of establishment and conversion.

Naming the Trinity in Genesis 1

Augustine sees in Genesis 1:1, "In the beginning God created heaven and earth," a reference to both the Father and the Son as establishing the creation from nothing. The subject of the sentence, God, is the name of the Father in the language of trinitarian doctrine.[31] Usually, one should understand the Father when Augustine refers to God.[32] Here, creation originates in the Father. The Father who is the source of the Son and the Holy Spirit in the Trinity and the Father who is the origin of creation are both similar and dissimilar to each other. The logical understanding of the inner trinitarian relationships reveals the Father as the source that itself has no beginning, while the Son is always from the Father and the Holy Spirit is from the Father principally and through the Son.[33] A similar trinitarian pattern holds here, where the creation's source is the Father who creates all creatures from nothing through his coeternal Son and Holy Spirit. However, if the creation has its origin in the Father, the Father's origination of the creation also is dissimilar to his origination of the Son and Holy Spirit. For, unlike the divine persons who are coeternal and equal with the Father, the creation is made from nothing and is not equal to him.

Augustine next argues that the remaining phrase of Genesis 1:1, "in the beginning," refers to the Son. This means that God the Father created everything in his Son (who is the beginning). He clarifies how the Son is understood as beginning in relation to God the Father when he writes, "[B]y the name of Beginning, [we understand] the Son, who is the Beginning, not for the Father, but first and foremost for the spiritual beings He has created and then also for all creatures."[34] Augustine attributes to the Son the name "Beginning" not in reference to the inner trinitarian relations, but rather in reference to the Son's relationship to creation.[35] The name "Beginning" refers to how God creates everything in his Son. This identification of the name of the Son with the name "Beginning" is not self-evident from the text of Genesis alone, but is justified by what Augustine finds said about divine creation in the Johannine prologue.[36] He notes John's claim that everything is created through the divine Word of God, who is the coeternal Son of the Father and not a creature of the Father.[37] The Son with the Father is at the beginning of all created things.[38] For Augustine, this suggests that the opening phrase of Genesis ("In the beginning") refers both to the Word of God and (indirectly) to the Father, since it is through God's Word that all is created, with God being the Father. If the Word is the Son, following John 1:2, then it follows that the "Beginning" of Genesis 1:1, in which everything is created by God, is also a reference to the Word, because the "Beginning" is set out as the means by which God the Father created everything—there is nothing that is not created in the Beginning. Anything not created in the Beginning is eternal and divine.

Similarly, Augustine identifies the Father and the Son in the work of conversion by explaining the phrase "God said" as referring to "the Word and the Father of the Word."[39] God is the Father, and this time, the Son is identified with the verb "said." What is "said," of course, is the Word that the Father speaks from eternity, the Word who is his Son.

Augustine makes the connection between the Spirit of God and the Holy Spirit in his interpretation of Genesis 1:2 when he writes, "[A]nd when Scripture says, *And the Spirit of God was stirring above the water*, we recognise a complete enumeration of the Trinity."[40] He goes one step further, though, in the next section, on the conversion of creatures, and identifies the Holy Spirit with God's love and goodness.[41] The identification of the Spirit with love and goodness also is made in relation to the establishment of creation. For example, in *The Literal Meaning* 1.7.13, he writes, "There is mention of the Spirit of God [*stirring above the water*], whereby the Divine Goodness and Love are to be understood." This explicitly links the Holy Spirit to the names Goodness and Love. Augustine continues in 1.7.13 to note that creaturely "love is generally needy and poor, so that its outpouring makes it subordinate to the objects that it loves." However, God's creative works are not to be taken as an indication of God's need for something to love, because God has no need of anything outside himself. To describe the Spirit as goodness and love, in light of this divine self-sufficiency, requires that the Holy Spirit be described as stirring above the creation, so as to indicate that God's love is poured out, or given, "out of the largeness of his bounty." God's love is not needy, but overflows from the divine being.

In another passage Augustine writes, "Certainly *the Spirit of God was stirring* above this creation. For all that He had begun and had yet to form and perfect lay subject to the good will of the creator. . . ."[42] The creator (the Father) has subjected the creation to his good will, which is an explanation of Genesis 1:2 about the Spirit of God stirring above the deep. Just prior to this passage, Augustine indicates that he understands the action of stirring above the deep also to designate the subjection of creation to God. When speaking of the creation being subject to the "good will of the creator" because the creation is under God's Spirit, Augustine is indicating that God's will is the communication of divine love (i.e., the bestowal of goodness upon the creation). The Holy Spirit is that divine will and love that bestows divine goodness upon creatures.[43] Creaturely existence is entirely dependent upon God, and there is no good thing except that which is subject to the divine goodness of the Spirit.

The naming of the Trinity in Genesis 1 is not simply an exercise in theological speculation for Augustine, as if he were testing his theory of the Trinity on a difficult text. Because he is convinced of the theological necessity of belief in the Trinity, he believes that God's activity must always be triune in shape. He does not simply identify the Trinity and then move on to talk about God's creativity without further reference to the Trinity. Rather, he enumerates the three in Genesis in order to be able to show the significance of the trinitarian nature of God for creation. In the next two sections we will look at how Augustine's discussion of the establishment and conversion of creation is elaborated and justified at greater length throughout the opening books of *The Literal Meaning*, and we will pay special attention to the trinitarian implications that the conversion of creatures has for his doctrine of creation. First, we will consider the establishment of the creation from nothing in the eternal reasons, and then how the founding phase is completed in the conversion of the eternal reasons into their material forms.

How the Trinity Founds the Creation

Creation originates because the Father forms it through the Son, his Word, and the Holy Spirit, his goodness, love, and will. The resultant creation is mutable in its spiritual and physical reality, thus distinguishing the creation from the immutable and perfect being of the Trinity.[44] Moreover, creation's dependence upon God is contrasted with God's independence from anything outside of the divine being.[45] The dependence of creation upon God is understood by Augustine to be the result of the creation not having existed apart from God's creative activity. For example, he writes, "[O]ur Catholic faith declares, and right reason teaches, that there could not have existed any matter of anything whatsoever unless it came from God."[46] Creaturely existence comes from God alone, not from some prior existing matter.

Returning again to the quotation from *The Literal Meaning* 1.6.12, we can consider how each of the divine persons is engaged in the establishment of the creation from nothing. According to Augustine, "[W]hen Scripture says, *In the beginning God created heaven and earth*, by the name of 'God' we understand the Father."[47] Genesis 1:1 does not refer to the creation of the physical earth and sky, for Augustine, but to the creation of spiritual and physical reality. Thus, as he explains elsewhere in *The Literal Meaning*, "by the expression 'heaven' we must understand a spiritual created work already formed and perfected, which is, as it were, the heaven of this heaven which is the loftiest in the material world."[48] This is a reference to the angelic realm, which is perfected to a degree greater than the physical world, just as the physical heaven ("sky," or "firmament") is used by human beings to refer metaphorically to that which is above and greater than the earth. Therefore, the spiritual realm is the "heavens of this heaven."[49] What this amounts to, for Augustine, is the idea that the Father is the creator of everything, both spiritual and physical. He will unpack this idea more when he turns to the next clause in 1.6.12, where he explains his understanding of everything being created in the Word of God.

That Augustine understands "Beginning" as a reference to the Son has already been noted. The Son is the "Beginning" in relation to the establishment of the spiritual and material creation, but not a beginning in relation to the Father (who is without beginning). He writes, "And by the name of 'Beginning,' [we understand] the Son, who is the Beginning . . . first and foremost for the spiritual beings He has created and then also for all creatures."[50] The creation is divided into two parts. The spiritual beings are the angels, and "all creatures" refers to the physical creation.

By explaining the Son's establishment of the creation according to spiritual and physical beings, Augustine is indicating that there is an order to the creation—the angels are the "first and foremost" beings that the Son creates. He thinks that Genesis 1:1 states a specific order in which God created: first was the heavenly or spiritual realm, and then the earthly or physical realm. Augustine specifies that the spiritual realm has a certain priority over the physical realm in the Father's and Son's establishment of them.[51] However, the division of the creation into spiritual and physical realms at their establishment, whereby the spiritual realm occupies a place above the physical realm, is not meant to denigrate the physical creation. It seems more probable that Augustine understands the ordering to refer to the degree of perfection that a created substance has. The mutability of a spiritual substance, like an angel or the soul, is limited to temporal change only, while a physical substance is subject to both temporal and spatial change. When the two are compared, Augustine finds that there is more perfection in a spiritual substance than a bodily substance, because the spiritual is subject to less change than the physical: "He established the spiritual creation above the corporeal, because the spiritual is changeable only in time, but the corporeal is changeable in time and place."[52] The immutable and eternal Son, who is the beginning of both the spiritual and the physical creation, is above both of them as the unchanging, absolute source of their being.

Augustine identifies the Holy Spirit in Genesis 1:2, where the Spirit is mentioned explicitly, "And the Spirit of God was stirring above the water." With this identification, he concludes that "we recognize a complete enumeration of the Trinity" in the work of establishing the creation.[53] Augustine explains the Holy Spirit's establishing work in two ways. First, in 1.5.11, he says that the reference to the Holy Spirit being *above* the creation is meant to convey the idea that the creation is "subject to the good will of the Creator." For the creation to be subject to the Holy Spirit means that creation is dependent on the Holy Spirit. The "good will of the creator" is the stirring presence of the Holy Spirit, who is the basis from which created matter is established "according to its capacity."[54] Created matter attains a certain capacity, or measure of being, from the Holy Spirit who stirs above it. In other words, the Holy Spirit is the will of God, bringing the creation to its fulfillment.

The second point Augustine makes about the Spirit "stirring above the water" concerns the meaning of "stirring."[55] He notes that whereas Greek and Latin translations of Genesis 1:2 refer to "stirring" (*superferebatur*), the Syriac version calls it "brooding" (translated into Latin as *fovebat*). This is a more suggestive term, pointing to how a bird will brood over its eggs, warming them so that the chicks inside may develop "through an affection similar to that of love."[56] Accordingly, he substitutes the idea of "brooding" for "stirring over," though he continues to use the word "stirring." For Augustine, the insight provided by the idea of brooding concerns the Spirit's fostering love, which creates the conditions for creation to attain the capacity to reflect the divine goodness and love that God willed for it through its participation in the "unchangeable and fixed exemplars of His coeternal Word and . . . His equally coeternal Holy Spirit."[57] In support of this he alludes to Luke 13:34, where Christ spoke of gathering Jerusalem under his wings just as a hen gathers her young, so as to help them grow to maturity.[58] The Holy Spirit's work in establishing the creation is to create in creatures the capacity for love—by brooding over them like a hen.[59] This divine love and support received from the Holy Spirit at the establishment of the creation is what creatures depend upon for their existence and development. Of course, creating in the creature a capacity for love, no more than creaturely existence and development themselves, is not solely the work of the Holy Spirit. God is at work in his Word, as well as in his Holy Spirit.[60] To speak of the Holy Spirit creating the capacity for love in creatures is to speak of the Father's work. And to speak of the Father's work is to speak of the Son's, since the Father "says everything" (meaning the Father's work) through his Word.[61] Moreover, remembering our discussion in chapter 2 of the unity of the Trinity in terms of a simple, indivisible substance, one would say that the Trinity works one divine action, not three discrete actions.

The establishment of everything by the Father in his Word and through the Holy Spirit is from nothing. We noted earlier that the general pattern of creation that Augustine develops begins with the creatures existing in the Word of God as eternal reasons, which are then formed into the creatures that now exist in created reality.[62] The establishment of substantial creatures, and their separation from the formless void in the conversion and perfection of creatures, is expressed in scripture as happening over a period of seven days. As mentioned, Augustine understood the seven human days to have been created all at once by God,[63] because "both the thing made and the matter from which it was made were created together."[64] What appears as two causal stages—the establishment of everything from nothing and the conversion and perfection of individual creatures from unformed matter—are temporally simultaneous (because time is a creature shaped from this unformed matter as well, as we have noted above), and also form one creative action by the Trinity.

As we now turn to a discussion of the conversion and perfection of creatures, we will see that Augustine understands the trinitarian activity of conversion to overlap with his understanding of the establishment of creation. This is so because the two stages are not two discrete activities carried out by the Trinity, with different aims and means of achieving those aims. Rather, the two stages are one divine activity that results in the making of a good creation. The work of conversion is not different from the work of establishment, but each is a mode of one creative work, so that the same trinitarian presence carries through both stages. In presenting God's activity as it is described in Genesis 1 as two stages, Augustine is able to work out the details of how the spiritual and physical creation comes into being in such manner that the order described in Genesis 1 is explained cogently. But by keeping the trinitarian nature of God's creative work in his explanation of the stages, he is also able to show that the stages form a unity that is both complex (that is, one can discern stages), and simple (that is, because the trinitarian persons carry out one activity that is indivisible, just as their nature or substance is indivisible). What is begun by the Trinity in the establishment of creatures from nothing is carried through to its divinely appointed ends in the conversion of those creatures into their manifold particularities. After we describe the conversion of creatures, we will then be in a position to consider at greater length how the two stages form a unity.

How the Trinity Converts and Perfects Creatures

The trinitarian conversion and perfection of creatures, as Augustine describes them in *The Literal Meaning* 1.6.12, covers Genesis 1:3–2:3. What he means is the conversion of creatures from the formless void mentioned in Genesis 1:3 to their particular, substantial forms over the six days of creation. He describes, it will be recalled, the trinitarian shape of the conversion and perfection of creatures in this way: "So in the conversion and in the perfecting of creatures by which their species are separated in due order, the Blessed Trinity is likewise represented: the Word and the Father of the Word, as indicated in the statement, *God said*; and then the Divine Goodness, by which God finds pleasure in all the limited perfections of his creatures, which please Him, as indicated by the words, *God saw that it was good*."[65] Specifically, the Trinity works "in the conversion and in the perfecting of creatures by which their species are separated in due order." As creatures are converted from the unformed matter, so that each creature is separated from the others and made distinct from the others, it is the Trinity shaping them.[66]

Before we examine the Trinity's work of converting and perfecting creatures, we need to establish what Augustine means by conversion and perfection. Augustine calls the shaping of each creature out of the formless matter a "conversion," because the creature is given its substantial form from the formless matter, and is thereby said to be perfected in its existence. For a spiritual or physical substance not to exist in the spiritual or physical form that it is intended for is to exist in an unconverted or imperfect state, which the formless void represents.[67]

As will be seen below in connection with the work of the Word of God, the process of conversion and perfection not only refers to the initial work of forming the creature from the formless void, but also to how conversion from formlessness is an ongoing work, since the creature is continually being "called back" to God by the Word.[68] Conversion and perfection are a continuing work, because a mutable creature "tends to nothingness,"[69] by which Augustine means it has a tendency to turn away from God, who is the source of creaturely being and form in the establishment of creation. Creation of the material forms from the formless matter is a "calling back," because the tendency to fall back into formless imperfection and nonexistence requires creatures constantly to depend on God's Word, who calls to them.[70]

A similar understanding of conversion and perfection as continuous work is related to the Holy Spirit by Augustine. Creatures are said to be perfected as God establishes and maintains them in their divinely intended individual forms, so that they rest in the "good will of the creator."[71] This is the Spirit's "loving endorsement of creation. . . . The Spirit's recognition of the goodness of all things reflects the Divine goodness which both wills and sustains created reality."[72] Above, we discussed how the Holy Spirit is part of the divine work of giving creatures their form according to their Beginning. Here, the perfecting work of the Holy Spirit is understood to maintain that form, just as being converted according to the Word also is a continual process.

Augustine names the Father and the Word together in the conversion of creatures, describing the Son as the speech by which the Father creates. He identifies the Father and the Word of the Father in Genesis 1:3, where he understands them to be "indicated in the statement, 'God said.' "[73] As above, in our discussion of the establishment of the creation, God is the Father and the source from which creation is made, and the Son is the Word that God speaks.[74] In the conversion and perfection of creatures in the six days, the Father and Son are presented as calling creatures into their particular forms on the appropriate day. In putting forward this interpretation of how the Father and Son are involved in the conversion of creatures, Augustine suggests that when the text of Genesis repeats the phrase "And God said, 'Let there be *x*' " for each day of creation, it does not mean that God spoke the words "Let there be *x*" time and again, but rather that "He begot one Word in whom He said all before the several works were made."[75]

What happens when the Father speaks "Let there be *x*" each day? God and his Word create each creature according to its proper form by converting unformed matter so that it imitates the Word, who in his relationship to the creature is the creature's exemplar.[76] Augustine defines the meaning of imitation in this way: "[I]t is when it [the creature] turns, everything in the way suited to its kind, to that which truly and always is, to the creator, that is to say of its own being, that it really imitates the form of the Word which always and unchangingly adheres to the Father, and receives its own form, and becomes a perfect, complete creature."[77] If a creature is not to tend toward nothingness, then it must turn—that is, be converted—to the creator of its being, so that it can receive its form. The creature is said to be turned toward, and receive form from, its creator, when it imitates the "form of the [Father's] Word." The Word's form is its unchanging adherence to its Father. Therefore, when the creature turns toward the Word in imitation of the Word's unity with the Father, it is said to receive its proper form, because by its turning toward the Word it is adhering to the Word. Just as the Word is eternally turned toward and joined to its Father, so the creature must be turned toward and joined with its creator, who is the Word of the Father. In saying this, Augustine understands the creature to be converted to its proper form. The Word gives existence to creatures by calling them into being from nothing and establishing them in proper forms, thus ensuring that the Father's creation takes shape according to the Father's will. The Word can do this because he is the command of the Father, spoken to the creation. The perfection of the creature is its conversion to its proper form by the Word, whose form of unity with the Father the creature imitates by being shaped by the Father's command, which is the Son.[78] It is in this sense of the Son being the Father's Word that creatures are called back to their proper form from the formless void.

The Holy Spirit's role in the conversion of creatures is important to Augustine's explanation of Genesis 1, and he discusses the Spirit's work at length as the divine goodness by which the Father sees the creation is good. After Augustine has identified the Father and Son in the phrase "God said," he then discusses how, in Genesis 1:3–2:3, the Holy Spirit is the ". . . Divine Goodness, by which God finds pleasure in all the limited perfections of his creatures, which please Him, as indicated by the words, *God saw that it was good*."[79] Augustine names the Holy Spirit as "Divine Goodness" in this quotation. That Augustine intends the reader to understand that the Holy Spirit is signified by the phrase "Divine Goodness" is shown by his making it the third point in his enumeration of the creative work of the Trinity in the conversion and perfection of creatures. Then, a few lines later, he makes the identification more explicit when he writes that "when there is mention of the Spirit of God . . . the Divine Goodness and Love are to be understood."[80] Augustine intends the references to love and goodness in *The Literal Meaning* to apply specifically to the Holy Spirit, as will now be shown.

The divine goodness is the means by which "God [the Father] finds pleasure in all the limited perfections of his creatures."[81] What is here translated as 'limited' is the Latin word *modulo*, which means a small or limited measure of something. The phrase "limited perfections" is a reference to the fact that God creates finite beings, whose very condition for existence is dependent upon the measure, number, and weight that he gives them, each according to the kind of being it is.[82] If God is the supreme good by which all other goods are created,[83] then the creatures God creates will share in that goodness according to the limits established by God.[84] God finds pleasure in their limited perfections because they embody the goodness that is from God "according to the largeness of His bounty."[85] In other words, God creates good creatures with a generous love, and enjoys the degrees of goodness exemplified in his creatures. We noted earlier how Augustine contrasts this divine love for creatures with creaturely love that "is generally needy and poor, so that its outpouring makes it subordinate to the objects that it loves."[86] God does not create out of need for love (which is perfect in God), but loves out of delight for the goodness of things that he creates by his generosity, which overflows as the work of creation.

What does the Holy Spirit do to make the creation's limited perfections a pleasure to the Father? According to Augustine, an indication of the work of the Holy Spirit in the conversion and perfection of creatures is found in Genesis 1:4, "God saw that it was good."[87] Augustine interprets the phrase "it was good" as a reference to the Holy Spirit, because it is through the Holy Spirit's work of converting and perfecting the creation's limited goodness that creation is seen by the Father to be good. This reflects the earlier discussion of the Holy Spirit's role in the establishment of the creation from nothing, where it was suggested that the Spirit creates in creatures their capacity for love (i.e., their proper rest in God). In both the establishment and the conversion of creatures, the Holy Spirit is the means by which creation is perfected, in order to exemplify the goodness it was created for by God.[88]

Later in book 2, Augustine again takes up the idea of God's finding "pleasure" in the goodness of creation when he writes, "Moreover, by the words, *And God saw that it was good*, we should understand that the Divine Goodness was pleased in the work of creation; and thus the work which God was pleased to make would continue in its existence as a creature, as indicated by the words, *The Spirit of God was stirring above the water*."[89] The divine goodness is the Holy Spirit, the one who is pleased with the work of creation that the Father creates through his Word. The Spirit's pleasure is also the way by which God the Father continues to bestow existence upon the creature. Elsewhere, Augustine specifies that the Father's pleasure in the creation is "in keeping with the benevolence by which He was pleased to create them."[90] The Father creates by means of his benevolence (goodness), who is the Holy Spirit. The continued bestowal of existence upon the creation is a free and generous act of love by God the Father, carried out by the Spirit stirring over the waters so that they might bring forth a creation that is a pleasure for God.[91]

One also finds a similar idea of the Holy Spirit described in terms of sight and goodness in *The Confessions* 13.28.43–13.31.46, where Augustine discusses the phrase "and God saw that it was very good" in Genesis 1:31. Augustine begins by affirming that each thing God the Father has made is good and that all things taken together are very good (*Confessions* 28.43). Augustine then goes on to draw a parallel between God's seeing and his own seeing. He says, addressing God, "I see those things which through my Spirit you see, just as I also say the things which through my Spirit you say" (*Confessions* 29.44). Here, alluding to how Genesis 1:31 describes God as seeing all things to be very good, Augustine now claims that what God sees is also through the Holy Spirit. We know that he means it is the Holy Spirit by which he sees, and not simply his own spirit, because it also is the Spirit by which God sees and speaks. For Augustine, God would not see or speak through a creature's mutable spirit, but through his coeternal Holy Spirit.

In *Confessions* 13.30.45, Augustine clarifies his understanding of how creatures are able to see the goodness of the creation because of the Spirit's perfecting work. There he contrasts the claim of Genesis 1:31 with the Manichaean view, which is a different (and for Augustine, false) understanding of the creation. The Manichaeans contend that not all things are created by God, and not all things are good in their original creation, because some things are created by an evil power that exists in opposition to God. The result is that the Manichaeans "do not see your works with the help of your Spirit and do not recognise you in them" (30.45). Here seeing the works of creation is the ability to recognize them for what they are—namely, good, because they are created by a good God. Seeing the goodness of the creation is possible because one's perception is conditioned by the work of the Holy Spirit, who enables such recognition. Seeing, then, is not simply a physical perception of the creation, but is an informed understanding of what the creation is, and is related to right knowledge. Seeing that the creation is good is possible because one has a right view as enabled by the Holy Spirit.

Augustine concludes his reflection on the Holy Spirit and creation's goodness in *Confessions* 13.31.46, by focusing on those who do see the works of creation to be good because those works are wholly from God the creator. "When people see these things [your works of creation] with the help of your Spirit, it is you who are seeing in them. When, therefore, they see that things are good, you are seeing that they are good. Whatever pleases them for your sake is pleasing you in them. The things which by the help of your Spirit delight us are delighting you in us."[92] Here he is pointing to the Holy Spirit as God's seeing and as the source of the creature's seeing that its existence is from God. People seeing how the creation is good do so because "your Spirit" (that is, God the Father's Spirit—Augustine does not name the Son here) enables them to recognize the creation's goodness. When people are enabled to recognize the goodness of the creation through the Holy Spirit's work of conversion, then "you are seeing that they are good," by which he means that God is seeing the fulfillment of his works ("And God saw that it was very good"), because they are taking shape according to God's good, creative intentions. When people delight in God's creation as good, it is because the Holy Spirit enables them to do so. Likewise, God delights in his creature's delight in God's goodness, because as they do so, they are manifesting what God created them for—namely, to be a good creation that recognizes (knows) its creator.[93]

In the conversion and perfection of creatures in the six days of Genesis 1, the Father and his Word convert the formless matter they have made from nothing into the creaturely forms that now exist by speaking the variety of species into being on each of the six days. Augustine establishes the presence of the Father and Son in the creative work by drawing out the implications of what it means for the creator God to speak his Word. The Holy Spirit converts creatures in their limited perfections so that they realize the goodness for which they have been made. Augustine establishes the Holy Spirit's presence in the work of conversion by explaining how the capacity for goodness that creatures have through the Holy Spirit is a delight to the Father, who sees the creaturely goodness through his Holy Spirit.

In Augustine's explanation of the triune nature of creation, the Son is the speech by which the Father creates, and the Holy Spirit is the divine goodness by which the Father sees that the creation is good. The Holy Spirit is God's seeing, just as the Son is God's speaking. As has been shown over the course of this chapter, in his trinitarian interpretation of the Genesis text Augustine develops his understanding of the relationship of God to his Word in the act of speaking, following the biblical concept of the Son as God's Word. The Holy Spirit is more difficult to identify in Genesis 1, however, since the verses that follow Genesis 1:2, where the Spirit is said to stir over the deep, make no further, explicit mention of the stirring Spirit. However, in God's declaration of the creation's goodness, Augustine finds the key that clarifies the Holy Spirit's identity. The work of the Holy Spirit in nurturing (which is how Augustine explains the work of stirring above the creation) and bringing about the goodness of creatures is distinguished from God's speech by linking that work to how God sees the creation's goodness. In Augustine's explanation of the creative work (the establishment and conversion of the creation) of the Trinity, the Father's creative activity is spoken in his Word and the divine goodness follows after the work of the Word. This pattern parallels his model of the inner Trinity where the Father is the fount of the Son and the Holy Spirit proceeds from both (but principally from the Father).[94] The order of the relations of the Father, Son, and Holy Spirit described in his trinitarian doctrine is also the order of the works of the Trinity as he interprets Genesis 1.

In bringing out the importance of the Trinity for Augustine's explanation of creation in Genesis 1, we have focused primarily on how he describes each of the three in the work of founding the creation. Nonetheless, the three are one God, and their work is one work as well. It should be possible to understand how the creative activity of the Trinity is one work, since the order of the creative activities of the three parallels the relations of origin in the doctrine of the Trinity. In order to understand how the activity of creating is one work, it should be noted that the eternal simplicity of the divine substance (a key for how Augustine understands what it means to speak of God as one) provides a framework to understand the activity of the persons as one activity, not three activities. In *The Trinity*, Augustine had argued, based on the revelation of the divine economy in scripture, that the divine substance is one and that each of the three is that one substance.[95] Part of his argument was that God's being (substance) is identical with any divine action, because God could not be different from his activity in the economy without the divine being changing.[96] As we have seen, Augustine connected the unity of divine being and action to the nature of the relations between the three persons, by putting forward examples of divine unity such as the Son eternally clinging to the Father and the Holy Spirit being the glue or friendship of the Father and Son.[97]

The conception of unity and distinction in the divine substance involves relative distinctions—relations of love between the persons where love is not different from any of the persons, but is the substance that each of the three persons is. Such an account of the Trinity brings out the dynamism of divine substance as charity.[98] In Augustine's understanding of the triune logic, these dynamic relations constitute the Godhead. Similarly, the distinct creative works he attributes to the Father, Son, and Holy Spirit are one activity. By keeping in mind the relations of the three persons in terms of cleaving to each other in the inner Trinity, one can see how his discussion in *The Literal Meaning* of the individual operations of the persons is congruous with the unity of the divine substance. The creative work of the Father is his speaking the creation into existence through his Word; and it also is through the perfecting goodness of his Holy Spirit, who unites the establishment and conversion of the creation in the Word to the Father by bringing creation's goodness to the Father's sight. While Augustine does not spell out in *The Literal Meaning* that in the creative activity God's speaking and seeing are not different from himself but are one with him, one can infer that this is the case, based on the logic of his doctrine of the Trinity, by which he conceives of the Son and the Holy Spirit as one substance with the Father.

The creative work of the three persons is one work, because the eternal activity of the three persons is not divided into temporal operations but is one simultaneous activity. The three modes of one action find cohesion in their source in the Father,[99] who is the source of the creation, speaking its ordering through his Word and seeing its completion and fulfillment in the operation of his Holy Spirit, who perfects its goodness.[100] Because the Trinity is eternal and immutable, the founding of creation does not happen in temporal stages, but all at once, according to the nature of the creator. The operation of the Holy Spirit in the act of creation is not temporally after the Word or the Father, nor is the Father prior to his Word and the Holy Spirit. The founding of creation from nothing in the Father's Word and Spirit is simultaneous with the founding of creation by its conversion and perfection from the formless void.[101] There is an order to the creative activity of the persons, but it is an order that is one activity undertaken by the Trinity.

The Word spoken is the creative power that gives creation its form and conversion to being from nonbeing. The Word spoken is the Father's Son carrying the Father's will toward its fulfillment. The Word is the very command of the Father fulfilled in its being spoken. The Word ensures that the Father's creation takes shape according to the Father's will, which is the same will as that of the Son.

The Holy Spirit does not come after the fact to finish the creation nor to speak a new word that declares the creation's goodness. There is only one Word of creation, and that is from the Father. The Holy Spirit's work also is from the Father, drawing the Father into the delight of his good creation that has found its form in the eternal Word of the Father. The Holy Spirit loves the creation and perfects it in accordance with the forms that the Word gives it. Just as the Spirit's charity in the Trinity unites the Father and Son in the bond of love, so in creation the Spirit is the fulfillment of the Father and Son's work, and the unity of the creation as one work. The Holy Spirit perfects the creation so that the Father's creative will, spoken through the Son, is seen in its goodness and is therefore a source of delight.

In the next chapter we will consider how the Trinity governs the creation, the second phase of Augustine's discussion of how he thinks of God's activity in relation to the creation. We will see that for Augustine trinitarian governance is explained in terms of divine providential care, because creatures are dependent upon God for their continued existence through participation in the Trinity. Creaturely dependence upon and participation in the Trinity are related to Augustine's conception of the Trinity's goodness and the trinitarian love for creation. This divine love for creation shapes Augustine's understanding of the nature of the divine governance of creation.

Chapter Five

Trinitarian Governance and Creaturely Participation in God

In the previous chapter we examined how Augustine's conception of the twofold nature of God's creative activity was rooted in his understanding of God as Trinity. It also was noted that he understood creation's existence as necessarily dependent on God; otherwise, the creation would cease to exist, because nothing can exist outside of God's sustaining Word, who gives form to the creation, nor apart from the Holy Spirit, who is God's good will, shaping and maintaining creatures.[1] This chapter will explore the implications of how creatures continue to exist because they are sustained by the triune God who enables them, by his providential government, to partake in him. We will begin with a general examination of how Augustine's understanding of the providential nature of divine government is based on his use of the concept of participation. Then, we will turn to an examination of two instances of how Augustine explained that creatures are governed through their ontological participation in God—namely, through motion, and through their having a certain measure, number, and weight. At the end of the chapter, we will address the question whether the interpretation of the conversion of creation from the formless void must require Augustine to understand God's creative work as the divine overpowering of created substance, or whether the ontological participation of creation in God allows for a different understanding of God's creative work. This chapter will set the stage for the next chapter, where we will turn to consider Augustine's understanding of human dominion as it is given to humanity on the basis of its being created in God's image according to Genesis 1:26.

Augustine's understanding of God's continued involvement with the creation after the founding work is an important component of his doctrine of creation, called divine governance or providence. As has already been described, Augustine interpreted the two creation stories of Genesis 1:1–2:3 and 2:4–3:24 as a two-part description of creation, where the first part refers to God's establishment of everything from nothing and its conversion into the spiritual and material forms that now exist; and where the second part refers to how God continues to work in the creation through providential governance.[2] As Augustine moves from Genesis 1:1–2:3 to 2:4–3:24, he explains that the rest attributed to God on the seventh day (2:2–3) does not conflict with the description of God's work as it is then depicted in Genesis 2:4ff.[3] Rather, it points to how God rests from creating new things after the six days of Genesis 1. Divine rest, then, denotes how God continues to govern his creation after the completion of the founding of creation. Divine rest also refers to how God rests in himself apart from all his created works, while the creation only finds its rest when it is led to repose in God, according to its measure, number, and weight.[4] The creation's rest is found only in God, which implies the creation's need for God is a need for God's providence, since no created good can exist apart from God, who is the source of all good. Thus, God's rest refers first to his rest in himself, and then to how creation must find its rest in God rather than in itself.

Governance indicates how God still works in the creation, so that creatures continue to exist. Through providential governance, "God moves His whole creation by a hidden power, and all creatures are subject to this movement: the angels carry out His commands, the stars move in their courses . . . animals are born and live their lives according to their proper instincts, the evil are permitted to try the just."[5] Providential governance is characterized by Augustine as a "double activity" of "the natural and the voluntary."[6] Natural providence refers to the way that God ensures that all creatures live and move and find their proper rest. For example, God's providential government makes trees grow according to their created capacity. Voluntary providence refers to how God governs souls, so that they are instructed, are able to acquire knowledge, are able to cultivate the land, and are able to live in harmony with others.[7] Also related to voluntary providence is God's power to accomplish his own good will despite the evil intentions of fallen wills.[8] "Hence it is that God . . . is over all creatures, that is, over natures that they may have existence, and over wills that they may do nothing without either His command or His permission."[9]

To underscore that God's providential government is a trinitarian work, Augustine refers to Paul's sermon to the Athenians (Acts 17:28), in which Paul says, "In him we live and move and have our being." Augustine explains that this verse confirms how God "works ceaselessly in the creatures He has made."[10] Rather than meaning that creaturely existence is in God in the same manner as "He has life in himself,"[11] it means that God's work of governance is the basis by which creaturely existence is maintained. This happens because God works through his wisdom (Son) and his good will (Holy Spirit), who keep creatures alive by holding all things together and by keeping them in motion.[12] If God's wisdom and good will did not reach out and cause creatures to continue to move toward God, then all things would cease to participate in God, and thus cease to exist.[13]

The concern of this chapter is largely with natural providence, by which all creatures continue in their existence through dependence upon God. We will explore natural providence in terms of how God has made creatures to participate in God, especially as it is expressed in terms of the motion of all creatures, and through their measure, number, and weight. We pointed out in the previous chapter that Augustine's explanation of governance overlaps with his discussion of the founding of the creation. As we discuss the motion of creatures, we will see that Augustine links God's providential care to the ongoing perfection of creatures. In our discussion of measure, number, and weight, we will see how Augustine portrays the Father to be the measure who limits creatures, just as he is the source of the creation from nothing; the Son is the number who gives form to creatures, which corresponds to the Word's founding work of forming creatures; and the Holy Spirit gives weight to creatures, just as in the founding of creation the Holy Spirit hovers over the deep, fostering the love in creatures that draws out their goodness.

In the next chapter, we will consider God's governance of creatures through voluntary providence and its implications for understanding the command for humans to exercise dominion over other creatures. We turn now to Augustine's characterization of creaturely dependence on God's governance in terms of its participation in God.

Participation in Augustine's Theology

Despite the importance of the concept of participation to Augustine's theology of creation, little scholarly attention seems to have been devoted to the topic in modern times. David V. Meconi has presented a survey of secondary literature and a preliminary analysis of the earliest writings in which Augustine uses the concept. He identifies three areas in which Augustine relies upon the concept: ontology, epistemology, and deification.[14] In this section, we will lay out a general picture of the concept of participation as Augustine employed it, using Meconi's three areas. We will look at each in turn, noting the way that the concept of participation enables Augustine to explain how the creation can be related to God, while also maintaining the distinction of God's transcendence over the creation and creation's dependence on God.

The first area where Augustine uses the concept of participation is to explain the ontological status of creation, by positing that all contingent created beings, and the qualities that they possess as existent beings, are dependent on God for their existence.[15] The most basic insight of the ontological dimension of participation theory concerns how creatures, unlike the divine being, are not their own perfections, but rather have their perfections through participation in the immutable perfections of the divine being.[16] For example, a creature, which by definition is mutable, is unable to be a "good-in-itself." Its goodness is through participation in a good that is immutable, or a "Good-in-itself."[17] That immutable good—namely, the supreme good, God—participates in nothing outside of itself. We have already seen that in Augustine's interpretation of Genesis 1, all creatures are said to be good by God when they are formed according to his Word and given their capacity for limited perfection through the Holy Spirit. They are good because they are created by God, who is the greatest good. The maintenance of creaturely goodness is God's trinitarian governance of the creature, by which it shares in the Goodness by which it is good.

To take another example, concerning "the Divine Word and Son of God," Augustine writes, "In His case not only is being the same thing as living, but living is the same thing as living wisely and happily."[18] This is contrasted with created beings, which are formless until the Word shapes them into creatures whose "being is the same thing as living, but living is not the same as possessing a life of wisdom and happiness."[19] After their formation by the Word, creaturely being is identical to its living—though only as far as God continues to maintain their being. Furthermore, the mutable perfections of their nature are only possessed by them through the work of God's Holy Spirit, who nurtures their "limited perfections,"[20] so that they "may exist" and "abide" according to the purpose of God's love.[21] As we will see below, a key way that Augustine explains the providential care of the Trinity is by describing how creatures are made to participate ontologically through their measure, number, and weight.

The second area in which Augustine relies upon the concept of participation, according to Meconi, is his understanding of epistemology. Augustine's epistemology is grounded in the concept of participation, because he understands rational beings to receive their wisdom and illumination from God's own wisdom.[22] Augustine touches upon this epistemological usage in *The Literal Meaning*. He explains the nature of the light that was created three days before the creation of the sun and moon (Genesis 1:3–13) thus: "[W]hen eternal and unchangeable Wisdom . . . enters into spiritual and rational creatures, as he is wont to come into holy souls . . . then in the reason which has been illuminated there is a new state introduced . . . [this state is] the light which was made when God said, *Let there be light*."[23] In this sentence, Augustine makes links between divine light of unchanging Wisdom (the Word of God) and spiritual (angels) and rational creatures (human beings). The links are forged because wisdom enters into these rational creatures "as he is wont" to do, so that creatures thereby are illuminated by the light of wisdom that shines through their reason. The Word of God is the source of intelligence, because God's wisdom illuminates these creatures.[24] This indicates that epistemological participation is not an act of the creature in an attempt to find wisdom in God, but rather, that such participation occurs because God enters into the creaturely being to make it able to shine with illuminated wisdom.

In the *Unfinished Literal Commentary on Genesis*, Augustine gives an explanation of the epistemological participation by which creatures become wise or chaste. He writes: "Now chastity is chaste without being so by participation in something, while it is by participation in her that any chaste things are chaste. And she is in God, where also is that wisdom which is wise without participation, but by participation in which any soul is wise that is wise."[25] Here Augustine refers explicitly to how creatures need to participate in God for their perfections, such as chastity and wisdom. Augustine begins with an example of participation, explaining how someone who is chaste participates in chastity. Being chaste is not the same thing as being chastity, however. Understood according to Augustine's concept of participation, chastity is by definition that which is chaste in itself. While someone is chaste through participation in chastity, it also is possible for that person to be unchaste by not participating in chastity; but chastity, being so in itself, is never not chaste.

Having put forward an example of chasteness and chastity, he then notes that chastity properly must be understood as a divine perfection: "And she is in God, where also is that wisdom which is wise without participation." Chastity is in God in the same way that wisdom is in God. What Augustine means is that God's wisdom is the same thing as being God. God does not participate in a wisdom that he does not have, because in God's simple being "to be is not different from to be wise, there wisdom is the same as being."[26] Likewise, if chastity does not participate in anything outside of itself but has chastity completely in itself, then it is complete in itself, which is only true of divine being. Contrariwise, created things are not complete in themselves, but are mutable and dependent on the God who has created them from nothing.

They do not have perfections in themselves, so that in order to have them they must participate in those perfections that are from God. The implication is that chastity is a divine perfection in the same way that wisdom is a divine perfection, since creatures can participate in it, but the divine being does not participate in anything outside of itself by which it has chastity. It has chastity in itself.

The wisdom of God is not different from God's being. Neither is chastity different from God's wisdom or from God's being. The link between chastity and wisdom is made by claiming that chastity is in God in the same way that wisdom is in God, because it does not participate in anything else, "but [it is] by participation in [it that] any soul is wise that is wise."[27] A soul is chaste by participation in chastity, just as a soul is wise through participation in wisdom. All perfections that persons can participate in—but do not have in themselves—are from God, who is those perfections in the wholeness of his simple being. Again, relying on Augustine's trinitarian explanation of divine creation according to Genesis, we can understand how epistemological participation is according to the Trinity. The Word, who is the Wisdom of God, forms creatures according to the Father's will, so that they are able to become wise or chaste; and, as well, the Holy Spirit shapes creatures so that they have the capacity to be perfected in their wisdom and chastity. Epistemological participation is not an act of the creature in its attempt to find wisdom or chastity in God; rather, such participation occurs because God enters into the creaturely being to make the creature able to shine with illuminated reason.[28]

The third area in which Augustine uses the concept of participation is his definition of deification. According to Meconi, not only does the human being necessarily participate in God for its being, but Augustine also speaks of Christ as the divine *particeps* in human nature. Creatures participate in God for their being because without God they would be nothing; and God participates in creation through Christ to enact creaturely redemption: "Only God is able to redeem because his ability to justify is his own and not by participation in another."[29] God's participation in creation "perfects us fully" without affecting God's own perfection, because by "becoming a sharer (*particeps*) in human nature, God has elevated our nature to his."[30] Participation describes the divine-human relationship, but not in any way that diminishes the complete dependence of creation on God, and God's independence from the creation. Bourke also notes the dual understanding of participation, where humanity participates in God because God participates in humanity "in the unique instance of the Incarnate Christ."[31] The difference is that humanity's participation is an ontological and spiritual necessity, while

God's participation in his creation is freely willed for the salvation of humankind. Creatures participate in God because they are dependent upon God, but God participates in creatures by causing their perfections of being and their redemption through the work of the incarnate Son.[32] In other words, to speak of God's participation in creatures through his Son is to speak of God's grace and mercy, by which creatures participate in God according to the fullness of their being.

These applications of the conception of participation by Augustine will help us as we now turn to his understanding of God's providential governance of creation; they provide a context for seeing how creation can be related to God without losing sight of his transcendence or the creation's dependence on God. In the rest of this chapter we shall examine two ways that Augustine explains the Trinity's providential governance within the framework of participation theory. First, divine providence draws creatures toward God through their motion, or movement. Second, all creatures are created with a certain measure, number, and weight, by which they can participate in the Trinity. In the next chapter, we will reflect on how human dominion over other creatures is through their participation in God through the image of God.

God's Providential Governance and Creaturely Motion

In this section we will explore Augustine's understanding of the creation's participation in God by considering how the creation's dependence through participation is manifested by its movement toward God's sustaining love—in fact, creaturely motion will be seen to originate from and be conferred by God's divine motion through his wisdom and Holy Spirit.

As we noted in the previous chapter, the conversion of creatures from the formless void involves shaping them so that they manifest the limited perfections that God intends for them. The limited perfection of a creature is the goodness of its mutable form in which God delights and declares it to be good. This conversion is brought about by God's Word, who forms creatures, and by the Holy Spirit, God's good will, who perfects them in their capacity for limited perfections.[33] Conversion is not only into the forms given by the Father through the Son and Holy Spirit at the founding of creation, but also is the continual attraction of the formed creature away from its natural tendency to "decay," "disappearance," and "loss of form," which are features of mutable creation.[34] Because creation is an eternal act of God, founding and governing creation are not separated by time, but are part of God's one creative act.

The conversion of the creature from formlessness to form in the divine Word and through the love of the Holy Spirit can be described both in terms of the start of creaturely existence in the founding of creatures, as well as throughout the duration of creation's existence under God's providential governance. In other words, Augustine's distinction between God's works of founding and governance is an exegetical explanation of the meaning of Genesis 1–2, but does not mean that he uses a strict terminological division. His language for the Word's forming and the Holy Spirit's brooding affection and perfecting also is used for explaining God's governance.[35] The perfecting of creatures is part of God's ongoing providential care.

In *The Literal Meaning*, as we noted earlier, Augustine describes God's providential government to be the ongoing source of the creation's existence by referring to Acts 17:28, in which Paul says "In him we live and move and have our being." For Augustine, Paul can be properly understood when one remembers that God "works ceaselessly in the creatures He has made."[36] To say that creatures live in God is not to be taken as indicating that creatures exist in God in the same manner as "He has life in himself,"[37] but, instead, that God's work of providential governance is the basis by which creaturely existence is maintained. This happens because God works through his wisdom (Son) and his good will (Holy Spirit), who keep creatures in existence by holding all things together and by keeping them in motion.[38] If God's wisdom and good will did not reach out and cause creatures to continue to move toward God, then all things would cease to participate in God, and thus cease to exist.[39] God's wisdom and good will rule creatures by keeping them in motion, "lest they forthwith lose the natural motions by which their actions and natural processes go on."[40] It is because the nature of existence is a "process" and "action" (or, perhaps better, an activity) that providential government is, in part, the conferral of motion. The limit of creaturely existence, which is mutability, since existence can change from coming-to-be into ceasing-to-be, signals that a creature moves from being given a form to losing its form (i.e., returning to formlessness). God's providence is the maintenance of that form within the limits he has set for a creature.[41]

Though God moves the creation through his Son and Holy Spirit, the Trinity is itself outside of the limits that frame creaturely motion. Augustine describes how God's Holy Spirit—who moves both spiritual and physical creatures through space and/or time—has no movement in time or space (having created them both) but "moves himself independently of time and space."[42] Likewise, God's wisdom, the Son, is also said to move the creation. In fact, "When Scripture says of Divine Wisdom that *It reaches from end to end mightily and governs all graciously* [Wisdom 8:1], and that Its motion is swifter and more active than all motions, it is quite clear, if we think well on the matter, that Wisdom, when It governs created things graciously, gives them motion beyond our powers to comprehend or describe, a motion we might call stable, if we can conceive of such a thing. And if this motion is withdrawn and Wisdom ceases from this work, creatures will immediately perish."[43] The motion that wisdom is said to confer upon creation, much like that of the Holy Spirit, is from its own motionless movement. In other words, the conferral of motion is "beyond our powers to comprehend," because it is conferred by wisdom whose own motion transcends creaturely notions and experience of motion. That is why it is a motion that might be called "stable," since, for Augustine, God is immutable, which indicates that God is free from all change as creatures know change (that is, as according to time and space).[44] In describing Wisdom as moving with a motion that is stable, Augustine also is letting the reader know that he is unsure exactly how to describe God as an unmoved mover of creatures.

One way that Augustine attempts to explain God's unmoving, or "stable," movement can be found in his discussion of the immanent Trinity. The relationship between the Trinity (the mover) and the creation (that which is moved) reveals a parallelism in Augustine's understanding of divine being and created being: both are dynamically conceived. With respect to the divine being, Augustine's description of the Trinity in terms of the relationship of the Father and the Son clinging to each other, and the Holy Spirit as the love between the Father and Son, suggests that divine being itself is a movement of one to another in charity.[45] And, as we have seen above, the divine persons move themselves (as opposed to needing something to move them) in this eternal clinging to one another. God moves toward creatures by creating them and delighting in their limited perfections, which conveys the idea of God's love being given to them at their establishment and conversion, in the work of the Son and Holy Spirit. In moving toward creatures by creating them and delighting in them, God also makes movement intrinsic to all aspects of created being—both the spiritual and the physical aspects. Creaturely life is moved by God, toward God, through the overflowing bounty of divine love that is the life of the Trinity.[46] This unmoved (i.e., simple, unchanging, and perfect) movement of triune love is both transcendent to the creation and conferred upon the creation through God's Word and Holy Spirit.

Augustine summarizes his conception of the movement of creatures according to divine, providential government in this way: "Without any distance or measure of space, by His immutable and transcendent power He is interior to all things because they are all in Him, and exterior to all things because He is above them all. Moreover, without any distance or unit of time, by His immutable eternity He is more ancient than all things because He is before them all, and newer than all things because He is also after them all."[47] Because the eternal God is outside of time, the creaturely experience of God's governance is such that he is at once before (that is, "more ancient than") and after (that is, "newer than") the creation.[48] God also is not confined by space—he is "exterior to all things" because of his transcendence of the creation. But God also is "interior to all things," because he has no distance from creatures, which is consistent with Augustine's conception of God always moving them in his wisdom (Son) and good will (Holy Spirit).[49] The work of God to move creatures originates in the divine transcendence of the creation, but that work also is immanent in the creation.

Divine conferral of motion on creatures is not conceived by Augustine in a generic sense of one movement for all. He recognizes that the variety of creatures made by God requires that God move each according to the limited perfections of their kind. In the quotation from *The Literal Meaning*, 4.12.23, what Taylor translates as wisdom's conferral of motion according to "gracious" government is more literally a conferral of motion by disposing creatures sweetly (*suaviter disponendis*), which highlights how each creature receives its particular type of motion according to the loving attention of wisdom. Creaturely motion differs according to how a creature has been made, so that "a soul moves in time, remembering what it had forgotten, or learning what it did not know, or wishing what it did not wish; but a body moves in space, from earth to heaven, or from heaven to earth, . . . or in similar ways."[50] The notion of creaturely movement applies to all creatures, then. An angel, being a spiritual substance without a physical body, only moves through time. A human being, though, has a soul and a body, and therefore moves through space as well as time. There also are those creatures that only have physical bodies and move in space and in time. In terms of simplicity, that which moves through time alone is "more excellent" than that which moves through both time and space (e.g., a human being).[51]

While human beings are said to move in space and time, like other creatures that have bodies and souls, Augustine also notes that there is uniqueness in human movement, because humans are created to the image of God, according to Genesis 1:26, "Let us make man to our image and likeness."[52] In *The Trinity*, Augustine gives particular consideration to how a human being moves toward God, which clarifies our discussion of movement. Being created "*to* the image" of God is not the same thing as being a perfect image, like the perfect image who is the Son. Rather, "*to* the image" refers to how the human being "*approaches* him [that is, the Trinity] in a certain similarity."[53] He then explains that "approaching" is not a motion across "intervals of place, but by likeness or similarity, and one moves away from him by dissimilarity or unlikeness."[54] What is the difference between the human image as movement and a movement across space? What Augustine means is that the rational nature of human beings is the factor that distinguishes them from other animals, in that they can know God through wisdom, which illumines and animates their minds.[55] To explain this difference, which Augustine finds in Genesis 1:26, he says, "Thus all things [are] through the likeness, but not all to the likeness."[56] It is by everything being created through the Word of God that all things receive their form of existence from the formless matter, but only human beings are created to the likeness of God, which is their rational nature.[57] All creatures, human or otherwise, are made in the likeness of God, and it is only possible for creatures to live, move, and have being as God rules over the creation by "the motion of Divine Wisdom"[58] and the motion of the Holy Spirit.[59]

Augustine's explanation of how a human being is made to the image (as opposed to being made through the likeness) is based on the idea that one "*approaches* him [that is, the Trinity] in a certain similarity."[60] On the basis of the description of God as an eternal movement of charity among the three persons,[61] Augustine describes human beings as creatures who approach the Trinity through a movement of likeness, by imitating the Son who clings to the Father in the bond of love—that is, through the grace of the Holy Spirit.[62] The imitation of Christ (God's wisdom) is motion that is enabled by God's Spirit (who confers God's grace). This movement to the image of the Trinity through the imitation of Christ by grace is the participation of human beings in the Trinity, which keeps the creation in motion. Humans, then, move like all bodies, through space and time. In their rational natures, though, they move toward God the Trinity in a certain similarity through the imitation of the Son's love through the Spirit's grace.

The parallel between the dynamism of the eternal Trinity that is a substance of love and humanity created to move to the image of God is most clearly seen in the biblical commandments to love God and one's neighbor.[63] In such love, one moves toward God, in fulfillment of God's creative intentions. When one is moved by rightly ordered love, then one imitates Christ according to God's grace. This dynamic of rightly ordered love will be taken up in the next chapter, when we consider the nature of human action as "use" and "enjoyment," and relate human action to the command to have dominion in Genesis 1:26.

Creaturely participation in God is through God's providential governance over the creation. Creatures are dependent upon God's governance, because if God does not keep the creation in motion it ceases to be—motion is necessary to creaturely being. The Trinity governs creatures by enabling the motion of creatures to imitate the Father's divine Word who has given creatures their form—and who himself eternally clings to the Father in their common love. Participation in God is to move toward God, according to his Word and Spirit. Augustine's view of both the founding of creation, discussed in the last chapter, and of its divine governance by the providential movement of creatures is marked by a dynamic relationship between the creation and God, where creatures exist as they are turned toward God. This Augustinian characterization of the divine-creature relationship finds its basis in the inner life of the Trinity, the persons of which are eternally turned toward one another. The nature of the movement that is granted to creatures by the Trinity will be expanded in our discussion of measure, number, and weight in the next section, and in our discussion of resting in God in the next chapter.

Participation in the Trinity through Measure, Number, and Weight

Another way to understand God's providential governance over creation through creaturely participation in the Trinity is to look at how creatures have been made so that this participation is possible. We have seen how a creature is made to live and move in God, and that participation involves a dynamic relationship with the Trinity, who is the source of all movement while being transcendent to the creation. Yet movement by itself does not fully explain the structure of creation so that it participates in God. What is it in creaturely existence that all creatures have from God and by means of which they participate by movement in the divine being, whether movement in time or in time and space? It is that all creatures have a certain measure, number, and weight by which they are able to participate in the Trinity. The Father is the measure who limits creatures, just as he is the source of the creation from nothing; the Son is the number who gives form to creatures, which corresponds to the Word's founding work of forming creatures; and the Holy Spirit gives weight to creatures, just as in the founding of creation the Holy Spirit hovers over the deep, fostering the love in creatures that draws out their goodness. Together, measure, number, and weight shape creaturely existence, so that it moves by God's providential care and thereby participates in the divine being that made it.

Augustine's understanding of divine governance as creaturely participation in the divine being through measure, number, and weight is based on Wisdom 11:20, where God is said to have "ordered all things in measure and number and weight."[64] In *The Literal Meaning*, he understands this verse to indicate two things about creation. First, it explains why Genesis 1 describes God as creating everything in six days. Second, it describes the pattern of being that all creatures exhibit and by which God rules them. For Augustine, measure points to how the creation has limits; number indicates how each creature fits harmoniously within the whole; and weight shows how creatures are drawn to live in a certain order or place.[65] We will consider how Augustine relates measure, number, and weight to his discussion of why God created everything in six days. In doing so, we will see again that the perfection of creation is maintained by God in providential government. Then we shall turn to his definition of measure, number, and weight, how all creatures are patterned after them, and how measure, number, and weight provide insight into God's trinitarian rule of creation.

Augustine's first extensive use of Wisdom 11:20 in *The Literal Commentary* forms part of his explanation of why creation happened in six days—namely, because six is a perfect number. He suggests the perfection of the number six "parallels the order of the works of creation," because six "rises in three steps from its parts" just as the works of creation also can be divided into three ascending phases.[66] In mathematics, a perfect number equals the sum of all of its factors (divisors). Accordingly, 6 is a perfect number since its factors are 1, 2, 3, and $1 + 2 + 3 = 6$. Augustine applies this pattern to the description of Genesis 1. The first ascending phase is the first day of creation, which brings light. The second phase comprises the second and third days of creation, in which the universe is completed—the second day, the firmament; the third, the earth and sea. The third phase comprises the fourth, fifth, and sixth days of creation, in which those things that are contained within the universe are made—the fourth day, the planets and stars; the fifth, the water creatures; and the sixth, the land creatures.[67] The creation of everything culminates in the symbolic perfection of the sixth day according to the pattern of the perfect number six.

Furthermore, the perfect number six reminds Augustine of the threefold ordering of creation—namely, according to measure, number, and weight—by which Scripture declares that everything is perfected by God. Since Augustine does not suggest that the number six is identical to measure, number, and weight, the perfect number seems to remind him of measure, number, and weight, because all are indicative of the perfections of the creation. The creation is perfected according to the perfect number six (six days of creation), and six is a perfect number because all perfections (including measure, number, and weight) are from God, who gives creatures form according to his perfect wisdom.[68] If everything is ordered according to measure, number, and weight, and since "before creation nothing existed except the Creator," one has to "in some way identify measure, number, and weight with Him, and say that the works of creation are, as it were, in Him by whom they are ruled and governed."[69] Augustine is making the connection between the creation of everything in six days and the creation's ordering according to measure, number, and weight, because both indicate the perfections of creatures that originate from God, and by which the creation participates in God as the Trinity governs them.[70]

The perfection of creation (both in the founding of creatures and in the governance of creation) by the number six and by measure, number, and weight does not mean that God is identical with them as they are understood within the creation, but rather that God is the source of these perfections in himself, and that he is above them as they are manifest in his creation.[71] One can understand this distinction between the perfections of six and measure, number, and weight as they are manifest in the creation and their origin in God by noting that Augustine argues in *Concerning the Nature of the Good* that God is the supreme good, while creatures are goods from God (mutable things made from nothing by the immutable God).[72] More specifically, all creatures are good within a hierarchy of goods and are equally dependent on God for existence.[73] Augustine then argues that all goods can be described according to limit, form, and order,[74] by which creatures possess their degree of goodness from God. However, "God is above every limit, above every form, above every order of the created universe" as the source of all three.[75] The limit, form, and order of all created things are the source of their goodness, and a creature's goodness comes from the supreme good who created it.

We shall now turn to Augustine's explanation of the structure of all creatures according to the pattern of measure, number, and weight. We will examine how he defined each term, and how the terms reveal the Trinity's providential rule of the creation by perfecting creatures so that they participate in the Trinity through them.[76] Augustine writes, "In so far as this matter can be grasped . . . we must understand that the words, *Thou hast ordered all things in measure and number and weight*, mean nothing else than 'Thou hast ordered all things in Thyself.' "[77] He reaches this conclusion by claiming that according to Romans 11:26 every created thing is "in Him by whom they are ruled and governed."[78] All creatures are in God insofar as they are ruled by God's ongoing providence. Measure, number, and weight are identified with God's providence as the means by which creatures are able to be in God. The three are perfections by which creatures are structured by God, and those perfections have their source in God who is "Measure without measure . . . Number without number . . . Weight without weight."[79] God makes his creatures have their limits (their measure, number, and weight) according to his creative purpose. God limits and upholds his creation according to them. As creatures participate in measure, number, and weight, they participate in God's providential governance.[80]

For Augustine, the Father is the measure who sets the limits outside of which no created things stray: "Measure places a limit on everything."[81] As Carol Harrison notes, just as the Father is the source who creates everything from nothing, so also in the governing of the creation the Father is the measure of creaturely beginnings and ends.[82] For Augustine, the Father creates everything to have limits by which they are measured through "a beginning and end to mutable time and existence."[83] The Father has created all things within the measure or limits of mutable existence, which, unlike God, not only change according to their measure but also cannot go beyond that measure, for beyond mutability and existence is eternity. Measure does not simply refer to the material creation, which can be measured according to its occupation of space and time, but also to the measure "of an activity, which keeps it from going on without control or beyond bounds."[84] Augustine is thinking of human activity, which is governed by limits that prevent one from doing things beyond the boundaries set for human action, so that humanity cannot do something that they could not then undo, or that would exceed all natural bounds within which they are created. Augustine points out that this measure or limit ("measure" and "limit" are synonymous terms for him) of creatures is itself "limited by another Measure. . . . There is a Measure without measure, and what comes from It must be squared with It, but It does not come from something else."[85] This measure that limits creaturely measure is the work of the Father, who is the source of the creation that he gives by means of his Word and Holy Spirit.[86]

The Son is number in that he "gives everything form."[87] Augustine already has shown that in the founding of creation the Word of God gives unformed matter its shape (form) by which it can be recognized according to its own kind.[88] This shaping or numbering also is true of all creatures in the Word's governing work. Material creatures have number in terms of mass and quantity. Spiritual creatures are governed by "the number of the affections of the soul and of the virtues, by which a soul is held away from the unformed state of folly and turned towards the form and beauty of wisdom."[89] The soul that is turned toward form and wisdom, as was shown above, is said to participate in wisdom (specified here through the number of the affections and of the virtues). The wisdom that a creature participates in is that which is wise in itself—namely,

God's Word. So then, all creatures have number, and "this number is formed by another Number . . . there is a Number without number, by which all things are formed, but It receives no form."[90] This is a direct reference to God's Word, the "Divine Exemplar, who is eternally and unchangeably united with the Father."[91] The Word is the form and number in which the creation participates so that it continues in wisdom rather than falling back to an unformed state of folly. If the Trinity were to cease from moving the creation, as we discussed in the preceding section, then it would fall back into its unformed state. When creatures are "held away" from such a fall, it is because their original formation and shaping according to number is maintained by the number without number.[92] In Augustine's thought, form and number are equal to each other, and they are created by the Word/wisdom of God who is their source. Form is given to creatures at the founding of creation, and is maintained as the Word governs the creation by making it possible to participate in wisdom.

The importance of the Word's governance of the creation, and of creation's participation in the Word, is also brought out in the *Tractates on the Gospel of John*.[93] In Tractate 1 Augustine develops the understanding of the Word we have already encountered, this time referring to Psalm 148:5, "He spoke and they were made; he commanded, and they were created." God creates through a Word that is eternal—its sound never fading.[94] More specifically, this invisible, eternal Word is Jesus Christ, the mediator between God and humanity, whose creative design is reflected in the "splendour," "abundance," variation," and "power" of the creation's structure. There is nothing that is not made through the unchangeable Word of God.[95] The divinely created world is built through the Word so that it has "weight, number, measure."[96] However, there is a disruption to the order of the world by sin.[97]

The disruption that sin brings to the order of the world requires a mediator who can reconstruct the world and direct it back to its stability in God. How does the Word, incarnate in Jesus Christ, do this? Augustine develops a picture of the Word's redemptive work by first drawing attention to the basic fact that "[t]hat which was made, in him is life."[98] This is explained using the image of the carpenter. The product made by a carpenter is the outcome of the design that is created in the carpenter's mind. The design exists invisibly, while the product exists visibly. Likewise, the corporeal world exists as a result of the Word being the creative knowledge (*ars*) that is called the wisdom of God. "You see the sky; there exists a sky in his creative knowledge."[99] As long as creatures participate in the divine, creative knowledge of the Word (through weight, number, and measure) they exist. The mediator, in the redemptive work, draws the creation back to its right order by calling it to return to the Word. In this sense the Incarnation represents a revelation of God's invisible Word that was spoken at the creation.[100]

That the creation participates in the Word become flesh is demonstrated in how the Gospels show Jesus to rule all nature—in other words, nature listens to its creator Word. This is important to Augustine, because the Word is the master builder who "constructs while infused in the world. He constructs while situated everywhere . . . he does not direct the structure which he constructs from the outside . . . by his own presence he governs what he has made."[101] As Jesus re-creates the world and brings it from the place of sinfulness to the divine presence, the creation witnesses that he is the eternal Word present among them. How does it acknowledge its creator? Augustine notes those instances where Jesus is described as ruler of nature in the Gospels. "The firmament gave witness from a star. The sea . . . carried the Lord when he walked. The winds . . . quieted at his command. The earth . . . trembled when he was crucified."[102] In developing this understanding of the incarnate Word, Augustine is careful to avoid implying that the Word is not always present in the creation; rather, "he never departs from you" as the governing Word in which all life holds together.[103] Thus, the invisible Word is also visible in the Incarnation. The creation by its very form, or number, responds to the eternal Word by which it is formed.

Finally, in Augustine's explanation of the structure of all creatures according to the pattern of measure, number, and weight, he explains how the Holy Spirit is the weight of creatures, by which they are drawn "to a state of repose and stability," so that they rest in the place for which they have been made.[104] Augustine understands the word "weight" to convey two meanings. First, with regard to physical objects, weight draws them to find rest in an appropriate space. For example, oil is "so constituted as to tend towards its proper place . . . and settle on the surface [of water]."[105] If oil's weight were heavier than water, then it would find rest under the water.

Second, a spiritual being has "the weight of the will and of love, wherein appears the worth of everything to be sought, or to be avoided. . . ."[106] Just as a physical object's weight draws it to rest in certain spaces, so a spiritual substance's weight also draws it to rest in certain spiritual conditions. As Augustine famously put it in *The Confessions*, "My weight is my love. Wherever I am carried, my love is carrying me. By your gift we are set on fire and carried upwards: we grow red hot and ascend."[107] Just as oil rests upon water, so the soul's love rests upon that to which it is attracted. The soul, by its will and love, is attracted to and seeks the form of beauty and wisdom, and wishes to avoid the folly of tending toward unformed and degenerate desires. The soul's ability to will and to love is at once its weight by which it finds rest in its proper place, and also is its weight because by the activities of willing and loving it is able to value (i.e., "weigh") things.[108] In both senses of the term "weight"—the weight something has, and the activity by which someone weighs the value of something else—the end is a "state of repose and stability."[109] In the first, the weight of a thing draws it to its proper place in the order of creation. In the second, the weighing of what is to be sought or avoided leads one to seek rest in one state rather than in another. Weight and order are often used interchangeably in Augustine's writings. For example, at the end of *The Literal Meaning* 4.3.7, in his explanation of Wisdom 11:20, Augustine paraphrases the verse this way: "He limits everything, forms everything, and orders everything." The equation of weight and order signals that when everything is properly ordered, then it has found the rest for which it is intended.[110]

As with measure and number, Augustine points out that creaturely weight is from "a Weight without weight"[111] to which creatures are drawn. To be drawn toward this weight is to find rest in that which gives everything weight and order.[112] The Holy Spirit is particularly associated with weight and order. It was noted in chapter 4 how the Holy Spirit's work in founding the creation is to establish creatures with a capacity for love by making them find their rest in God's love.[113] Augustine's understanding of creaturely love is that it is properly drawn toward God's love, which is manifest in the work of the Holy Spirit. We have already noted how, in *The Confessions* 13.10.10, he writes, "Wherever I am carried, my love is carrying me. By your gift we are set on fire and carried upwards. . . ." He continues, "There we will be brought to our place by a good will, so that we want nothing but to stay there for ever." In this quotation, he speaks of his love carrying him upward because his heart has been set on fire by God's gift, and then lifted to its place by God's good will. Both terms, "gift" and "good will," already have been linked to the work of the Holy Spirit.[114] Here God's gift is the source of the soul's love, carrying it to the place where it lacks nothing; through God's good will, the spiritual fire warms the soul so that it might rise upward to its proper place, an image of it finding its place in the order of creation for which it has been created. It rises to that place by the Spirit's fire. The weight of the soul is such that it rests in the place for which it has been designed; and it finds that place through the Spirit who gives creatures their weight and also is the rest toward which they are drawn by their weight.

Measure, number, and weight are not three independent ways in which creatures may exist according to God's providence. Rather, God makes creatures according to measure, number, and weight, which is the basis for all creaturely unity. In *On Genesis: A Refutation of the Manichees* Augustine writes, "There is not a single living creature, after all, in whose body I will not find, when I reflect upon it, that its measures and numbers and order are geared toward a harmonious unity."[115] By this, Augustine is referring to how "all these things are beautiful to their maker and craftsman, who has a use for them all in his management of the whole universe. . . ."[116] Everything God creates exhibits a particular measure, number, and weight according to his wisdom and will. And though Augustine cannot explain why there is such an abundance of creatures, or what is the purpose of each one,[117] he does think that the answer to a creature's unity lies in its originating from God, who is "the supreme measure and number and order which are identical with the unchanging and eternal sublimity of God himself."[118] The Father's will and wisdom are not different from the Father—each is God and God is each.[119]

Just as the triune God is one and three, so he is the source of creaturely unity through his threeness that is one. Every creature is made by the three who are one; and when each creature properly exhibits measure, number, and weight, it is a unified and harmonious whole in the unity of the Trinity's perfect work. While Augustine describes the correspondence of measure/limit with the Father, number/form with the Son, and weight/order with the Holy Spirit, one should not assume that Augustine restricts the work of measuring, numbering, and weighing creatures to each respective divine person. What the Father has, so have the Son and the Holy Spirit in themselves, and all three have them together in perfect unity.[120] The Trinity governs the creation by ordering everything to measure, number, and weight. When Augustine identifies the individual terms with the persons of the Trinity, he is not contradicting the oneness of the divine work, but is showing how the Trinity, which is three in one and one in three,[121] is identified as three persons at work in the divine governing. Moreover, we already have pointed out that Augustine's explanation of governance overlaps with his discussion of founding the creation, which suggests that the founding and governing of creation, while distinguished by Augustine, nevertheless also form a certain unity. Just as the three persons' work in the founding of the creation is one work, so it is in the governing of creation; and, the two together—the founding and governance of creation—are one work by the Trinity.

Formless Matter and the Question of Passivity

We have tried to show, thus far, that Augustine's interpretation of God's creative work in Genesis 1 is thoroughly trinitarian in regard to its founding and its governance. Moreover, the governance of God over the creation is described in such a manner that creation is moved toward God according to each creature's measure, number, and weight. However, questions have been raised as to whether Augustine's understanding of God's relationship to his creation really is as dynamic as it appears, or if it is not instead best described as authoritarian and dominating, like an arbitrary will.[122] Does not the conversion of creatures from a formless void (Genesis 1:2) in Augustine's interpretation indicate that God's actions are in fact the imposition of form upon an inert or passive substance? If so, does this not confirm the suspicion that the creation from its very beginning is simply under the domination of its divine maker?[123]

To answer this claim that God's relationship to creation is authoritarian and oppressive, we need to think about how Augustine characterizes the formless matter in the founding work from which everything is shaped, which he does in *Concerning the Nature of the Good*. We also need to attend to how Augustine's description of God's governance and creaturely participation are presupposed in that description of the forming of the formless matter.

Michael Hanby has addressed the question of the nature of the formless void from which creatures are shaped and its supposedly passive quality in his *Augustine and Modernity*. In *Concerning the Nature of the Good*, section 18, Augustine identifies the formless void of Genesis 1:2 with the Platonic term *hyle*. Hanby admits that Augustine's definition of *hyle*, by itself, could be taken to indicate God's domination of a passive substance: "I mean by *hyle*, as did the ancients, a sort of matter utterly formless and without qualities, and out of which are formed the qualities which we perceive."[124] However, Augustine adds to this definition a clarification concerning the goodness of the *hyle*, because it was created by God with the capacity for receiving form (which is a good): "We must not term evil that *hyle* which not only cannot be perceived through a visible form, but can scarcely be conceived of on account of its all-embracing privation of visible form. Even this has the capacity for forms. . . . If form is a good . . . doubtless the capacity for form is likewise a good."[125] For Augustine, according to Hanby, the *hyle*'s capacity for good, among other things, denotes its capacity to receive form by its "participation in the good."[126] It has this capacity for participation in goodness because God created it (from nothing) to be open to goodness even in its formlessness. Participation in goodness (namely, the Trinity) is not simply introduced into Augustine's understanding of governance, but also is presupposed in the conversion of creatures from the formless void as well.

The capacity to receive form through participation is the means by which the conversion of the formless matter into the variety of creaturely forms happens. In Hanby's explanation, the *hyle* is "interposed in the interval between the Father's intention of and delight in the Son and the Son's response to and vision of the Father, and it is by virtue of this location that the *hyle*, along with formed matter . . . can be understood to participate in the conversion to form."[127] According to Hanby, creaturely participation is grounded in a twofold understanding of the Father-Son relationship: on the one hand, creaturely participation is grounded in God's intention of love for his Son, who is the Word by which he creates; and, on the other hand, the Son's response to that intention of love from the Father is to speak forth the creation as the Father's Word. Creation is understood as arising out of this mutual relationship of the Father and Son, because "In the beginning, God created." When the creatures (the individual goods that are made) are formed from the formless void, according to Hanby's account, that conversion is best characterized as the response of the formless void to the love between the Father and Son (Word), by which the formless void becomes actually (being formed by the Word) what it only was potentially when it was formless.[128]

In support of the contention that Augustine understands the creation to be active from its very beginning because of its place between the Father and Son, Hanby cites a portion of *The City of God* 11.24.[129] There Augustine writes, "For it is the Father of the Word Who said, 'Let it be.' And that which He spoke was beyond doubt made by means of the Word. Again, when it is said, 'God saw that it was good,' it is thereby sufficiently signified that God made what He made not from any necessity . . . but simply from His goodness: that is, so that it might be good. And this was said after the created thing had been made, so that there might be no doubt that its existence was in harmony with the goodness for the sake of which it was made." Hanby is arguing, again, that in this passage the activity of creating reflects the relationship of the Father and his Word. On the one hand, the Father is the origin of his Word and its result (the creation that was spoken by the Father in his Word). On the other hand, the Word's response to the Father is to make that which the Father intends (i.e., the creation) when he creates in his Word by saying "[L]et it be." So, the relationship of the Father and the Son in eternity is the basis for the creatures that are formed (from the formless void, though Augustine does not mention that explicitly in this passage). They are a product of the mutual goodness of the Father and the Son,[130] which, according to Hanby, is a movement of love—that is, the Father's loving "intention" and the Son's loving "response." In other words, because Augustine calls the *hyle* good in *Concerning the Nature of the Good*,[131] and because he understands creation's goodness to originate in the Father-Word relationship (which is goodness itself), the *hyle* itself reflects the active intention and response of the Father and the Son. The good *hyle* could only reflect this active intention if it participated in the good of the supreme good—which is the Trinity. Hanby's argument makes sense when one understands that, for Augustine, participation in the supreme good is one of active response (movement) toward that goodness.

Hanby's argument could have been strengthened if he had continued his quotation from *The City of God* 11.24 just one sentence further, so as to include "And if this goodness is rightly understood to be the Holy Spirit, then the whole Trinity is revealed to us in the works of God."[132] By doing so, Hanby could have noted that the goodness of the *hyle* is also shaped by the Holy Spirit, who is the movement over the formless void, nurturing its perfections and potential.[133] The Holy Spirit, the charity between the Father and the Son,[134] who hovers over the creation so that it is loved to perfection, is integral to Augustine's trinitarian understanding of creation's founding. The founding of the creation (including the *hyle*) in the interval between the intention and response of the Father and Son is where God's goodness and love are located: "God made what he made . . . from His goodness [namely, the Holy Spirit]."[135]

Rowan Williams points out that Augustine's conception of God's Word forming the formless void is important for grasping his understanding of creation.[136] The Word forms created matter. That should not be taken to imply that formless matter is dominated by that Word of the Father, by forcing matter into the form it has. Rather, as Williams puts it, "The action of form on matter is not the imposition of one thing on another, let alone one system on another: it is simply the process of actualization itself, the process by which organization appears."[137] Williams is pointing out that Augustine's idea of formless matter is not simply an idea that two "things" are engaged in an activity where one overcomes the other, but rather that formless matter is matter that is open to the potential for which God has created it.[138] As God's Word forms the formless matter, that matter is able to achieve its potential for having form. The *hyle* is not evil matter, nor is it matter that is neither good nor bad, but rather it is matter created by God to become what God has intended it to become, by being converted from formlessness to form, and from potentiality to actuality. Whatever God creates is good,[139] so that formless matter is already good, though it can achieve a greater goodness as it realizes its potential through God's forming Word.

We noted, at the beginning of this chapter, that Augustine described divine providence as God moving "His whole creation by a hidden power, and all creatures are subject to this movement."[140] We then explored some aspects of the movement by which God providentially governs creatures.

Noting first of all that for Augustine the conception of participation is basic to his understanding of the God-world relationship, we explored how participation helps him to express the dependence of the creation's motion upon God. As creatures partake in God for their perfections, they manifest their being as God intends it for them. The perfection of creatures is described by Augustine in this way: "[W]hen creatures remain in the state in which they have been created, possessing the perfection they have received . . . they are good individually, and all in general are very good."[141] Any perfection that belongs to a creature (and different creatures have different sets of perfections by which they are called perfect)[142] is given by God, so that the creature may be in a state of perfection with regard to its being and its perfections may contribute to the overall goodness of the creation. God providentially governs the creation by moving creatures to participate in God's perfections, so that their perfections may be good. God's providence, then, is life-giving, by moving the creation toward the goodness of existing as a creature in the supreme good.[143]

The participation of creatures in measure, number, and weight is the ontological structure that Augustine uses to describe how creatures participate in God (in whom they live and move and have their being)—that is, how they are subject to divine providence. When created beings participate in measure, number, and weight according to the divine intention, they reveal the goodness of God's work. Augustine's description of measure, number, and weight corresponds to his understanding of how each of the divine persons is at work in the creation. Measure, by which creatures receive their limit, is related to the Father, who is the beginning of the creation. Number, by which creatures receive their individual forms, is related to the Son. Weight, by which creatures are moved to their proper place in creation, is related to the Holy Spirit. Williams describes measure, number, and weight in this way (using the word "proportion" instead of "number"): "Measure and proportion govern the reality of things that are made to change, and 'weight' is what pulls them to their proper place."[144] The structure of reality has been designed by the Trinity so that all creatures move toward their proper place. This is not surprising, since Augustine's understanding of the immanent Trinity is itself dynamic: the Father eternally begetting the Son who clings to the Father in the charity of their Holy Spirit. Divine governance reflects that dynamic life of the Godhead. The participation of creatures through measure, limit, and weight is a participation in the Trinity, which is an eternal relationship of divine persons.

At the same time, creatures are not God, and participation in God is not the same as being God. The creation is made in the finite, mutable likeness of God.[145] The relationship between creator and creature, though founded on God's goodness and love, never is fused ontologically. The creature is always from nothing and without God's governance would return to nothing. God's governance, then, maintains the creation in its goodness, so that it might move toward the perfect ordering of everything according to measure, number, and weight. God's governance brings about the perfection of goods that are finite and mutable.[146]

Over the course of the last two chapters we have seen how God, as triune creator, is described by Augustine. Augustine is careful not to compromise his understanding of the eternality, simplicity, and immutability of the Trinity; he does this by distinguishing the creation from God's being and by making the creation of everything from nothing central to his explanation of the founding of creation. The conversion of creatures from the formless void, too, is described in trinitarian terms, whereby the Trinity's eternal life of love (with the Son clinging to the Father in the Holy Spirit) is manifest in the economic activity of shaping creatures through God's forming Word and brooding Spirit of goodness and love. Augustine also makes clear that God's governance of creation, through his ongoing providential work, enables the goodness of created being to be maintained and fulfilled by moving toward its rest in the Trinity through the creature's participation according to its measure, number, and weight.

In the next chapter, we will examine how Augustine understood the relationship of creatures among themselves, in light of the triune God's governance of creation. It is here that the moral consequences of God's governance will be discerned, which is a major concern to ecological theologians. Of particular note will be how Augustine conceives the way human beings, created in the image of God, are to exercise their dominion in the universe.

Chapter Six

Resting in God, the Image of God, and Dominion

In chapter 4, we explored Augustine's understanding of the founding of creation and showed it to be trinitarian in shape, with the Father creating everything that exists through his Word and Holy Spirit. This trinitarian delineation of the divine work, as we have seen, corresponded in form to Augustine's doctrine of the immanent relations of the Trinity, set out in chapters 2–3. In chapter 5, Augustine's conception of God's governance was described in terms of God's providential work of sustaining the creation's existence and order, which lives and moves in God through participation in him. In particular, the creation's participation in God through its measure, number, and weight helped Augustine explain how creatures realize the goodness for which God had created them—that they might live and move in God. All creatures depend on the work of God the Trinity for the goodness of their being and fulfillment.

We now turn to consider Augustine's understanding of human dominion as it is given to humanity on the basis of their being created in God's image, according to Genesis 1:26. Human dominion within the order of creation is understood by Augustine to be one of the human works that lead to rest in God—which means, simply, that human beings fulfill the good ends for which God has created them according to God's goodness and love when they exercise dominion well. This, as we have seen in chapter 1, is a reading of Augustine that goes against that of some modern commentators, who see in Augustine, and more generally in the classical theological traditions of the East and West, the promotion of a dominating role for humanity over the creation, a domination based on a deficient conception of God that is not trinitarian. In order to find the link between Augustine's conception of the Trinity's creative work and governance of creation as we have described them in the previous chapters, and his understanding of the work of human dominion as it is commanded in Genesis 1:26, we shall first look at another way in which

Augustine conceived of the participation of creatures in God—namely, the resting of the creation in God. The conception of resting in God follows naturally from the discussion in the previous chapter of participation as movement and as the measure, number, and weight of a creature. The movement of creaturely being, by God's providential government, which is according to its measure, number, and weight, is toward the end of resting in God. We will turn, after discussing Augustine's understanding of creaturely rest, to the question of how one can know one's activities lead to rest in God by looking at Augustine's distinction between use and enjoyment as a way of properly conceiving of good human action. From there we will turn to his understanding of the image of God. The image of God is the proper movement of human beings toward rest in God's love. Augustine conceives of human dominion as the rule of creatures according to the image of God, which is a seeking of God's love in the right use of the creation.

Resting in God

We considered in chapters 4 and 5 Augustine's explanation of God's resting from creation (Genesis 2:2) as a reference to how God creates no new creatures after the founding of creation in Genesis 1.[1] God's rest also is thought, by Augustine, to describe the state of divine independence from the creation, on the grounds that God has no need of creation.[2] The creation is a work of God's goodness, and is a delight to God precisely because it is a good created by God, who is the supreme good.[3] God's rest from creation is not indicative of divine mutability or even of his need to create.[4] As we look at Augustine's understanding of creaturely rest in this section, we will see that his concept of rest is closely related to his understanding of happiness. Human beings' likeness to God manifests itself through proper rest, which follows after the good works for which they have been created. To find rest in God is to find one's happiness in God in all things, including the works for which one has been created. One of those works is dominion, which we will consider in light of the idea of resting in God.

Divine rest implies the creation's need for God, since no created (mutable) good can exist apart from God's providential work. As we saw, Augustine's reference to a creature's being in God is based on Paul's description of humanity existing in God (Acts 17:28). Augustine develops this idea of creaturely being in God when he writes, "For the perfection of each thing according to the limits of its nature is established in a state of rest . . . in Him to whom it owes its being, in whom the universe itself exists."[5] The finite limits of a creaturely nature are its measure, number, and weight. Just as God rests in himself, apart from all created works, so the creation only truly rests when it is led to repose in God, according to its measure, number, and weight. Thus, God's rest refers first to his rest in himself, and second to how creation must find its rest in God rather than in itself.

Augustine expands on this understanding of rest, as it applies to creatures, by observing that creaturely rest is like and unlike God's rest. "The repose of God, by which He rests in Himself and is happy in the Good which is identified with Himself, has no beginning and no end for Him."[6] In God is eternal rest, having no beginning or end, unlike creaturely rest that has its beginning and ending in the creative work of the Trinity. God's rest also is identified with the indivisibility of the divine being. God is not made of parts, such that happiness is somehow different from God's rest. Rather, God's rest "is happy in the Good which is identified with Himself."[7] Augustine creates a synonymy between rest, happiness, and goodness on the basis that God has all three indivisibly in himself. The argument for the synonymy follows this reasoning: God's happiness is found in himself, rather than outside of the divine being;[8] God's happiness is in his unchanging goodness, which is the source of all true happiness;[9] and, since God is happy in his own goodness, God's rest, which also is his happiness,[10] is his repose in his own goodness.

Creatures, in contrast, find the perfection of their limited, mutable being not by resting in themselves, but by resting in the immutable God: "For the perfection of each thing according to the limits of its nature is established in a state of rest, that is, it has a fixed orientation by reason of its natural tendencies, not just in the universe of which it is a part, but more especially in Him to whom it owes its being, in whom the universe itself exists."[11] In this quotation, Augustine makes a passing reference to the physical rest toward which creatures are oriented "in the universe." For example, oil rests on water because God has created oil to have such a physical nature that its weight is less than water.[12] The main point that Augustine wishes to make, however, is that not only does oil rest on top of water, but it also rests in God because it only exists as a creature of God. The mutable nature of created being cannot find rest in itself, because all creatures are created from nothing and would fall back into nothingness, except that God upholds the creature's being. A creature's perfections are understood in relationship to God, not only in relation to the creature itself. Augustine has already linked the perfection of happiness in God to God's self-rest. He also thinks that the happiness of creaturely natures resides in their rest in God's goodness.[13] Human beings find their rest in God by imitating Christ, who eternally clings to the Father.[14] Just as with nonsouled creatures, the tendency of a human soul toward its proper place of rest in God indicates the means "by which it maintains its nature and identity."[15] Because it is created out of nothing, like all other creatures, its nature is only maintained in its rest in God, not in itself.

Human rest, like that of other creatures, is an "inclination that might be called an appetite of their weight, and when they find it they are at rest."[16] The "place" that all creatures find their rest in is God. However, Augustine admits, "I have not used this term 'place' in the literal sense."[17] A literal sense of creaturely rest in its intended place implies the physical space it occupies. Yet, as Augustine observes, even in physical space bodies do not always "remain in place."[18] They may move about. If literal "rest" is not God's intention for creatures, then "rest" has more to do with the creature's need to fulfill its appetite, what was described in the previous chapter as its ontological participation in God, who is the source of creaturely existence. In this sense, the motion of the universe is not toward stasis, which would be the literal understanding of rest at a particular, fixed place. Rather, the motion of the universe is toward the completion of its perfections according to God's will—that is, having its appetite fulfilled through ontological participation. One infers from this that creatures' lack of resting is a sign that they can only find rest outside of themselves, rather than in themselves. Their temporal composition means that they cannot achieve literal rest. Their final rest can only be in God, who is their true end—the source of their goodness and happiness.

Augustine also relates this orientation to rest in God in human beings to the moral quality of holiness, which is part of the human likeness to God:[19] "Our likeness to God cannot be holy if we wish to be like Him in such a way as to rest in ourselves from our works as He rested in Himself from His works. For we must rest in an immutable Good, that is, in him who made us . . . and this is what we must desire after our good works, which, though taking place in us, we recognise as His. Thus, He also rests after His good works, when He bestows rest in Himself upon us after the good works we have done when justified by Him."[20]

Human beings' likeness to God manifests itself through proper rest, which follows after the good works for which they have been created. We shall deal specifically with the right use of God's creation and the work of human dominion later in this chapter. Likewise, the unique form of human likeness to God—being created to the image of God—will be taken up in the discussion of dominion. At this point it is sufficient to recognize that the likeness to God is manifest in the desire for rest in God's immutable goodness, which is both the source of all good works and the rest that is bestowed after all good works, as we shall see below.

Augustine's argument is that God rests in himself because he is the immutable good and therefore, by implication, is the only stable source of rest. Because God is immutable goodness, human beings can only rightly find rest after their works in God's unchanging rest, which he bestows through justification.

The first sentence of the above quotation, from *The Literal Meaning* 4.17.29, provides a picture of the relationship between works and rest. God has made human beings to do works (such as exercising dominion) that are holy—that is, in accordance with God's will. Human works done properly are not performed with the desire to delight in them as if one were self-sufficient in one's abilities apart from God. Rather, human works are done properly in dependence on God who is the source of all good works and the rest to which they lead in God.[21] That one would want to find rest within oneself rather than in God is part of humanity's sinfulness, expressed in human nature as pride.[22] Human pride leads to the idea that happiness may be found outside of God and in one's ability to do good and delight in that good apart from God. However, as Augustine continues in the next sentence, "[W]e must rest in an immutable Good. . . ."[23] The only good works that a human being can delight in are the works and subsequent rest that come from God's goodness, who is the source of good works. All good human works, in fact, are part of God's creation and therefore ultimately are God's works.[24] Human works follow from God's creative activity in the beginning, and must find their culmination in God's gift of rest[25] (who is perpetually at rest in himself, apart from the creation).[26] Therefore, though God rests apart from his creation, human works manifest God's continual working, which is his providential governance.

By beginning with a discussion of how God has created the world so that all creatures may find their rest in him, we have set up a context in which to understand Augustine's discussion of human dominion. Human dominion is one of the works that God intends for humanity, and is a good and holy work when performed in dependence upon God. Human works should be part of the movement by which God providentially leads humanity to its rest in God. As part of the movement of creation toward God, they are a means by which humanity participates in the Trinity, in whom everything lives and moves and has its being. In other words, the triune nature of Augustine's concept of participation and movement, as discussed in the previous chapter, extends as well to human works, which are explained by Augustine within the framework of divine providential government.

Human works can be carried out and true rest found when, as understood by Augustine, one has a proper understanding of how to use and enjoy things. In the next section we will consider how Augustine describes the proper objects of human use and enjoyment. In doing so, we will see that the fulfillment of human goodness is the enjoyment of God, in whom humanity finds true rest.

Use and Enjoyment

Human works are good when they lead to rest in God, because God is the source and end of all things.[27] How can one know whether one's works lead to rest in God? Augustine provides an answer to such a question in his discussion of use and enjoyment. One's works, in Augustine's estimation, reveal the object of one's love and where one desires to find rest. By looking at use and enjoyment as a measure of one's love, one is able to see how human works point forward to that place where one seeks rest (i.e., "in God"). In taking account of how Augustine conceives of use and enjoyment, we can then turn to a related idea—namely, how the image of God in humanity, which Augustine relates directly to human dominion in Genesis 1:26—is to be worked out in relation to God as the proper object of enjoyment.

Augustine understands the scriptural commandments to love God completely and one's neighbor as oneself as central to the formation of a good soul.[28] One way that he attempts to explain the relationship between these two loves is by employing the terms "use" and "enjoyment." This distinction is given an extended treatment in *On Christian Teaching*,[29] but also is present more generally in his subsequent works as a way of understanding how Christians are to love both God and neighbor.[30] He defines his terms thus: "To enjoy something is to hold fast to it in love for its own sake. To use something is to apply whatever it may be to the purpose of obtaining what you love—if indeed it is something that ought to be loved."[31] The enjoyment of something is directed at the thing itself as the source of love, but by using something, one recognizes that it is not a source of love in itself, but points beyond itself to another love. Augustine identifies God alone as the proper source of enjoyment, because only God is perfect and unchangeable.[32] One should not use God, since God is the source of all that is good, and all created things only have their goodness from God.[33] However, Augustine recognizes that one can love one's neighbors without making them the object of that enjoyment which only belongs to God.[34] In other words, the biblical commandment that one ought to love one's neighbor need not lead to a potentially idolatrous enjoyment whereby one confuses the proper limits of one's love of neighbor with one's love for God.[35]

Augustine's conception of the use that can be made of the things of the world (including people) is not intended to be understood in terms of using something as merely a means to an end, which is the negative way that one might conceive of the term.[36] Rather, as Rist puts it, Augustine's employment of use "is merely a standard Latin locution—found also in earlier English, e.g., 'He used him well'—indicating how people are to be treated; the notion of 'exploitation' is not to be read into it."[37] The proper use of something is so that God may be enjoyed (loved) fully.[38] In sum, then, God gives creatures being—that is, gives them goodness, since to be is to be good—for the ultimate end of enjoying God. As we shall see, the work of human dominion is a command to use something not in order to exploit it, but in order to love God more fully, and thus to find one's rest in him.

In order to make sure that the use of people is not misconstrued, Augustine also refers to the commandment to love one's neighbor as the enjoyment of another "in God."[39] He then defines such "enjoyment" as to "use with delight."[40] One's ultimate enjoyment, which is fellowship with the Trinity,[41] provides a limit on how one might enjoy one's neighbor, because the proper enjoyment of one's neighbor leads to one's ultimate end in God. One's enjoyment of others is not that ultimate end, but an enjoyment along the way toward one's final end of enjoying God, just as one can enjoy a trip without forsaking the end of that trip.[42]

In addition to explaining how one's love of one's neighbor is both a form of "enjoyment" and "use," it should be clarified that loving others in God is not only in reference to enjoying their souls, but to enjoying their whole being—body and soul.[43] Thus, Augustine does not separate the physical dimension from the spiritual dimension in his understanding of good behavior, but actually emphasizes the unity of the spiritual and the physical.[44] This unity of the physical and the spiritual dimensions of the human being provides a clear enough clue that the physical is not to be neglected or merely used as a means to another end. Augustine's affirmation that the corporeal can be used well echoes his understanding that the whole creation finds its rest in God, and that the whole, rather than just the spiritual aspects of the creation, is "very good."[45] The physical universe is not denigrated or given short shrift by Augustine, but is a part of God's good work of creation.

The distinction between use and enjoyment provides Augustine with a way in which he can distinguish between the proper goals of human actions in relation to God (enjoyment) and to other creatures (use), with human beings occupying a middle ground because of their constitution as physical and spiritual beings (thus they are to be enjoyed, but only in

God—in other words, enjoyment is a form of use when directed toward human beings). Augustine's distinction between use and enjoyment serves to clarify how human actions can be good and lead to their intended eternal ends of human beings loving God. As such, the distinction gives a more concrete way of delineating what it is that leads to the rest that humanity has been designed to seek—that human use is conditioned by the enjoyment (love) of God. Inasmuch as one's participation in the Trinity involves a conversion of the soul toward God so that one finds one's rest in God, as discussed in the previous chapter, Augustine's understanding of use and enjoyment is assumed to be trinitarian in shape. It is through the soul's measure, number, and weight that one is drawn to love things properly in the Holy Spirit, according to the form given through the Word and according to the limits of creaturely existence that are set by God the Father. That is, to use some things and to love others is possible when one participates in the Trinity that draws the soul toward those things that should be used and enjoyed. In the next section we will employ Augustine's conception of how human beings should act, according to proper use and enjoyment, to explore his understanding of dominion as the practical expression of how human beings are the image of God.

The Work of Human Dominion and the Image of God

The work of human dominion over nature, which will be our focus in the remaining sections of this chapter, is one of the ways that Augustine understands humanity to be distinct among created beings. He argues that the idea of dominion, as understood in Genesis 1:26, is able to clarify the description of humanity as being created to the image of God.[46] Augustine understands human works to be holy when they lead to rest in the supreme good, who is God.[47] He specifies the reason for this relationship between human works and rest when he describes human rest in God as reflecting the special human likeness to God. Rather than resting in oneself instead of the creator, the human being shows its likeness to God by depending on God with complete devotion—that is, by desiring rest in God as the proper end of human works.[48] It is because humanity has been created in God's image that its works are to be holy. Moreover, human works are not for the enjoyment of the works in themselves, but for the end of enjoying (loving) God. Dominion is one of those human works that reflects the right use of the creation so that God may be enjoyed. The relationship between dominion and human likeness to God is rooted in a conception of human works as revealing the proper object for one's love—namely, God's immutable goodness, the greatest good, which orders the creation, giving it rest and final fulfillment.

As we saw in chapter 4, Augustine believed that God created everything according to a certain order. As well, as we have just seen, part of that ordering involves how one uses or enjoys something, so that God is the proper object of enjoyment, and other people (with the qualifications that we also noted) and the world are to be used. So, in the *City of God*, for example, Augustine describes how the order of the heavenly city is best because it leads to peace: "The peace of the Heavenly City is a perfectly ordered and perfectly harmonious fellowship in the enjoyment of God, and of one another in God."[49] God created humanity to have its end in the enjoyment of God, where people also can enjoy each other in God according to God's conferral of peace upon its citizens. However, Augustine does not limit his conception of harmony to the enjoyment of other human beings in God. He continues, "The peace of all things lies in the tranquillity of order."[50] Just as use and enjoyment, when rightly practiced toward other humans in God, produce harmony, so the right order of all creatures within the creation produces peace for the whole creation. For humanity, this requires that creation is used rightly.

This context of the moral use of others is crucial for understanding Augustine's interpretation of God's command in Genesis 1:26 that humanity is to exercise dominion over the world. He understands dominion as the rule by human beings of nonhuman creatures through the exercise of their rational capacity. However, this should not be misunderstood as a rule for merely human ends and enjoyment. His framework for speaking of the use and enjoyment of others "in God" helps to explain his understanding of human dominion over nature. All human works are to be done in reference to God, and not merely as ends in themselves. The use of something is in order to love God. The orientation of human works, when set within the larger picture of the goodness of all creation and its participation in God, suggests that the commandment to exercise dominion is supposed to mandate the rule of nature not for human enjoyment, but for upholding the divine ordering of reality in its goodness.

Augustine does not devote much space to explaining what dominion means in Genesis 1:26. Primarily he understands it as part of the statement that human beings are made to the image of God, and accordingly believes that the verse bears a trinitarian stamp. The passage in Genesis reads: "Let us make mankind to our image and likeness; and let them have dominion over the fish of the sea, the birds of the air, all the cattle, and all the earth, and all the creatures that crawl on the earth.' And God made man, to the image of God."[51] Augustine explains that this verse, on the one hand, begins with a plural pronoun, "Let us make," thus indicating the plurality of persons in the Godhead, so that making "mankind to our image" is not the work of one divine person (e.g., the Father) making human beings to the image of another divine person (e.g., the Son).[52] On the other hand, it ends with a singular subject, "God made," indicating the unity of the Godhead, whose work is one work, not three works.[53]

He then suggests that because humanity's dominion over the animals is mentioned directly after the first clause, "Let us make mankind to Our image and likeness," but before the affirmation that God did so ("And God made man, to the image of God"), one should understand that the part of human nature that is the basis for dominion—namely, "his reason"—is what is meant by "to the image of God": "From this we are to understand that man was made to the image of God in that part of his nature wherein he surpasses the brute beasts. This is, of course, his reason or mind or intelligence, or whatever we wish to call it."[54] A person's mind is at once the aspect of human nature that allows it to exercise authority over other earthly creatures, and also that which is specifically made to the image of God the Trinity. In Sermon 43.3, he also answers the question of what the basis for human dominion is in Genesis 1:26: "What gives him this authority? The image of God."[55] He then continues to explain, in this sermon, what the image is by showing how human beings are different from other creatures: "We have existence in common with sticks and stones, life in common with trees, sense in common with beasts, understanding in common with angels."[56] Human beings are different from other creatures because of their rationality. The image of God in human beings lies in their exercise of reason. And it is the exercise of reason that gives them authority, or dominion, over animals. Given this close relationship between the image of God and human dominion, we shall briefly unpack Augustine's understanding of the image of God as a movement of the human being toward knowing God. In the previous chapter, while considering the governance of divine providence, we noted that Augustine's understanding of participation sometimes was expressed in terms of how creatures move in God. Our focus on the image of God here will dwell on how Augustine speaks of the image in terms of the moral participation of humanity in God as they move toward him. In grasping this aspect of Augustine's conception of the image of God we will be in a position to clarify how the exercise of dominion according to that image is envisaged by him. [57]

Immediately after linking the exercise of dominion to the image of God in *The Literal Meaning* 3.20.30, Augustine cites Paul's argument about how a person's mind is renewed by the putting on of the "new man, who is being renewed unto the knowledge of God, according to the image of his Creator" (Ephesians 4:23–24; Colossians 3:10), as a justification for his interpretation of the image of God as human reason. His point is that Paul points to the mind, as opposed to the body, as that part of the person in which renewal happens according to the image of God.[58] By citing Paul, Augustine brings out a parallel between God's work of creation and redemption. In both cases God is the subject and creatures are the objects of the divine work. The person created by God is also redeemed by God. In redeeming creatures, God's activity arises from his love of creation; in creating, God's works arise from his love, which is the nature of his being.[59] The external activities of God—the works directed toward his creation—come from the Trinity of eternal persons whose indivisible substance is love.[60]

When Augustine cites Paul in order to indicate that the image of God is one's mind, he is likely thinking of this relationship of love between God and the creation. In *The Trinity*, Augustine also cites Ephesians 4:23 and Colossians 3:10 as part of his explanation concerning the renewal of the image from sin. There he describes the process of renewing the image "*in the recognition of God* (Colossians 3:10), that is *in justice and holiness of truth* (Ephesians 4:24). . . . So then, the man who is being renewed in the recognition of God and in justice and holiness of truth . . . is transferring his love from temporal things to eternal, from visible to intelligible, from carnal to spiritual things. . . . But his success depends on divine assistance. . . ."[61] One is renewed in one's image, which is the mind, in the recognition of God, when one's love is directed toward God. The recognition of God, in terms of his justice and holiness, is revealed in how one directs one's love toward God. Augustine is portraying one's knowledge of God "as operational and vital," because the mind must return to—or better, move toward—God in love.[62] As one's mind is renewed, the person recognizes God as the immutable source of holiness and justice, who has called that person back to that person's proper love. This moral renewal of the image is rooted in the redemption of a person from sin, since in sin human beings do not participate in such moral perfections as they ought to (because they have transferred their love from God to "temporal things," "visible" things, and "carnal" things). But when the image is renewed, then a person can know and participate in justice and holiness inasmuch as he or she is in God, who is perfect in justice and holiness.

The identification of the image of God with "the reason, mind, or intelligence"[63] by which humanity has dominion over other creatures implies the superiority of humanity over other creatures.[64] Of course, even that part of human nature that is the basis for the image of God, and that differentiates humanity from other creatures, must participate in God just as all creatures do. One of the key aspects of Augustine's conception of participation, discussed in the last chapter, is its dynamic quality. Williams brings out the importance of Augustine's description of the image as movement. He describes Augustine's understanding of the image of God as a person's maturing understanding that he or she is loved and known by God: "We come to 'image' God by grasping that our reality exists solely within his activity of imparting wisdom and justice, and thus letting that prior gift form our conscious reflection and decision-making—which of course is not done by our effort but by the receiving of the grace of Christ which reconnects us with our vocation to be God's created image. The image of God in us might be said to entail a movement into our createdness, because that is a movement into God's own life as turned 'outwards.' "[65]

Williams's description of Augustine's understanding of the image of God as a movement toward knowing God, especially God's wisdom and justice as they are known through one's redemption by the grace of Christ and the Holy Spirit, and his emphasis on letting that knowledge form one's consciousness clarify how the image of God is a dynamic intelligence. It is about knowing who God is through a "movement into God's own life" as God turns "outwards" toward his creatures.[66] Augustine describes this movement of creatures into God as the movement of creatures toward their proper end or rest.[67] Likewise, Williams's reference to God's life turned outward is in keeping with Augustine's explanation of trinitarian creativity in Genesis 1–2—namely, that the Father's Word and Holy Spirit shape and uphold the creation in God's love.[68] Williams rightly calls Augustine's conception of the image of God a "vocation," by which he means one's ongoing movement toward a deeper knowledge of God and God's creation. Such a movement happens according to the "corporate charity" that is given to the human being by the Trinity, originally at the creation and then later through the redemptive work of the Trinity in the economy of salvation.[69] Another way to put this idea, in the context of our discussion of God's governance of creation, is that one is the image of God the Trinity as one is dependent upon God's work according to the proper use of creation and enjoyment of God.

The image of God, according to Augustine, concerns persons moving toward God particularly through the exercise of their intellects, which enable them to pursue knowledge of God's love. As we also have seen, the exercise of human dominion is through the intellect, by which human beings are above other creatures (which do not have intellects).[70] The image of God, then, functions as a limiting concept for how dominion may be understood. For example, dominion (following Augustine's understanding of it as the exercise of the image of God in creation) does not refer to the imitation of God's rule over the creation, but rather to the realization of the image through the vocation of seeking and knowing the triune creator's love.[71] A proper understanding of the work of dominion should take into account how it leads to rest in God. Put another way, dominion over other creatures is not an ultimate source of enjoyment for humanity; it is supposed to lead the person toward rest in and enjoyment of God. The enjoyment of God is the experience of God's love as it is known by a person through the image of God. It is this idea of dominion that we must work out in the rest of the chapter.

Dominion and Power

Though the verb *dominor* means to rule, primarily in the legal sense of a ruler in government, Augustine did not simply read a Roman, patriarchal, dominating political authority into his interpretation of the commandment for humanity to have dominion in Genesis 1:26. Instead, he understood dominion to be the rule of reason, which, as we have just seen, is understood properly when reason is conceived as an orientation to the knowledge of the love of God. Because of the close connection between the image of God and dominion, the latter needs to be understood within the larger context that Augustine has described concerning the image, which is directly related to how human beings participate in God and enjoy (love) God. In this section, we will take up the question of how the power exercised in human dominion can be understood according to this enjoyment of God and the right use of others. We will do this by first considering some of the ways in which God's power is described by Augustine in his portrayal of God's governance of providential care and redemption. Then, we shall link Augustine's conception of how the human being is to respond to God's power (which we will describe in terms of a loving worship of God) with how human dominion is described within the context of use and enjoyment.

Augustine does not describe God's power to rule over creatures (God's governance) as a dominating power. Rather, he sets God's rule within the context of wisdom: "For He is all-powerful not by arbitrary power but by the strength of wisdom."[72] God's wisdom is his Word,[73] who, with the Holy Spirit, founded and converted the creation and holds it together so that its goodness might be a delight to the Father.[74] Augustine recognizes God's will as omnipotent, but clarifies that omnipotence is not to be defined as an unrestrained, arbitrary power that is thoughtless in its application, but rather as the power of God's wisdom and goodness. As we have seen, the Word and the divine goodness create out of God's love and govern the creation so that the creation will find rest in that love.

An excellent example from Sermon 43 of how God's power is manifest is the work of redemption, which is the foundation from which Augustine developed his doctrine of the Trinity. The redemptive work of Christ saves humanity from bondage to sin and is revealed as God's powerful mercy and justice on the cross.[75] This merciful and just redemption, "[which we needed] just as we needed a creator," is an expression of God's governance.[76] It is from the God who created and governs the world that the redemption of fallen humanity also comes. To distinguish God's wise, omnipotent power from the idea of power that leads creatures boastfully to use (and even abuse) their authority over others, Augustine goes on to note how God's power is revealed through humble means, such as the apostle Peter, who witnesses to God's saving revelation in Jesus Christ: " 'Give me,' he says, 'that fisherman, give me a common man, give me an uneducated man, give me one whom the senator doesn't deign to talk to, not even when he's buying fish. . . . The fisherman isn't in a position to boast about anything except Christ. Let him come first, to give a salutary lesson in humility. Let the fisherman come first; the emperor is best brought along through him.' "[77] God's omnipotent power is revealed through the example of humility, not only the humble witness of Peter, but supremely through God's own incarnate Son.[78] Through this humility even those who have great authority will be brought back to God. God's lordship is an omnipotent power, but also is simultaneously merciful, just, and humble.

The rule of God is not sheer dominating power, but instead is a rule of wisdom, such as is revealed through the humility of Christ's redemption, and also through God's delight in creating all things to be good through participation in the Father's Word and goodness. The basis for human dominion rests in the human being's uniqueness of being created to the image of God, so that through its mind it seeks understanding and rest in God, according to the movement of love in which all creatures partake according to divine providence. While Augustine does claim that having dominion over animals means they are "subjected to us,"[79] because Genesis 1:26–27 implies "that reason ought to rule the irrational life,"[80] it is a rule that should reflect the vocation of the image of God. One can infer that for Augustine the vocation of humanity to know and love God, who created the world out of his goodness and love, does not warrant the wanton destruction of God's creatures. In fact, such license is an act against the goodness of God and oneself, since "the peace of all things lies in the tranquillity of order."[81]

For Augustine, the natural use of creatures, such as for food, is not a violation of the command to have dominion. It is a fulfillment of God's design that those nonrational forms of life might supply the necessities of physical life, not only for human beings but for one another. Thus, concerning why animals consume one another, Augustine explains that "one animal is the nourishment for another. To wish otherwise would not be reasonable. For all creatures, as long as they exist, have their own measure, number, and order. . . . [E]ven when one passes into another, [they] are governed by a hidden plan that rules the beauty of the world and regulates each according to its kind."[82]

The predatory nature of animals, including human beings, is justified as the natural state of affairs by which God has ordered the world. Augustine goes on to indicate that the answer to why God created things in this way—so that some animals eat other animals for nourishment—is only dimly grasped by most people.[83] Part of the problem is that sin has obscured human ability to understand the purpose of God's creation, so that good things that God has created now appear to be evil, when in fact they are still good, but also function as a punishment for human sin: "Since . . . all things are ordered in the best possible way, which seem to us now adverse, [evil, which is the penalty of sin,] has deservedly happened to fallen man. . . ."[84] In fact, though God has made everything to be good, sin not only makes it difficult to see how everything is good, but it also leads to good things being a punishment for humanity. "Since . . . it behooves us to be good not of necessity but voluntarily, it behooved God to give the soul free will. But to this soul obeying His laws, He subjected all things without adversity, so that the rest of the things that God made should serve it, if also the soul itself had willed to serve God. But if it should refuse to serve God, those things that served it should be converted into its punishment."[85] As we noted above, Augustine understands that the predatory nature of animals is normal. However, he also suggests that sin, which has disordered God's good creation, has made humanity's dominion less effective than it is supposed to be. The world seems to be against people's interests as a result of sin.

The fact that predation is a natural state for animals—that they eat one another—does not mean that Augustine thought God had relegated nonhuman animals merely to serve as food or for some other utility at the hands of humanity. As Augustine puts it in *The City of God*, one of the problems of calling nonhuman creatures displeasing or evil is that "men consider them not in themselves, but only with reference to their utility. . . ."[86] This surely suggests that for Augustine dominion, whatever utility may properly be included in its exercise, is not first or foremost to please human beings "in themselves." He goes on to write a few lines later, "It is not with respect to our comfort or discomfort, then, but with respect to their own nature, that created things give glory to their maker."[87] He affirms animals as having their own intrinsic goodness that can be appreciated by people in relation to God's creative work. Similarly, in *The Literal Meaning* 8.23.44, Augustine argues that all creatures that are without free wills are not simply subordinate to those beings with wills without any qualification. Rather, the ranking of creatures is set within limits according to a specific "order established by the justice of the Creator."[88] The rule of some creatures over others is to be guided by the providential government of God, who delights in all the things he has made.

Observing animals' desire for life, which they cling to instinctively, Augustine also sees their beauty and praiseworthiness.[89] The harmony of measure, number, and order produces in an animal a beauty that amazes Augustine, especially the beauty of animals "doing their utmost . . . to protect the material and temporal life which has been given them by their position in the lower ranks of creatures."[90] The protection of life and the fight for survival is an example of the right use of life and its goodness, in which creatures properly delight when they use and protect life according to the measure that God gives them.[91] Preaching on Psalm 144, Augustine says that the beauty, goodness, power, and utility of the creation should always lead people to the praise and celebration of God: "I want the creator to be glorified in all he has made."[92] The perfections of the universe are to lead people to love God and praise him, just as the rest of creation confesses and praises God in their being, which is ordered according to God's goodness.[93] It follows that the exercise of dominion is not merely to delight in the use that a creature provides for human needs, but that the creator might be praised. Animals, then, have their part in the beauty of God's plan, according to which things are to delight in life according to their measure, number, and order. This part, or role, in God's plan is more than merely serving as a product for human consumption, but is a form of worship of the creator.[94]

In Sermon 68, Augustine says, "Observe the beauty of the world, and praise the plan of the creator. Observe what he made, love the one who made it . . . because he also made you, his lover, in his own image."[95] In saying this, Augustine makes clear that if one recognizes in forms of life that are not made in God's image the signs of God's good plan for creation, then they who are made to God's image should love God because of his good works. Since all forms of life are good and therefore reveal God's greatness, their use by humanity should be to lead to humanity's worship and enjoyment of God, "Others, in order to find God, will read a book. Well, as a matter of fact there is a certain great big book, the book of created nature. Look carefully at it top and bottom, observe it, read it. God did not make letters of ink for you to recognise him in; he set before your eyes all these things he has made. Why look for a louder voice? Heaven and earth cries out to you, 'God made me' . . . Observe heaven and earth in a religious spirit . . . [but those who have done so] . . . *while recognising God, they did not glorify him as God* (Romans 1:21)."[96] According to Augustine, it was on account of the Athenians having read the book of creation, which speaks to any who would read it concerning God's creative work, that Paul affirmed that they had an understanding of the creator, which enabled them to write concerning God, "For in him we live and move and have our being" (Acts 17:28).[97] Just like one who reads scripture with understanding, Augustine goes on to state, so one who observes the book of nature ought to be led to glorify God (though the Athenians did not). It would seem reasonable to infer, because his theology of creation leads to the affirmation that God is to be glorified for his goodness and love, that the proper use of creatures in the exercise of human dominion leads to an increase of one's love of God. It was noted above how Augustine connected the enjoyment of God to the maintenance of the harmony of God's ordering of creation.[98] "Understanding the divine ordering of creation—according to a creature's measure, weight, and number—and promoting that harmony by which each creature fits into God's beautiful plan" is an apt description of how humankind properly is to exercise dominion and to use creatures.[99]

In fact, knowledge of how God has ordered the creation according to a hierarchy of creatures, and subjected some to others can lead to two possible ends: to the wisdom of knowing God and loving him (i.e., using others to know and love God better), or to the folly of thinking oneself to be higher than others in the hierarchy (i.e., enjoying or loving oneself because one can exercise one's intellect at the expense of others). For example, in *On Christian Teaching* 2.38.56, Augustine notes that there are some who study arithmetic; indeed, they do so with "shrewd and sagacious minds." Nevertheless, it would be wrong if they claimed that the immutable rules of arithmetic were instituted by human beings. He then writes: "However, take someone who loves knowing all these things [including learning why some things are mutable and other things are immutable] just so that he can give himself airs among the uneducated . . . and who does not turn all this to the praise and love of the one God from whom he knows it all proceeds; such a person can seem to be very learned, but in no way at all can he be wise."[100] In this passage, Augustine argues that the knowledge of truths in creation (through secular education) in terms of their degrees of mutability and immutability only can be called wisdom when it leads to the praise and worship of God. However, it is vanity when such knowledge does not result in worship, but instead leads one to a sense of superiority over others who do not recognize such structures in reality. Put in the terms Augustine used to describe divine providence, such a sense of superiority happens when one tries to rest in oneself, rather than in God. If dominion is exercised in the hierarchy of beings, following Augustine's understanding of creation in Genesis 1–2, it is not because human beings are able to institute their rule over others through sheer strength of arbitrary power or will. Rather, dominion is given to human beings because they are created to the image of God. And, as a result of being created to the image of God and in light of God's trinitarian governance of the creation through providential care, Augustine's conception of dominion should be one that leads to a deeper worship of God by those who exercise that dominion in order to enjoy God.

In this chapter, we have gotten to our main topic of how Augustine's trinitarian doctrine of creation describes God's providential care of the creation, and how this relates to the commandment of Genesis 1:26 that human beings are to exercise dominion over other creatures. It will be recalled how Gunton claimed, "In Augustine's theology of creation . . . the Christological element plays little substantive role, and the pneumatological even less. The result is that the way is laid open for a conception of creation as the outcome of arbitrary will [of the Father]."[101] Chapters 4–5 showed how thoroughly trinitarian Augustine's conception of creation and governance is in his understanding of Genesis 1–2. In those chapters we discovered how the founding and governance of creation are portrayed as arising out of the goodness of the Trinity and resulting in the Trinity's delight in the creation's goodness. The Trinity's creative works and governance of creation are not susceptible to the criticism that they are simply the result of the Father's arbitrary will, as Gunton suggests.[102] As we have seen, Augustine explains that God's providential care, while omnipotent, is not arbitrary: "For He is all-powerful not by arbitrary power but by the strength of wisdom."[103] More specifically, the order of creation under God's governance is according to God's wisdom and divine goodness, in order that the creation might participate in God.

We have seen how all creatures are created to have their rest in God. Outside God there is nothing to rest in, for the Trinity is the source of all created being. Rest in God was not conceived by Augustine as a static or motionless existence, like a rock at rest, since everything is in motion.[104] The rest creatures have in God is their movement toward God, who is ever working in the creation that it might continue to exist. While God is always working in creation, so that it might not fall back into nonbeing, God also is said ever to be at rest in himself apart from the creation, because while creation is dependent on God, God is not dependent on creation. God rests in himself, apart from his works, in the eternal relationship of love that is the Father, Son, and Holy Spirit. This conception of God's self-rest as the divine love of the Trinity is seen in Augustine's doctrine of the Trinity as the Son clinging to the Father, and in the Holy Spirit who is the glue of love between them.[105]

In the proper ordering of creation, according to Augustine, all creatures are turned toward their creator, according to their measure, number, and weight. Humanity has been given a special place in this ordering of creation toward God, because it has been created to the image of God—which is manifest in the vocation of knowing God's love. To understand Augustine's explanation of how a person grows in the image of God, we have noted how he distinguishes between use and enjoyment. Human beings should find their enjoyment in God alone, and the proper use of something is so that God may be enjoyed (loved) fully. Every human action is understood in relation to God, whose worship is the end of all things for Augustine.

Dominion, which is the exercise of authority or rule over creatures, is given to humanity through its possession of the image of God. However, dominion is not an authority that is meant to be exercised apart from God's love of the whole creation. Just as the creation has been created and providentially ordered by God according to his goodness and love, humankind's exercise of dominion also should reflect God's rule of goodness and love. Dominion, in this respect, is a form of use (not enjoyment), since it uses creation to know better God's goodness and love, which is the goal of the proper exercise of the image of God. When dominion is exercised well, it contributes to the "peace of all things . . . in such a way as to give to each its proper place."[106] In order to give each thing its proper place, one must know its place (and one's own) in the divine order, and thus must know the God who has ordered all things according to the divine goodness of the Holy Spirit and the formative Word, the eternal Son of God. That is to say, one's view of the world must be shaped according to the divine love for the creation, which is also the divine love for humanity, made according to God's image.

Conclusion

The impetus for our study of Augustine is connected to modern religious responses to the need for ecological ethics, as they were described in the introduction. While the religious responses to the data that ecological science has produced are varied, there has been particular interest in positioning religious responses according to the theme of the interrelatedness of creatures. There also have been frequent attempts to link the ecological problems of today to antecedent causes that stem in part from earlier religious views of the world and the human place in it. In particular, several evaluations of traditional Christian beliefs have been critical of Augustine's theology. We have attempted to show that Augustine's theology is not as one-sided as it is portrayed by critics in theology and environmental ethics. Is Augustine's view of the creation as a community of interrelated, equal components? No. Does his understanding of creation contain positive resources for developing a positive view of the world, and acting in it within an ecological framework? That answer can be more positively affirmed, within limits, if we concentrate on the themes that emerge in his attempt to explain the world as he knew it and interpreted it through the lens of faith. We shall consider six ways in which Augustine's trinitarian doctrine of creation might be understood to contribute positively to ecological and ethical concerns today.

Unity and Diversity of Creation and Ecological Interrelatedness

Augustine's trinitarian interpretation of Genesis sees the world—indeed, the entire universe—as a unified whole whose status in the eyes of God is good with regard to all of its particular creaturely components, and very good in its wholeness. He recognizes that there is a certain tension in how one views reality. Sometimes he is amazed by the variety of creatures and their individual complexity.[1] Then, again, he is struck by how everything holds together, maintaining its own space but also revealing a unity that he describes as a big book—a metaphor that brings a storylike quality to how he saw the world.[2] Not only is there a unity of creatures in space, but there is a unity of creatures moving through space in time. That unity of movement is not a random jostling, but a movement of creatures toward their source of existence in God through the guidance of the Holy Spirit and the Word of God. This unity of movement is toward an end that is profoundly meaningful and satisfying: finding rest in the creator. Augustine can turn again to the variety of creatures and see how they individually manifest this movement, each holding on to the measure, number, and weight that God has given it with tenacity, and moving through space and time by the providential care of God's governance. Augustine's recognition of the unity and diversity of the world does not favor the unity over the diversity, nor collapse particularity into monism.

He writes about the unity and diversity of creation while admitting that he often can see neither the rhyme nor the reason of the book of nature.[3] However, one of the means that he has available to him for recognizing that the unity and diverse particularity of the creation is good is the doctrine of the Trinity. As we have seen, he does not reduce the Trinity to a logical problem of how three persons can be made to fit a more basic commitment to a divine substance that takes priority over threeness. Rather, he explains the Trinity as a three-in-one divine nature (substance), and one divine nature that is three. The unity that he recognizes most clearly in his writing on the Trinity is that of love, which he identifies with God's substance or nature. In his account of how God creates the world in Genesis, he falls back on this understanding of God as love by describing the creation as resulting from God's love pouring "out of the largeness of his bounty."[4] God's love overflows from the divine being, and it flows out as an action of the three divine persons, who act in concert, just as in their eternity they cling to one another.[5] The ecological significance of this recognition of unity and diversity is important to note. Augustine observed reality as holding together in unity without losing its particular beauty through diversity. His observations found their justification in the revelation of how God is portrayed as creating in Genesis 1, and he interpreted it according to the trinitarian theology he had received through the church's doctrine of the Trinity. Modern ethical concerns about ecological ethics see the issue of interrelatedness as highlighting how human decisions cause reverberations throughout an ecosystem. To be ethically sensitive requires that decisions be made that take seriously such causal power and incorporate the valuation of other ecosystem components into decision-making. Augustine is not concerned about the cause and effect of decisions in that sense, but his understanding of the nature of reality also does not undermine the ecological urgency that requires such moral valuation of interrelatedness today. In fact, Augustine's theological interpretation of reality is a worldview that would justify such moral valuation of interrelatedness by linking the particular goodness of individual creatures to the unified goodness of the creation via the love of God. Everything is part of God's good creative work, and therefore is connected by a common origin and destiny in God.

The Hierarchical Structure of Reality

The goodness of creation in its unity and diversity does not mean that Augustine describes reality as egalitarian or nonhierarchical. He does have a conception of the equality of creatures, but it is nothing like the equality that is usually discussed in modern writings about ecological ethics. The equality that all creatures share is the equality of being creatures of God. Such equality is important, however, since the ability to perceive goodness and value its manifold expression in the diversity of creatures is possible because of the world's origin in God's creative work. God has made insects to exist, just as he has made human beings, rocks, and angels. All hold the same goodness of being that the others hold because of their origin in God. Nevertheless, each creature holds that goodness differently, according to the limited capacity that the unlimited God has given it.

If all creatures hold an equality of being because of their origin in God's creative work, their variety of expressions of being according to their measure, number, and weight suggests that God has ordered the creation. That ordering of creatures according to their particular capacities of being is described along many different lines by Augustine. For example, there are creatures which are purely spiritual (i.e., angels) and others that are material (i.e., rocks), and yet others that hold both spiritual and material properties (i.e., human beings).[6] Another way that he describes their ordering is according to the simplicity of their being, so that spiritual creatures are only temporally mutable, while humans and material creatures are materially finite and temporally mutable. That there is a difference in the simplicity of created substances suggests for Augustine that some are better than others according to the limits of their mutability.[7] Yet another way to describe the ordering of creatures is through his observation that some creatures provide nourishment for others.[8] As well, there is the ordering of creatures by which human beings are given to rule over other earthly creatures.[9] He explains this ordering as an instance of how human beings are created to the image of God, but describes it according to the observation that human beings can rationally observe and act upon their observations in ways that other animals do not seem to act. Regardless of whether Augustine's observations are all scientifically justified or not, he has observed that creatures are ordered in relation to one another in various ways.

The problem of hierarchy, as presented in ecological ethics or theological critiques of classical thought, is usually expressed as one of valuing the spiritual over the physical, the human over the nonhuman, the male over the female, and the eternal over the finite.[10] Thus, the idea of heaven as a spiritual realm means that the physical world is disdained as transitory and therefore expendable. The eternal by definition is superior to the finite because the one continues (usually without change) while the other is in a constant flux that eventually dissipates and ends in absolute death. Human beings, because they partake in spiritual qualities, such as having hope of eternal life in heaven, therefore naturally are superior to merely earthly creatures that have no such hope. Some combination of these pictures of classical religious hierarchies often ends up being expressed by the idea that the one is given priority and power over the many. Thus, Boff and Gunton are both critical of the classical expression of the doctrine of the Trinity in its Western formulation, and are critical of Augustine in particular, because of his favoring of oneness over threeness in his doctrine of the Trinity. Boff and Gunton trace such a conception of God to an acceptance that human power ought to be modeled on divine power, via the image of God.[11]

As we have shown, though, Augustine's trinitarian theology does not reflect such a negative commitment to hierarchy, nor does it find expression in his doctrine of creation. He does not value the spiritual over the physical, but regards their ordering in terms of the degrees of change that occur (temporal or material and temporal) to distinguish them. In the face of death, eternity is preferable to finitude, but he sees all creatures as being subject to finitude. That is part of the essence of creaturely being. That there is hope for eternal life does not mean that there is no eternal body, since being embodied is part of being a creature. That the body may become spiritual in the resurrection does not disqualify the goodness of bodies.[12] Rather, it amplifies the fact that God loves bodies. Indeed, God loves bodies so much that his Son became incarnate in order to bring redemption to the creation. That is the foundation upon which Augustine builds his doctrine of the Trinity.[13] Indeed, Augustine's description of nature as a book that can be read to see the goodness and greatness of God, as we discovered in the last chapter, not only is a clear statement of the beauty and goodness of creation, but also is a condemnation of those who look at the creation but fail to see its goodness and fail to praise God as a result.[14] This is hardly a hierarchy of power, where the many are reduced to subservience by God or by those few with enough power to dominate others. We shall return to the nature of hierarchy again in subsequent points. Here we have set out the fact that Augustine's view of created hierarchy is ontological in form, not one that is meant to devalue other creatures. The hierarchical understanding of the created order that Augustine works with also does not destroy the sense of interrelatedness that is expressed through Augustine's vision of creatures that are good and that together compose a creation that is very good and a delight to the Trinity.

Divine Providence and the Dynamic Structure of Reality

One of the problems that we saw recited by Boff and Gunton in chapter 1 was that the classical church was seduced by Greek philosophical categories that promoted abstraction from the constantly changing world and a logic rooted in the changelessness of eternity. This affected the doctrine of the Trinity by neglecting the foundational accounts of God's trinitarian activities in creation in favor of speculative metaphysics. For Gunton, Augustine's dislike of the material creation corresponded with this philosophical bent toward abstraction, thus removing God from the creation and devaluing the material world. However, our analysis of Augustine's understanding of creation shows that abstract logic is not at the root of Augustine's theology. Most important for our purposes is his theology of divine providence. The blending of conceptions of creaturely motion, with the capacity for a limited measure, number, and weight, and of the desire for rest in God helps Augustine to understand how creatures have been created, and how the divine persons are at work in the providential governance of the world. As we observed, the dynamic and interrelated nature of the creation can be explained in part by Augustine's doctrine of the Trinity, which itself reflects the dynamic motion of the divine substance that each of the divine persons is—namely, love.

This understanding of the creation's dynamic movement provides a context in which to define the meaning of creation. Creatures are not only given their value by being God's good creatures, but their meaning is always in relation to God's care for every creature by making it, sustaining it, and drawing it to its natural end in God. While Augustine quoted Paul to explain how humanity has its being in God, he understood all creatures to be in God, who never withdraws from sustaining the creation.[15] That the dynamic movement of creation is in God means that there is a purpose that is exemplified in that very motion that is natural to creaturely being. It is the movement of divine love that brings creation into being and causes it to move in its own limited perfections to find rest in the triune God of love. If the dynamic purpose of creation is to find its end in God, then the acting out of the human vocation will need to be in keeping with God's delight in creation as it moves toward God. The goal of human existence is not to overcome change and finitude; rather, change and finitude are the means by which existence is affirmed and celebrated as from God, who is an eternal movement of love in three persons. Moreover, the end that all creatures have in God is described as peace.[16] Since the peace of the creation, not only of humanity, is part of God's providential structuring of reality, Augustine's moral interpretation of human activities in terms of achieving peace as part of the creation only makes sense. It is that moral aspect of Augustine's view of creation to which we now turn.

Use, Enjoyment, and Consumption

Moving from the themes pertaining to Augustine's worldview and the shape it takes according to his trinitarian understanding of creation, we also find that Augustine understands the necessity for human activity to be guided by the trinitarian understanding of creation. The most basic theme is that of loving God and one's neighbor as oneself. In describing how this work of love is to be carried out, Augustine developed a terminological distinction between use and enjoyment. As we saw in the last chapter, Augustine described, on the one hand, enjoyment as the love of something in itself, which should be directed to the stable, unchanging source of perfect goodness and love, God. In this respect, to enjoy another creature is to attach oneself to something as an end in itself, something that is not the reliable source of perfect goodness and love in itself, since only God is the true source of love. Use, on the other hand, is a form of love and valuation that is properly directed toward one's neighbor, valuing them for their goodness and how they refer one to love of God. This is true not only of other human beings, but also of creatures. To use a creature is to love the goods that it refers one to, but not to fixate on those goods as originating in the creature. For example we might use and value the sun for its light, warmth, and beauty. But the sun is not to be enjoyed as an end in itself, because it and the good effects of it come from God and not from the sun.[17] To love the sun in itself would be similar to idolizing it, or at least coveting it for the sake of one's own greedy consumption. A person's greed for food or money would be a similar bad employment of enjoyment for something that only ought to be used. In *The Trinity* he explains that what he means is "not that the creature is not to be loved, but if that love is related to the creator it will no longer be covetousness but charity."[18] Deciding how to act, then, requires discerning what a right action is. If nature is indeed a book that tells us about God, then we need to learn how to read it. The proper use of creatures is possible because we can read nature and see who the subject of their story is, and enjoy that story in all its goodness because of its author.

The right use of creation is first and foremost a type of love and valuation that sees God as the true source of all goodness. How does this relate to modern ecological concerns? The major cause of much of the ecological trouble we face is the human use of the world without respect for the complex natural relationships by which it has been composed and the balance that it exhibits. In some respects that use could be described as covetousness and greed for material pleasure, perhaps even an addiction to consumption without any boundaries. This may be an example of using something because it pleases us, and we are content to find ultimate love in ourselves and our own pleasures; or it could also be an example of using the world as an end in itself, seeing it as an end in itself. Either way, there seems to be no external reference by which it is possible to judge how one ought to use (love) the creation well. Augustine's employment of use and enjoyment is able to provide an external rule by which use can be evaluated as beneficial or detrimental. This is not a universal rule, inasmuch as it is a theological argument based on a Christian worldview that contextualizes the proper forms of love and their appropriate objects. However, it is useful for showing that there are good and bad ways to love creatures within the Christian context. The proper use and enjoyment of the world opposes the tendency to destructive, unlimited consumption. The limits it places on consumption are fitted to respect the goodness of creation that Augustine finds in his trinitarian understanding of creation and providence.

Dominion and Domination

Building on the basic distinction between use and enjoyment as a means to judge what and how one ought to love, Augustine's discussion of dominion should be understood as about a human work exercising the proper use of creation. It has been made clear already that use is not to be thought of in terms of using something as a means to an end (which, if baldly followed as a principle, would amount to covetousness or idolatry), but rather as loving something by valuing its goods always in reference to the enjoyment of God. Dominion is the exercise of rule that human beings can carry out in the world because God has given to humanity the capability of reasoned action. For Augustine dominion in its most practical form is represented by vocations such as shepherding and farming, as well as the political rule that enables societies to flourish in peace.[19] The danger of dominion from an ecological perspective is that it represents the domination of human reason over the world, the license to exercise arbitrary will without restraint. This possible interpretation of the meaning of dominion, based on the term's historical associations with the absolute rule of kings and despots and the rhetoric of modern science conquering the world and exposing its mysteries and secrets, certainly is capable of limiting its ethical value. Modern theological critiques, such as we have seen in Boff's and Gunton's work, of how concepts of God were formulated in conformity to politically motivated ideologies also have made it difficult to find positive grounds on which to promote the continued usage of a term like dominion. It seems freighted with too much questionable baggage.

Despite our natural hesitation to use the word "dominion" in light of some of its history, there must also be latitude extended to the term's validity. It is impossible not to deal with a term that has such a long history, even an authoritative stature, in theological history. Augustine does use the term, and therefore it is imperative to know how he used it. Rather than being guilty of exercising an arbitrary will and excising the term and Augustine's use of it, we have traced its place in Augustine's thought and found that it has a rather positive role to play in understanding how human beings are to carry out their works vis-à-vis other creatures. Dominion, or rule, is to reflect the human vocation of being the image of God in the world. To be the image of God, for Augustine, is to seek out God and cling to him in the Son and Holy Spirit in the particular way that God has made humanity (without losing sight of the fact that the purpose of existence and the end of all creatures is to find rest in God according to divine providence).[20] Dominion as a reflection of the image of God is the rule of the generosity of love, which makes it possible for others to know the love of God (the example that is to be followed in this regard is the incarnate Son who died on a cross for the sake of the creatures he made).

Keeping in mind Augustine's moral reading of the significance of God's creative work, the dominion of the land or animals is the exercise of human reason not merely to use animals or the land as ends in themselves (idolatry) or because humanity is to enjoy itself through others (covetousness, greed, sin). It is the exercise of human reason to use (love) God's creation as God's, and thereby to love God as the proper end. If human domination of the land and animals actually destroys the creation and causes harm that need not arise, then it can hardly be called dominion (except in a perverse way). God did not create the world to enjoy its diminution and to delight in its domination and abuse. Human beings, which are some of the creatures that God has created in a universe of creatures, are called to love God and love the way that God loves, which they can know and do through the providential and redemptive work of God. One can imagine Augustine saying that farmers have dominion over the land by explaining that through their use of creation they will know its goodness according to the proportion it ought to be known, and praise it for the glory it reveals about God and his delight in creating and preserving (through divine governance) good things. And, inasmuch as peace is the end of all creatures, one must respect the need for a certain interdependence of creatures by which peace is to be found, not by domination.[21]

Dominion and Stewardship

The account of dominion that we have drawn out from Augustine's trinitarian understanding of creation does not amount to a clear definition of stewardship as it is put forward in contemporary theology and ecological ethics. Models of stewardship are spelled out now in the face of an ecological devastation that requires certain nuances of stewardship that would be novel to Augustine's contemporaries. Nevertheless, an Augustinian understanding of dominion can still contribute to the contemporary discussion about dominion as stewardship. His ability to draw out a clear relationship between God's creative work and its moral implications for human works provides a way that one can assess theological attempts to define stewardship. There is a clear thematic connection between God's creative work and redemptive work; it is spelled out by Augustine using the doctrine of the Trinity as the bridge. This trinitarian connection between creation and redemption carries over into his moral theology about humanity being created to the image of God, about use and enjoyment, and about dominion. The effect of this is to provide a basis for doctrine and moral theology in God's economic work through the Son and the Spirit. This gives theological definitions of stewardship a richer vocabulary that brings together scriptural texts within a trinitarian worldview.

It is clear that Augustine did not develop his theological work in terms that favored a Greek metaphysics of static, timeless existence, built upon an abstract logic that avoided the reality of a diverse and changing world. In fact, contrary to many popular accounts, his doctrine of creation grows out his understanding of the doctrine of the Trinity, a doctrine that itself was developed out of the biblical story of redemption of the world through the divine economy. The conception of God as an arbitrary will that funded a justification for an Augustinian portrayal of humanity as rulers of the earth through dominating power also falls short of the reality that one finds in Augustine's writings. He has a rich exposition of God as love and how that is displayed in the creative work of God. The ecological significance of Augustine's trinitarian theology is its development of a trinitarian worldview that provides a clear and substantial account of the relationship between God and the world as it is found in the scriptural and doctrinal traditions. This is achieved through the unifying theme of the doctrine of the Trinity, which is how Augustine is able to explain God's providential care for the creation. In addition, he extends the comprehensive picture that he captures in his theological worldview to its implications for the Christian life by relating God's work to the moral nature of existence. Augustine's doctrinal work and the ethical themes that arise out of that work provide a strong basis for dialogue and debate about the development of the doctrine of creation in modern trinitarian accounts of ecological ethics.

Notes

Introduction

1. Colin Gunton, *The One, the Three and the Many: God, Creation, and the Culture of Modernity* (Cambridge: Cambridge University Press, 1993), 54.

2. Leonardo Boff is a proponent of "perichoresis" as a key term for bringing traditional theological concepts such as the Trinity into contemporary dialogues about political, social, ecclesial, and ecological issues. See, for example, *Cry of the Earth, Cry of the Poor*, trans. P. Berryman (Maryknoll, NY: Orbis Books, 1997), 164ff. For a critical reflection on the use of perichoresis in theology, see R. E. Otto, "The Use and Abuse of Perichoresis in Recent Theology," *Scottish Journal of Theology* 54 (2001): 366–84.

3. Lynn White, "The Historical Roots of Our Ecologic Crisis," *Science* 155 (1967): 1203–7.

4. We will not tackle the contemporary historical-critical debates about the meaning of dominion in the text of Genesis 1:26–28. It will suffice to note that scholars have delved into the substance of these debates and have produced helpful summaries and applications for discussions about religious approaches to ecology. See, for example, Jeremy Cohen's historical survey, *Be Fertile and Increase, Fill the Earth and Master It: The Ancient and Medieval Career of a Biblical Text* (Ithaca, NY: Cornell University Press, 1989); William P. Brown, *The Ethos of the Cosmos: The Genesis of Moral Imagination in the Bible* (Grand Rapids, MI: Eerdmans, 1999), esp. chap. 2; Ronald A. Simkins, *Creator and Creation: Nature in the Worldview of Ancient Israel* (Peabody, MA: Hendrickson, 1994); Michael Welker, *Creation and Reality*, trans. J. F. Hoffmeyer (Minneapolis, MN: Fortress Press, 1999), 60–73; and J. Richard Middleton, *The Liberating Image: The Imago Dei in Genesis 1* (Grand Rapids, MI: Brazos, 2005). The application of the command to have dominion, while sometimes interpreted negatively as a license for domination, is understood in most current literature as a command to exercise care, or stewardship, for the earth. Our concern is what the term meant in light of Augustine's theological conceptions of God and creation.

5. For example, see Cohen, *Be Fertile*, who finds little in the history of classical and medieval interpretation on dominion that relates to stewardship or caretaking of the earth. What he does find is that many theologians understood dominion primarily as a way to interpret the claim that human beings are made

in the image of God; usually it implied exercising a rational rule over nonrational creatures.

6. Rosemary Radford Ruether, *Sexism and God-Talk: Towards a Feminist Theology* (Boston: Beacon Press, 1983); idem. *Gaia & God: An Ecofeminist Theology of Earth Healing* (San Francisco: HarperSanFrancisco, 1992); and idem, *New Woman/New Earth: Sexist Ideologies and Human Liberation* (New York: Seabury Press, 1975).

7. Anne Primavasi, *From Apocalypse to Genesis: Ecology, Feminism and Christianity* (Minneapolis, MN: Fortress Press, 1991); and idem, "Ecology and Christian Hierarchy," in *Sacred Custodians of the Earth: Women, Spirituality, and the Environment?* ed. A. Low and S. Tremayne (New York: Berghahn Books, 2001), 121–39.

8. Boff, *Cry of the Earth*, for example, relies on their critiques of the concept of dominion and how traditional theologies used it for his own interpretation of the history of the doctrine of the Trinity.

9. G. E. Likens defines an ecosystem as "a spatially explicit unit of the Earth that includes all of the organisms, along with all components of the abiotic environment within its boundaries." Likens, in *The Ecosystem Approach: Its Use and Abuse*, (Oldendorf/Luhe, Germany: Ecology Institute, 1992), quoted in the Ecological Society of America, "The Scientific Basis for Ecosystem Management," September 15, 1997, http://www.epa.gov/ecocommunity/tools/ecosysmn.pdf.

10. The essay noted above by the Ecological Society of America, "The Scientific Basis for Ecosystem Management," is part of the literature that the United States Environmental Protection Agency makes available on the discipline of ecology, for the purpose of promoting the development of an environmental ethic of management. The EPA essay assumes that a relationship exists between scientific research and ethical practices, beginning with the guiding statement: "We should manage so as not to deny future generations the opportunities and resources we enjoy today." This clearly sets out moral implications that arise from scientific research—namely, the promotion of the moral good of enjoyment for present and future generations. The science of ecology is important for ethically sound management. While leaving the moral ramifications of the research to others who wish to make use of it, they do make an effort to present their research as part of the solution to larger moral questions about the world. Ruether, in *Gaia & God*, goes beyond this cautious attempt to link science and ethics, stating simply that science is to be used "as normative or as ethically prescriptive" (47). Her claim is that the earth (Gaia) is an evolving consciousness through human evolution and human consciousness. Conscience, which is part of human consciousness, is also part of earth-consciousness, through evolution. Therefore, science, which tracks evolution, is a key part of the description of consciousness and conscience. Scientific knowledge must be taken into account as one attempts to understand what is ethically prescriptive.

11. Thus, Roderick Nash, *The Rights of Nature: A History of Environmental Ethics* (Madison: University of Wisconsin Press, 1989). An example of how ecosystems can be characterized in an environmental ethic using terminology that includes "community" and "health" is Conrad Brunk and Scott A. Dunham, "Ecosystem Justice in the Canadian Fisheries," in *Just Fish: Ethics and Canadian Marine Fisheries*,

ed. H. Coward, R. Ommer, and T. Pitcher (St. John's, NF: ISER, 2000), 9–33.

12. James Nash, *Loving Nature: Ecological Integrity and Christian Responsibility*, (Nashville, TN: Abingdon, 1991).

13. Ibid., 18.

14. Ibid., 95.

15. Ibid., 63–67.

16. Ibid., 67.

17. E.g., the significance of the Incarnation of Jesus Christ for creation (ibid., 108–11), the work of the Holy Spirit in creation (111–16), and the idea of human responsibility toward nature as expressed in the command to have dominion in Genesis 1:26–28 (102–8).

18. E.g., by means of his definition of Christian love in ibid., chaps. 6–7.

19. Douglas John Hall, *The Steward: A Biblical Symbol Come of Age*, rev. ed. (Grand Rapids, MI: Eerdmans, 1990); and idem, *Imaging God: Dominion as Stewardship* (Grand Rapids, MI: Eerdmans, 1986).

20. Catherine Roach, "Stewards of the Sea: A Model for Justice?" in *Just Fish: Ethics and Canadian Marine Fisheries*, ed. H. Coward, R. Ommer, and T. Pitcher (St. John's, NF: ISER, 2000), 67–82.

21. Jürgen Moltmann, *God in Creation: An Ecological Doctrine of Creation*, trans. M. Kohl (Minneapolis, MN: Fortress Press, 1993), 236–40.

22. Ibid., 240.

23. Sallie McFague, "A Square in the Quilt," in *Spirit and Nature: Why the Environment Is a Religious Issue, an Interfaith Dialogue*, ed. S. C. Rockefeller and J. C. Elder (Boston: Beacon Press, 1992), 49ff., has contended similarly that the historical Christian expression of God as a king exercising dominion over creation, does two things. First, it makes God appear distant and untouchable, like a human monarch who rules, at best, through a kind of disinterested benevolence (understood to be the price of understanding God as transcendent and uninterested in the creation), or, at worst, through an exercise of dominion that is tantamount to sheer domination. Second, the expression of God as king fails to take seriously God's relationship to the whole creation. According to McFague, a human monarch, while claiming dominion over lands, nonetheless is concerned primarily with the rule of human beings. From a monarch's point of view, other creatures are largely irrelevant apart from their utility for human purposes. At the very least, McFague's description of kingly rule lacks nuance.

24. Moltmann, *God in Creation*, 240–42.

Chapter One

1. An articulation of this division is found in T. R. Martland, "A Study of Cappadocian and Augustinian Trinitarian Methodology," *Anglican Theological Review* 47 (1965): 252–63. M. R. Barnes has traced the roots of this assumption and some of its unfortunate consequences for the interpretation of classical writings in "Augustine in Contemporary Trinitarian Theology," *Theological Studies*

56 (1995): 237–50. Barnes argues that the division took hold in the nineteenth century, and has since become normative, although it remains without sufficient justification.

2. Leonardo Boff, in *Holy Trinity, Perfect Community*, trans. P. Berryman (Maryknoll, NY: Orbis Books, 2000), 121, defines monarchy as "the unique causality of the Father; it is the Father alone who generates the Son and spirates (as the Father of the Son) the Holy Spirit: a characteristically Greek Orthodox expression." See T. F. Torrance, *The Christian Doctrine of God: One Being, Three Persons* (Edinburgh: T. and T. Clark, 1996), 141.

3. Athanasius played a key role in developing a theological understanding of the Father as the origin of the Son and the source of divine unity. See Peter Widdicombe, *The Fatherhood of God from Origen to Athanasius*, rev. ed. (Oxford: Clarendon Press, 2000), 174–75. Likewise, in post-Nicene orthodoxy the Cappadocians maintained the emphasis on the Father as the "sole *archē*," see B. Studer, *Trinity and Incarnation*, trans. M. Westerhoff, ed. A. Louth (Collegeville. MN: Michael Glazier, 1993), 146.

4. Examples of how the concept of monarchy was used by Hippolytus and Tertullian to indicate the Father as the beginning of the Son and the Holy Spirit are noted in J. N. D. Kelly, *Early Christian Doctrines*, rev. ed. (San Francisco: HarperSanFrancisco, 1976), 111–12; B. de Margerie, *The Christian Trinity in History*, trans. E. J. Fortman, Studies in Historical Theology, vol. 10 (Petersham, UK: St. Bede's, 1982), 81–85; and J. Pelikan, *The Christian Tradition: A History of the Development of Doctrine*, vol. 1, *The Emergence of the Catholic Tradition (100–600)* (Chicago: University of Chicago Press, 1971), 36ff.

5. Pannenberg, for example, still assumes that the Father's monarchy is necessary for explicating the doctrine of the Trinity. Wolfhart Pannenberg, *Systematic Theology*, trans. G. Bromiley (Grand Rapids. MI: Eerdmans, 1991–98), 1.324–27.

6. Leonard Boff, *Trinity and Society*, trans. P. Burns (Maryknoll, NY: Orbis Books, 1988), 7, 81–83.

7. Ibid., 4, 47–49.

8. Boff, *Holy Trinity, Perfect Community*, 43–44.

9. Boff, *Trinity and Society*, 5–6.

10. A summary of such a danger for different aspects of society is described in Boff, *Holy Trinity, Perfect Community*, 7–9. He uses the terms "totalitarianism," "authoritarianism," "paternalism," and "machismo" to explain what is here covered by the term "patriarchalism." In *Trinity and Society*, 15, he refers to the focus on the Father over against the other two persons as manifesting itself in society as patriarchalism.

11. Boff, *Trinity and Society*, 21, 82, 120–22, and 172–73. Boff is suspicious of a potential, lingering subordinationism despite his recognition that the egalitarian language and definitions of the ecumenical and Roman councils stressed how none of the persons is inferior to the others (81).

12. Which Boff refers to as the Thomistic theme of the Western church (Boff, *Trinity and Society*, 79–80).

13. Which Boff refers to as the Augustinian theme of the Western church (ibid., 80).

14. Ibid., 4. One sees this assumption also in Thomas Marsh's historical survey in *The Triune God* (Mystic, CT: Twenty-third Publications, 1994), 132.

15. Boff, *Trinity and Society*, 17–18.

16. For Boff, Rahner's axiom—that the immanent Trinity is the economic Trinity and vice versa—in conjunction with a socially informed ontology of "history, process, and freedom" provides a more adequate method for the development of the doctrine of the Trinity (Boff, *Trinity and Society*, 112).

17. Boff, *Trinity and Society*, 46–47.

18. Ibid., 80.

19. Ibid., 112, 117–18.

20. *Holy Trinity, Perfect Community*, 31.

21. Boff, *Trinity and Society*, 16–17.

22. Ibid.

23. Boff points to studies that argue for a direct correlation between classical Christian theologies and patriarchy, such as M. Daly, *Beyond God the Father* (Boston: Beacon Press, 1973); and Jürgen Moltmann, *The Trinity and the Kingdom*, trans. M. Kohl (San Francisco: Harper and Row, 1981), 118–22.

24. Boff, *Trinity and Society*, 169. Cf. Moltmann, *God in Creation*, 236–40.

25. Boff, *Trinity and Society*, 11.

26. Ibid., 20–23. Boff cites the example of Genghis Khan's claim to authority based on monotheism, "In heaven there is but one God, and on earth but one Lord, Genghis Khan, the Son of God." Qtd. in J. Moltmann, "The Inviting Unity of the Triune God," trans. R. Nowell, *Concilium* 177 (1985), 51.

27. Boff, *Trinity and Society*, 16–17.

28. Ibid., 25–26. The gradual recognition, revealed over time, of the three persons of the Godhead fits well with Boff's understanding of the evolution of all knowledge in a cosmogenic process, an understanding that informs his own ecological theology. The Trinity chose to reveal itself gradually, as humanity evolved in its capacity to know. See Boff, *Holy Trinity, Perfect Community*, 100–101, and idem, *Cry of the Earth*, 163ff.

29. On the importance of the economy as a foundation for the doctrine of the Trinity, see Boff, *Trinity and Society*, chap. 2, and 76–84.

30. Ibid., 10–16.

31. Ibid., 11.

32. Boff, *Cry of the Earth*, 13–20.

33. Ibid., chap. 3.

34. Several of Gunton's texts will aid us in understanding Gunton's argument: *The Promise of Trinitarian Theology* (Edinburgh: T. and T. Clark, 1991), chap. 3; *The One, the Three, and the Many* (Cambridge: Cambridge University Press, 1993); *The Triune Creator: A Historical and Systematic Study* (Grand Rapids, MI: Eerdmans, 1998); "Between Allegory and Myth: The Legacy of the Spiritualising of Genesis," in *The Doctrine of Creation*, ed. Gunton (Edinburgh: T. and T. Clark, 1997), 47–62; and "The End of Causality? The Reformers and Their Predecessors," in *The Doctrine of Creation*, ed. Gunton (Edinburgh: T. and T. Clark, 1997), 63–82.

35. In this Gunton builds upon similar moves by other theologians, such as Robert Jenson, whose own discussion of the rise of the doctrine also follows the

division between East and West, though with less enthusiasm for the triumphs of the Eastern model. See his *The Triune Identity* (Philadelphia: Fortress Press, 1982), 118–19. Similarly, Catherine Mowry LaCugna argues that Augustine departed "from the biblical and patristic doctrine of the monarchy of the Father." LaCugna, *God for Us: The Trinity and Christian Life* (San Francisco: HarperCollins, 1991), 99.

36. Gunton, *Promise of Trinitarian Theology*, 32.

37. Ibid., 54.

38. Ibid., 55.

39. Ibid., 33–34.

40. Ibid., 34–35.

41. Thus, Gunton cites Augustine, *Trinity* 3.27, 4.31.

42. Gunton, *Promise of Trinitarian Theology*, 35–36.

43. Ibid., 44.

44. Ibid., 42–45.

45. Ibid., 39.

46. John Zizioulas, *Being as Communion: Studies in Personhood and the Church* (Crestwood, NY: St. Vladimir's Seminary Press, 1985).

47. Gunton, *Promise of Trinitarian Theology*, 39.

48. As evidence, Gunton cites *Trinity* 5.10, where Augustine complains about the confusion caused by the terms *hypostases* and *ousia*, which when translated into Latin can both refer to nature or substance.

49. I.e., Augustine, *Trinity*, trans. E. Hill, Works of Saint Augustine, pt. 1, vol. 5 (Brooklyn, NY: New City Press, 1991), 7.11.

50. Gunton, *Promise of Trinitarian Theology*, 39–41.

51. Ibid., 42.

52. Ibid., 53.

53. Ibid.

54. Gunton, *One, the Three, and the Many*, 2.

55. Ibid., 54–56.

56. Ibid., 2–3, 54–56.

57. Ibid., 2. Also see Gunton, *Triune Creator*, 76–79.

58. Gunton, *One, the Three, and the Many*, 2–3, and repeated on 56 n. 21.

59. Ibid., 58. Gunton, in "Between Allegory and Myth," 49, also comments, "It is with this theologian [Augustine] that there comes into theology the notion of creation as the product of abstract omnipotence, inadequately related to the economy of salvation."

60. Gunton, *Triune Creator*, 180–81.

61. Ibid., 83–84; and idem, "Between Allegory and Myth," 56.

62. Gunton, *One, the Three, and the Many*, 58.

63. Ibid., 140.

64. Ibid., 83. For Gunton, what confirms his concern that finite, changing things are less than good is Augustine's claim in *The Confessions*, trans. H. Chadwick, (Oxford: Oxford University Press, 1991), 12.7 that all material things are "close to nothing" (Gunton, *The Triune Creator*, 78–79).

65. Gunton, *The Triune Creator*, 76.

66. Gunton again refers to Augustine, *Confessions* 12.7. According to Gunton, in *Triune Creator*, 74–75, Augustine's statement of the Christological nature of divine creation is limited to a few brief statements: *Confessions* 12.7, 13.2; *City of God* 11.32; and the *Literal Commentary* 1.3. In fact, the reference to the *Literal Commentary* 1.3 should actually be to the *Unfinished Literal Meaning of Genesis* 1.2 and 3.6. The latter reference Gunton confusingly does not call the *Unfinished Literal Meaning of Genesis*, but simply the *Literal Commentary*.

67. Gunton, *The Triune Creator*, 74–75, also cf. 53.

68. Ibid., 75–76.

69. For Gunton, one of the most significant contributions to a trinitarian doctrine of creation is found in the Cappadocian understanding of the Holy Spirit: "According to Saint Basil, the distinctive feature of the Spirit is to perfect the creation, and we can interpret this as meaning to bring to completion that for which each person and thing is created. In that respect, the distinctive work of the Spirit is eschatological. One way of expanding such an insight theologically would be to say that the Spirit's peculiar office is to realize the true being of each created thing by bringing it, through Christ, into saving relation with God the Father" (Gunton, *One, the Three, and the Many*, 189–90).

70. Gunton, *One, the Three, and the Many*, 120.

71. Ibid., 137–38.

72. Ibid., 159 n. 5.

73. Ibid., 55–56.

74. Ibid., 205; and Gunton, "End of Causality?" 67.

75. Marsh, *Triune God*, 132. Later in the chapter (p. 137), in criticism of the "double procession" of the Holy Spirit, Marsh quotes from Augustine, *Trinity* 15.29 regarding the Father being the principal source of the Son and the Holy Spirit. He notes that this is one of the "rare" occasions that Augustine acknowledges that tradition of the Father's monarchy. Marsh is suggesting that Augustine does not follow the Nicene tradition because he does not state it frequently. Of course, such a critique is suspect, since how rarely one says something also can be an indication of the degree that it has become an assumption that need not be frequently stated.

76. Augustine, *Trinity* 1.5.

77. Augustine, *Trinity* 1.7.

78. Marsh, *Triune God*, 140–42. K. Rahner, *The Trinity*, trans. J. Donceel (Wellwood, UK: Burns and Oates, 1970), 10–12, reaches a similar conclusion—that Christian piety loses its connection to the Trinity beginning with Augustine's doctrine of the Trinity.

79. Augustine, *Trinity* 1.7.

80. On the authoritative value of the scriptures for understanding who God is and God's works of creation, providence, and redemption, see Augustine, *The Literal Meaning of Genesis*, trans. J. H. Taylor, Ancient Christian Writers, nos. 41–42 (New York: Newman Press, 1982), 4.21.38 (unless otherwise indicated, all citations of *The Literal Meaning* in the book are to this translation). There Augustine indicates

his belief in the trustworthiness of the scriptural witness: "[T]here can be no error in Scripture. . . ." He also understands the origin of scripture to be related to the work of the Holy Spirit, "But as much has been told as was judged necessary by the Holy Spirit as He inspired the writer, who put down those things . . ." (5.8.23). In *The City of God Against the Pagans*, trans. R. W. Dyson (Cambridge: Cambridge University Press, 1998), 11.3, Augustine writes, that Jesus Christ "established the Scriptures. . . . These have the most eminent authority, and we trust them in all matters of which it is not expedient for us to be ignorant but which we are not capable of knowing for ourselves." The scriptures reflect the trinitarian nature of their origin, and their authority for understanding the nature of the trinitarian God is essential to Augustine. For further reflections on the importance of history and scriptural faith for Augustine, see Basil Studer, "History and Faith in Augustine's *De Trinitate*," *Augustinian Studies* 28 (1997): 7–50.

81. For example, the importance of the Nicene Creed in the patristic church centered around the controversial and nonbiblical term *homoousion*, which was associated with Greek philosophical tradition (though Augustine rarely referred specifically to the Nicene Creed in his argumentation), as shown in J. N. D. Kelly, *Early Christian Creeds*, 3rd ed. (New York: Longman, 1972), 242–62.

82. On the influence of philosophical traditions on Augustine, see C. N. Cochrane, *Christianity and Classical Culture: A Study of Thought and Action from Augustus to Augustine* (New York: Oxford University Press, 1957), 376–98, and chap. 11, where Cochrane discusses Augustine's trinitarian theology and Platonism. That Augustine was influenced by philosophical thought cannot be denied, as one sees throughout his *Confessions*, where he describes his journey to conversion as including the influence of several philosophical writers, including Cicero and Plotinus. However, to speak of their influence is not the same thing as to say that they were more foundationally critical to his method than his faith in the risen Christ and the biblical explanation of God's work of salvation. With regard to the philosophical and theological resources in Augustine's method of inquiry in *The Trinity*, see R. D. Crouse, "St. Augustine's *De Trinitate*: Philosophical Method," in *Studia Patristica 16*, ed. E. A. Livingstone (Berlin: Akademie-Verlag, 1985), 501–10. Some related comments are found in E. Muller, "The Dynamic of Augustine's *De Trinitate*: A Response to a Recent Characterization," *Augustinian Studies* 26 (1995): 65–91. The possibility that Augustine's understanding of the relationship of philosophy and faith was balanced, with each accorded its proper place (as opposed to the assumption that he simply downplayed the theological-biblical traditions of the church in favor of philosophical method), is briefly outlined by J. M. Rist, *Augustine: Ancient Thought Baptized* (Cambridge: Cambridge University Press, 1994), esp. 5–10. Rist's book provides a bibliography of sources for those interested in Augustine's philosophical foundations.

83. Michel R. Barnes, "Exegesis and Polemic in Augustine's *De Trinitate* I," *Augustinian Studies* 30 (1999): 43–59. He uses a detailed analysis of the scriptural passages Augustine focuses on in the first book of *The Trinity* to develop a picture of "homoean" theologies, on the theory that Augustine develops his argument in the first seven books according to the polemical climate of the time. He also compares Augustine's defense with earlier homoean writings, and with those of pro-

Nicene theologians such as Hilary. Also helpful is Michel R. Barnes, "The Arians of Book V, and the Genre of *De Trinitate*," *Journal of Theological Studies*, n.s., 44 (1993): 185–95; and idem, "The Fourth Century as Trinitarian Canon," in *Christian Origins: Theology, Rhetoric, and Community*, ed. L. Ayres and G. Jones (New York: Routledge, 1998), 47–67. For the wider historical context, see R. P. C. Hanson, *The Search for the Christian Doctrine of God* (Edinburgh: T. and T. Clark, 1988), 557–97, who provides a detailed picture of Homoean Arianism up to 381.

84. While Augustine does use the term 'substance' (*substantia*) throughout *Trinity* 5–7 to refer to God's "being," he typically prefers other terms such as *essentia*. In *City of God* 12.2, Augustine explains that *essentia* is a relatively new Latin technical term to express the meaning of the Greek *ousian*. Lewis Ayres, "The Fundamental Grammar of Augustine's Trinitarian Theology," in *Augustine and His Critics: Essays in Honor of Gerald Bonner*, ed. R. Dodaro and G. Lawless (New York: Routledge, 2000), 51–76, points out that Augustine preferred the terms "essence" (*essentia*) or "divinity" (*divinitas*) to express the meaning of the Greek term, instead of "substance" (*substantia*), which he thought could be misleading if one thinks of substance as a "unitary 'reality' apart from the three persons" (62). Michael Hanby, *Augustine and Modernity* (London: Routledge, 2003), concurs with this idea, noting that "though Augustine is notorious for lacking a technical vocabulary and sometimes refers to God colloquially as *substantia*, in non-colloquial speech he explicitly rejects the designation of *substantia* as improper, instead preferring *essentia*, since the former term implies that 'God subsists, and is a subject, in relation to his own Goodness' " (154). *Substantia* potentially can be thought to be different from the three persons, which is precisely what Augustine wants to avoid (e.g., *Trinity* 7.5.10). Thus, one needs to be careful to recognize that Augustine's use of the term to speak about God's being is done with full awareness of the potentially improper ways that it might be used.

85. E.g., Augustine, *Trinity* 1.7–8.

86. E.g., Augustine, *Trinity* 1.8–10.

87. Augustine, *Trinity* 1–4.

88. Augustine, *Trinity* 5–7. The modalist problem is one that is not taken up exclusively in these books. Rather, Augustine attempts to lay out, throughout the first seven books, ways of understanding the Trinity that do not subordinate the Son and Holy Spirit. Arianism is the primary object of Augustine's arguments. Nevertheless, he does argue, especially in *Trinity* 5–7, against a position where the three are indistinct from a prior divine substance, and where the Son and Holy Spirit are not clearly distinct from the Father (7.9).

89. Augustine, *Trinity* 1.7.

90. Augustine, *Trinity* 1.7.

91. See Lewis Ayres, *Nicaea and Its Legacy: An Approach to Fourth-Century Trinitarian Theology* (Oxford: Oxford University Press, 2004), 364–83, where he discusses the philosophical roots of Augustine's trinitarian thought, as well as his commitment to the received tradition of Nicaea.

92. The importance of the inseparable, common activity of the three persons for Augustine's understanding of the Trinity is discussed in Lewis Ayres, " 'Remember That You Are Catholic' (Serm. 52.2): Augustine on the Unity of

the Triune God," *Journal of Early Christian Studies* 8 (2000): 39–82. M. R. Barnes links Augustine's use of this conception of common activity to the Nicene tradition (and especially to the Cappadocians) in "Rereading Augustine's Theology of the Trinity," in *The Trinity: An International Symposium on the Trinity*, ed. S. T. Davis, D. Kendall, and G. O'Collins (Oxford: Oxford University Press, 2002), 145–76.

Chapter Two

1. Augustine, *The Trinity*, trans. E. Hill, Works of Saint Augustine, pt. 1, vol. 5 (Brooklyn, NY: New City Press, 1991), 1.14. The importance of the passage in Philippians for Augustine has been commented on by J. Pelikan, "*Canonica Regula*: The Trinitarian Hermeneutics of Augustine," in vols. 12/13 of *Proceedings of the PMR Conference at Villanova University* (Villanova, PA: Augustinian Historical Institute, 1987–88), 17–29.

2. Augustine, *Trinity* 1.14. The rule therefore is supplemented by other principles of interpretation. For example, at 2.4 he suggests that if one cannot decide, in a passage that talks of the Father sending the Son (e.g., John 7:16), whether it should be understood according to the rule of being less in the form of a servant or according to the rule of equality because he is from the Father, then either can be affirmed.

3. Augustine, *Trinity* 1.14.

4. Augustine, *Trinity* 2.2.

5. See E. Hill, introduction to *The Trinity*, by Augustine, trans. E. Hill, Works of Saint Augustine, pt. 1, vol. 5 (Brooklyn, NY: New City Press, 1991), 47–48; a brief discussion of the importance of the theophanies in the apologists' discussions of the Father-Son relationship is presented in J. N. D. Kelly, *Early Christian Doctrines*, rev. ed. (San Francisco: HarperSanFrancisco, 1976), 96–97.

6. As Hill notes in Hill, introduction, 47–48.

7. Augustine, *Trinity* 2.7.

8. Augustine, *Trinity* 2.12.

9. Cf. Augustine, *Answer to Maximus the Arian*, in *Arianism and Other Heresies*, trans. R. J. Teske (Brooklynm, NY: New City Press, 1995), 2.14.9. Here Augustine argues against Maximus's characterization of the Father commanding the Son as one commands a servant.

10. Augustine, *Trinity* 2.17–35 is a sustained discussion of whether one can identify particular theophanies with particular persons. Augustine's conclusion is that one should never be dogmatic about who is manifest in a theophany, because the Old Testament texts tend to be ambiguous about the identity of the particular divine person involved.

11. Augustine, *Trinity* 2.35.

12. He will also introduce his understanding of the Holy Spirit being given to the church as a proper mission in book 4.

13. Augustine, *Trinity* 3.27.

14. Augustine, *Trinity* 3.22–27.

15. Augustine, *Trinity* 1.11–13.

16. Augustine, *Trinity* 4.30. Note the centrality of the monarchy of the Father for Augustine's taxonomy of relations of origin.

17. Augustine, *Trinity* 1.12, 1.25, 2.9.

18. Augustine, *Trinity* 4.12–4.23.

19. Augustine, *Trinity* 4.4.

20. This reasoning, found in Augustine, *Trinity* 15.46, is only alluded to in 4.29.

21. Cf. R. Canning, *The Unity of Love for God and Neighbour in St. Augustine* (Heverlee-Leuven: Augustinian Historical Institute, 1993), esp. pp. 301–30, which deals primarily with Augustine, *Trinity* 6, 7, and 15.

22. Augustine, *Trinity* 4.29.

23. Augustine, *Trinity* 5.15.

24. Augustine, *Trinity* 5.15.

25. Augustine, *Trinity* 4.29. Again, we see how the Father, who is never sent, is the source of the missions of the Son and the Holy Spirit, just as he is the sole beginning of them in the immanent Trinity. The taxonomy is ordered according to the Father's monarchy.

26. See Augustine, *Answer to Maximus the Arian* 2.14.1. Here Augustine is clear that the Father's monarchy is the basis by which the divine relations of origin are to be understood.

27. Augustine, *Trinity* 5.15.

28. Augustine, *Trinity* 4.29.

29. In Augustine, *Answer to Maximus the Arian* 2.17.4, where Augustine explains John 1:1, "In the beginning was the Word," Augustine describes the origin of the Son and Holy Spirit from the Father, but in such a way that the three are one beginning of the creation they have made: "The Father then is the beginning without beginning, and the Son the beginning from the beginning. Both together are not two, but one beginning, just as God the Father and God the Son are both not two gods, but one God. Nor will I deny that the Holy Spirit who proceeds from each of them is the beginning. Rather, I say that these three together are one beginning just as they are one God." The generation of the Son and the procession of the Holy Spirit from the Father (who is the "beginning without beginning") is eternal, and the three are one beginning (of the creation) with the Father. Augustine says this because the Father is not a beginning before the beginning (i.e., the Son), which would contradict his understanding of the eternal nature of the Father and the Son. Another way to make this point is to remember that one aspect of divine eternity is simultaneity, since the indivisible nature of the divine being excludes the idea that the eternal nature is able to be broken down into constituent parts. One understands the begotten Son to be from the Father in eternity, because being begotten requires the Son to be from the Father but not vice versa. This eternal begetting of the Son does not substantially prioritize the Father over the Son or put him before the Son, but describes the relationship of the Son from the Father (i.e., the relations of origin in the monarchy of the Father). However, when turning to the creation's beginning in God's creative work, the eternal Trinity is the one creator. The three

persons are a simultaneous beginning of the creation, not the Father creating before or after the Son. And the Holy Spirit is one beginning with the Father and the Son, thus implying the Spirit's coeternity with them as well.

30. For example, in Augustine, *Trinity* 4.28, he writes, "That he [the Son] is born means that he is from eternity to eternity—he is *the brightness of eternal light* (Wisdom 7:26). But that he is sent means that he is known by somebody in time." In this quotation, Augustine is noting that the eternal nature of the Father, from whom the Son is begotten, provides the context by which one can understand the eternal begottenness of the Son. The message of the New Testament about the Son's being sent into the world, however, is not a reference to the eternal begetting of the Son, but to the human experience of the Son's being sent in the mission of redemption. Whereas the eternal begetting is understood according to the nature of eternity, the biblical revelation of the Son's sending is presented as an experience by a creature of the Son's being sent into the creation. They are two different contexts, and so the sending is not confused with the eternal begetting, though the sending does provide the basis for the knowledge of the eternal begetting.

31. Building on the correspondence of the Son's begetting with his being sent, Augustine points out in *Trinity* 4.28 that "of the Holy Spirit he [wisdom] says, *He proceeds from the Father* (Jn. 15:26), but the Father is from no one." According to Augustine, the Holy Spirit sent to the disciples as the Advocate in John 15:26 is sent by the Son (named "Wisdom" by Augustine). However, when the Holy Spirit is sent by Jesus in this passage, Augustine notes how the Holy Spirit is described by Jesus as proceeding from the Father. This is the eternal procession of the Holy Spirit, rather than the sending of the Spirit. Thus, he has shown that both the Son and Holy Spirit are revealed to be from the Father in eternity, and also that the Son has sent the Spirit. He then notes, in *Trinity* 4.29, how scripture not only describes the Spirit as the Spirit of the Father (an eternal relation), but also as the Spirit of the Son (Galatians 4:6, "the Spirit of his Son"). Therefore, he understands the Spirit to be from the Father and the Son, as well as being sent by the Son. Finally, at the end of *Trinity* 4.29, he completes the correspondence of begetting/proceeding with sending by showing how scripture also states that the Father has sent the Spirit (John 14:26, the Holy Spirit, "whom the Father will send in my name").

32. Augustine, *Trinity* 4.28. The Son and the Holy Spirit, however, are both said to be sent.

33. This saving knowledge from the eternal God, who is above the sinfulness of creatures, could not be attained by creatures in their finitude. That is why Augustine's argument in book 4 emphasizes how the Son came as the mediator sent by the Father. If the equality of eternal divinity were not his, just as he received it from the Father, then he could not impart the saving knowledge that creatures need, because he also would be a creature. This is summed up in Augustine, *Trinity* 4.24–26.

34. As Basil Studer puts it in "History and Faith in Augustine's *De Trinitate*," *Augustinian Studies* 28 (1977): 39, in his summary of the argument of books 1–4 of *The Trinity*, "In a word, the fact [is] that the Father was not sent, that

the Son was sent only from the Father, and the Holy Spirit was sent from the Father and the Son demonstrates their eternal status."

35. Augustine, *Trinity* 4.32.

36. In *The Trinity* Augustine employs these terms at 4.29, 5.14–15, 6.3, 15.29, and 15.47. A similar passage is in Augustine, *Answer to the Arian Sermon*, in *Arianism and Other Heresies*, trans. R. J. Teske (Brooklyn, NY: New City Press, 1995), bk. 17. He also uses other terms that have a similar meaning, such as in *Trinity* 7.4 where he refers to the Father as the fount of life.

37. See Augustine, *Trinity* 6.8–9.

38. Augustine, *City of God Against the Pagans*, trans. R. W. Dyson (Cambridge: Cambridge University Press, 1998), 11.10.

39. An in-depth analysis of how simplicity functions in Augustine's conception of God is found in Lewis Ayres, "The Fundamental Grammar of Augustine's Trinitarian Theology," in *Augustine and His Critics: Essays in Honor of Gerald Bonner*, ed. R. Dodaro and G. Lawless (New York: Routledge, 2000). A helpful, condensed analysis of Augustine's trinitarian logic is found in John Milbank, "Sacred Triads: Augustine and the Indo-European Soul," *Modern Theology* 13 (1997): 451–74.

40. See further explanation, including commentary on Letter 120, in Ayres "Fundamental Grammar," 61–62.

41. Letter 120.2.7 in Augustine, *Letters*, trans. W. Parsons, vol. 2, Fathers of the Church 18 (Washington, DC: Catholic University of America Press, 1953), 305–6.

42. Letter 120.3.16 in Augustine, *Letters*, 2:313.

43. Ibid.

44. As is the case in the new translation of Letter 120.3.16 in Augustine, *Letters 100–155*, trans. R. J. Teske, Works of Saint Augustine, part 2, vol. 2 (New York: New City Press, 2003).

45. In a footnote to Augustine, *Confessions* 13.3.4, Chadwick defines Augustine's reference to God's "absolute simplicity" in this way: "The concept of 'simplicity' for Augustine and the Neoplatonists means freedom from any element of distinction between substance and accidents or attributes, and has overtones of being without need. Goodness is therefore no attribute of Plotinus' One, but is inseparable from the One." H. Chadwick, in *The Confessions*, by Augustine, trans. Chadwick (Oxford: Oxford University Press, 1991), 275 n. 4. Chadwick's use of the classical philosophical term "accidents" is the same as our use of "qualities." Chadwick uses "goodness" to explain how this distinction relates to creatures and to God. Whereas a human being can be said to be good at some point, but also not good (or without the quality of goodness) at some other point. God's being is goodness, and therefore is not an attribute. It is not something God possesses at one moment but potentially does not possess at another moment. Divine simplicity, then, refers to how the divine nature is not divisible into parts, so that one cannot distinguish between substance and accidents in the way that one can do with a human being.

46. See Augustine, *Trinity* 7.1. Basil Studer, *The Grace of Christ and the Grace of God in Augustine of Hippo: Christocentrism or Theocentrism?* trans. M. J.

O'Connell (Collegeville, MN: Liturgical Press, 1997), 104–9, provides a brief but helpful explanation of how the distinction between talking about "common" and "proper" attribution helps Augustine develop his trinitarian logic.

47. The identity of substance and wisdom is spelled out in Augustine, *Trinity* 7.2

48. Augustine, *Trinity* 4.29, 5.14–15, 6.3

49. Augustine, *Answer to Maximus the Arian* 2.14.7. We shall describe the context of this work later in this chapter, when we take up the question of hierarchy in Augustine's thought.

50. Augustine, *Answer to the Arian Sermon* 34.32 indicates that Augustine does not hold that the Son is the same as the Father: "The Sabellians say that the Son is the same one as the Father; we say that the Father who begets and the Son who is born are two persons, but not two different natures. Hence, the same one is not the Father and the Son, but the Father and Son are one."

51. Some of these arguments are similar to the exchanges he had with Arians in letters from the same (or slightly earlier) period. He began *The Trinity* in 399 and corresponded with two Arians, Pascentius and Elipidius, between 395 and 404. Thus, Arianism was fresh in his mind during the writing of *The Trinity*. On dating the letters, see A. Fitzgerald and J. C. Cavadini, ed., *Augustine through the Ages: An Encyclopedia* (Grand Rapids, MI: Eerdmans, 1999), s.v. "Epistulae."

52. Sabellianism, rooted in modalistic monarchianism, is discussed in J. Pelikan, *The Christian Tradition: A History of the Development of Doctrine* (Chicago: University of Chicago Press, 1971), 1:176–82.

53. Modalism can lead to other problems, like patripassianism. This is the claim that the Father suffered on the cross, rather than Christ, who is distinct from the Father. In *Heresies* 41, in *Arianism and Other Heresies*, trans. R. J. Teske (Brooklyn, NY: New City Press, 1995), Augustine describes patripassianism as part of Sabellianism.

54. Jenson, *The Triune Identity* (Philadelphia: Fortress Press, 1982), 118–19.

55. Ibid., 118.

56. Augustine, *Trinity* 6.9.

57. Augustine, *Trinity* 6.9.

58. Augustine, *Trinity* 6.9.

59. "But anyone united to the Lord becomes one spirit with him." This passage is also taken up in Augustine, *Answer to Maximus the Arian* 1.10; 2.10.2, and 2.22.2.

60. In Letter 241, in Augustine, *Letters*, trans. W. Parsons, vol. 5, Fathers of the Church 32 (Washington, DC: Catholic University of America Press, 1956), 213–14, Augustine makes the same argument to Pascentius, but notes that the idea of Christ "clinging" to the Father is not the ideal language, since there never was a time when Father and Son were not joined, nor could they ever be separated by distance. Thus, he is constantly aware of the need for analogies that are spiritual in nature and avoid the idea of a separation or division of the divine being into temporal or corporeal parts.

61. This change, whereby a creature who cleaves to its creator is made better, follows Augustine's conception of the creature's fulfillment—receiving its "form and conversion"—from participating in God the creator. See the description of how the Trinity works in giving the creature its form and conversion in Augustine, *Literal Meaning of Genesis*, trans. J. H. Taylor (New York: Newman Press, 1982), vol. 1, 1.5.11. For a definition of participation in Augustine's usage, see Vernon Bourke, *Augustine's View of Reality* (Villanova, PA: Villanova Press, 1964), 117–23.

62. It has been noted how Gunton is concerned that Augustine's assumption that God is an indivisible (and unchanging) substance makes the relations of the divine persons merely logical rather than real and dynamic in the Godhead. Colin Gunton, *The Promise of Trinitarian Theology* (Edinburgh: T. and T. Clark, 1997), 38–42. In this quotation, though, we see Augustine describing their unity in terms of the Son cleaving to the Father, which is hardly an abstract, logical, or static description of divine relations. Furthermore, the cleaving of the Christian to Christ, which leads Augustine to then speak about Christ's cleaving to the Father, is taken from the Pauline discussion of the sexual cleaving of a man and woman. Augustine takes over this language of cleaving to describe the Father-Son relationship. This is not to suggest that the Father-Son relationship is one of sexual love, but rather that the dynamic language of cleaving is not eschewed by Augustine. It can be used to talk about different orders of relationships, including human relationships, human-divine relationships, and the inner trinitarian relationships. By itself, Augustine's discussion of the Son cleaving to the Father in *Trinity* 6.9 is not sufficient to explain what the relationship between the Father and the Son is—a relationship of love, which is the essence of God. (The divine substance has already been asserted to be love at *Trinity* 6.7. Also, note *Trinity* 8.11–12.) However, the passage does indicate that even in his discussion of the logic of the triune relations, those relations are more than the speculative logic concerning some abstractly conceived substance, because love is an activity between the persons whose unity of being is in their relations of origin in the Father. On this see Rowan Williams, "*Sapientia* and the Trinity: Reflections on the *De Trinitate*," in *Collectanea Augustiniana: Mélanges T. J. Van Bavel*, ed. B. Bruning, J. van Houtem, M. Lamberigts (Leuven: Peeters, 1990), 323. For more on the divine essence as love in Augustine, see Lewis Ayres, "Augustine, Christology, and God as Love: An Introduction to the Homilies on 1 John," in *Nothing Greater, Nothing Better: Theological Essays on the Love of God*, ed. Kevin J. Vanhoozer (Grand Rapids, MI: Eerdmans, 2001), 67–93.

63. The Son and Holy Spirit have the same substance, which is from the Father, but not in any manner that alters that substance (e.g., by degree). Thus, he avoids the Arian understanding of the Son and Holy Spirit as originating from the Father in such a manner that they are less than the Father in substance. Instead, the three are equally one and also distinctly three.

64. Augustine also relates this relational description of the inner Trinity to the problem of modalism in his *Answer to Maximus the Arian*. There he responds to Maximus's conception of how the Father is related to God's divinity (which

Maximus apparently understood as distinct from any of the persons): "You say, 'Then God the Father is part of God.' Heaven forbid!" Augustine's counterexplanation is to explain the equality of the three and unity of substance using 1 Corinthians 6:17. At the conclusion of his argument he sums up his understanding of the usage of substance for speaking of the three persons thus: "In the Trinity, then, which is God, the Father is God, and the Son is God, and the Holy Spirit is God, and these three are all together one God. One is not a third of this Trinity, nor are two of them a greater part than one, and all of them are not something greater than each of them, because their greatness is spiritual, not corporeal" (*Answer to Maximus the Arian* 2.10.2). This conclusion is consistent with those nonmodalist descriptions of substance cited above in Letter 120 and *The Trinity*. The image of cleaving between the believer and Christ is contrasted with that of the Father and Son, because a change in the substance of the Father and Son is not possible without dividing them into parts, which in this conclusion he describes by the terms "thirds," "parts," and "wholes," which are corporeal in nature and thus misleading in application to an incorporeal Trinity. Instead, one should understand the language of substance and oneness as referring to the spiritual nature of God as perfect wholeness. The cleaving of believer to Christ raises up the believer into a oneness of spirit that perfects him or her, but the cleaving of Father, Son, and Holy Spirit to one another is the perfection that is called God. But if the Father, Son, and Holy Spirit are God, then none is less than either of the others or the whole, since perfect divinity is indivisible.

Chapter Three

1. Leonardo Boff, *Trinity and Society*, trans. P. Burn (Maryknoll, NY: Orbis Books, 1988), 20–23.

2. Sallie McFague, "A Square in the Quilt," in *Spirit and Nature*, ed. S. C. Rockefeller and J. C. Elder (Boston: Beacon Press, 1992), 49ff.

3. For example, see Boff's concerns about anthropocentric and androcentric attitudes toward the world, and the use of the world as primarily a source for human pleasure. See Leonardo Boff, *Cry of the Earth, Cry of the Poor*, trans. P. Berryman (Maryknoll, NY: Orbis Books, 1997), 71–75.

4. Basil Studer, "*Deus, Pater et Dominus* bei Augustinus von Hippo," in *Christian Faith and Greek Philosophy in Late Antiquity: Essays in Tribute to George Christopher Stead*, ed. L. Wickham and C. P. Bammel (New York: Brill, 1993), 190–212.

5. Studer notes the work of S. Poque, *Le langage symbolique dans la prédication d'Augustin d'Hippone*, 2 vols. (Paris: Études Augustiniennes, 1984), 1.193–224, as supporting his thesis that Augustine's use of the Roman concept of father does not undermine his theological work, nor uniformly force him into patriarchal ideas.

6. For more background on the work, see R. J. Teske, introduction to *Arianism and Other Heresies*, trans. R. J. Teske (Brooklyn, NY: New City Press, 1995).

7. Augustine, *Answer to Maximus the Arian*, in *Arianism and Other Heresies*, trans. R. J. Teske (Brooklyn, NY: New City Press, 1995), 2.14.8.

8. Augustine, *Debate with Maximus the Arian*, in *Arianism and Other Heresies*, trans. R. J. Teske (Brooklyn, NY: New City Press, 1995), 15.14.

9. Cf. Augustine, *The Trinity*, trans. E. Hill (Brooklyn, NY: New City Press, 1991), bks. 1–2.

10. This is a brief development of the idea also found in Augustine *Trinity* 4.28.

11. Augustine, *Answer to Maximus the Arian* 2.14.8.

12. Augustine, *Answer to Maximus the Arian* 2.14.8.

13. The dependence of the creature upon God for its existence will be discussed more when we turn to Augustine's interpretation of Genesis.

14. Augustine, *Answer to Maximus the Arian* 2.14.8.

15. Augustine, *Answer to Maximus the Arian* 2.14.9.

16. Augustine, *Answer to Maximus the Arian* 2.14.9.

17. Augustine, *Debate with Maximus the Arian* 15.14.

18. Augustine, *Answer to Maximus the Arian* 2.14.9.

19. Augustine, *Answer to Maximus the Arian* 2.14.9.

20. The eternal perfection of the begotten Son's divine nature is his simplicity.

21. See the whole of Augustine, *Answer to Maximus the Arian* 2.24.

22. Augustine, *Debate with Maximus the Arian* 15.24.

23. Augustine, *Answer to Maximus the Arian* 2.24.

24. Many of Augustine's earlier arguments against subordinationism are rehearsed throughout *Answer to Maximus the Arian*. In the passage under consideration he assumes the equality of the Father and Son so that he can demonstrate how their equality of being points to their equality of love for each other.

25. Augustine, *Answer to Maximus the Arian* 2.14.8–9.

26. Augustine, *Answer to Maximus the Arian* 2.24.

27. Augustine, *Answer to Maximus the Arian* 2.24.

28. Thus, Augustine implies that if one refers to the Son receiving the Father's words or commands separate from his being begotten, this would indicate the Son is indeed of a different nature than the Father, and therefore is less than the Father. This is what Maximus does.

29. Lewis Ayres, "Augustine, Christology, and God as Love: An Introduction to the Homilies on 1 John," in *Nothing Greater, Nothing Better: Theological Essays on the Love of God*, ed. Kevin J. Vanhoozer (Grand Rapids, MI: Eerdmans, 2001), 88.

30. This quotation from Ayres is part of his summary of results from his exegesis of Augustine's homilies on 1 John. We are using the quotation as a helpful summary of what lay behind Augustine's assumption about the equal love of Father and Son in his comments against Maximus. It informed his thought in *The Trinity* as well.

31. Augustine, *Trinity* 7.1–4. In Letter 170.8, in Augustine, *Letters*, trans. W. Parsons, vol. 4, Fathers of the Church 30 (Washington. DC: Catholic University of America Press, 1955), 66, Augustine writes to Maximus concerning Christ:

"All He has and can do He attributes to his Father, not to himself, because He is not of himself but of the Father. For he is equal to the Father and this also He received from the Father, but He did not receive His being equal as if He had previously been unequal and was born equal, but, as he is always born, so he is always equal. "Similarly, the Son's and the Father's mutual love is equal. The Father receives nothing from the Son that is not already the Father's. That the Son receives everything he has from the Father is not a sign of his lacking anything in himself. Instead, it is to be understood as the proof of his having everything in eternal fullness because he has it from the eternal Father.

32. Augustine, *Trinity* 7.6.

33. Augustine, *Trinity* 6.6.

34. Augustine, *Trinity* 6.7.

35. Augustine, *Trinity* 6.7.

36. Augustine, *Trinity* 6.7, 7.6. Lewis Ayres, *Nicaea and Its Legacy: An Approach to Fourth-Century Trinitarian Theology* (Oxford: Oxford University Press, 2004), 370–72, argues that Augustine inherited this idea of the Holy Spirit as the communion of the Father and Son from the received tradition.

37. Augustine, *Trinity* 7.6. Augustine continues the quotation with "and subjoining us to them." This addition helps us to see that it is in the human experience of the divine economy of salvation that the understanding of the eternal Godhead is made possible. The Father and Son's work of uniting humanity to God through the Holy Spirit is the basis on which humanity can begin to grasp the person of the Holy Spirit in relation to the Father and the Son.

38. Augustine, *Trinity* 7.6.

39. Augustine, *Trinity* 5.12.

40. On the Spirit as gift, see Rowan Williams, "*Sapientia* and the Trinity: Reflections on the *De Trinitate*," in *Collectanea Augustiniana: Mélanges T. J. Van Bavel*, ed. B. Bruning, J. van Houtem, M. Lambereigts (Leuven: Peeters, 1990), esp. 327–29. Williams brings together Augustine's discussion of the Spirit in books 4–7 of *The Trinity* (which we are focusing on here and in what follows), and some of Augustine's reflections in books 14–15, which strengthens the points being made here.

41. Augustine, *Trinity* 5.13.

42. Augustine, *Trinity* 7.6.

43. Augustine, *Trinity* 6.7. He quotes Ephesians 4:3 in support of this: "They keep the unity of the Spirit in the bond of peace." The Father and the Son keep their unity that is "of the Spirit" in a bond of peace. Augustine seems to understand "peace" to be the divine love that is the unity of the Spirit. The verse in its original context refers to the relations of members of the Ephesian church, not to the Godhead. On the assumption that the "unity of the Spirit" refers to the Holy Spirit's work in the Ephesian church, Augustine is consistently following his principle that the divine economy reveals the eternal Godhead by also showing how it refers to their eternal relations.

44. Augustine, *Trinity* 6.7. Participation is the means to explain how creatures have their being by dependence on something outside of themselves—namely, God. God, however, has no need of anyone else, since the divine being is simple,

and therefore indivisible, eternal, and entirely self-sustained. The importance of the concept of participation will be taken up in subsequent chapters.

45. Augustine, *Trinity* 6.7.

46. Augustine, *Trinity* 6.7. We have already encountered this idea in the previous chapter, especially in Letter 120.3.16, where Augustine notes that the simplicity of the divine substance requires human language about qualities to apply to the divine substance, because unlike created beings, in God qualities are the divine substance.

47. The opposite case would be human friendship and love, because human beings can be unfriendly and without love. The Holy Spirit's love that unites the Father and the Son is not something that can be absent from Father, Son, or Holy Spirit. Rather, the love of the Holy Spirit for the Father and the Son is also the love that the Father has for the Son and vice versa.

48. Augustine, *Trinity* 6.7. Also see Augustine, *Trinity* 13.14, where Augustine cites a favorite verse: Romans 5:5, "The charity of God has been poured into our hearts through the Holy Spirit which has been given to us."

49. As if two things are stuck together by a third object, like two pieces of wood united by glue. Such a passive image conveys no sense of the activity of loving that happens between the three persons.

50. See Augustine's definition of friendship in *Confessions* 4.4.7, where he also attributes true friendship to the work of the Holy Spirit, who bonds two persons who cleave to each other (again he cites Romans 5:5). On the connections Augustine made between friendship and love as substance terms in the Godhead, and their unique attribution to the Spirit as derived from his understanding of the divine economy of salvation, see Joseph T. Lienhard, " 'The Glue Itself Is Charity': Ps. 62:9 in Augustine's Thought," in *Augustine: Presbyter Factus Sum*, ed. E. C. Muller, R. J. Teske, and J. T. Lienhard (New York: Peter Lang, 1993), 375–84. Indirectly related to this topic is Lienhard's article on human friendship, "Friendship in Paulinus of Nola and Augustine," in *Collectanea Augustiniana: Mélanges T. J. Van Bavel*, ed. B. Bruning, J. van Houtem, M. Lambereigts (Leuven: Peeters, 1990), 279–96.

Chapter Four

1. For examples of Augustine's understanding of the trinitarian nature of scripture, and its authority and trustworthiness for constructing doctrine, see our discussion in chapter 1.

2. One way that Augustine's trinitarian project might fall apart, for example, would be if he failed to attend to (or at least minimized) the threeness of God in the act of creation because of a more basic commitment to monotheism. A potential for this in classical theology was described by Boff, as we noted in chapter 1. Also see Colin Gunton, *The One, the Three and the Many: God, Creation, and the Culture of Modernity* (Cambridge: Cambridge University Press, 1993), 54, 120–21, and 138, for more criticisms of Augustine as a monotheist who gives negligible attention to God's threeness.

3. In the final three books of the *The Confessions*, for instance, he included a reflection on God as creator that covered the first chapter of Genesis. Books 11 to 12 of *The City of God* also treat aspects of the creation story. On the dating of these works, see *La Genèse au sens littéral en douze livres (I–VII)*, trans. and ed. P. Agaësse and A. Solignac, in *Œuvres de Saint Augustin*, vol. 48, (Paris: Desclée de Brouwer, 1972), 25–31. For a further and very thorough treatment of the range of works in which Augustine discusses the doctrine of creation, see M. A. Vannier, *"Creatio," "Conversio," "Formatio," chez Augustin*, Paradosis 31 (Fribourg: Éditions universitaires, 1991), 83–89.

4. *The Literal Meaning* differs from his *Unfinished Literal Commentary on Genesis*, as Augustine points out in *The Retractions*, trans. M. I. Bogan, Fathers of the Church 60 (Washington, DC: Catholic University of America Press, 1968), 1.17, because he did not yet have the knowledge to address the questions raised in such a commentary, in part due to his lack of time for research as a result of his pastoral duties. Therefore, he did not finish his first attempt at a literal commentary on Genesis. Six years later, having developed a greater understanding of the issues and the types of answers that could be applied to interpreting the text literally, he again set about the task of writing a commentary. He considered his first attempt at a literal commentary unsuccessful, but did not reject the results of it as being without merit. Thus, rather than destroying the work, he made an emendation at its conclusion, and left it for those who might find some of its ideas helpful. That emendation concerns one of the significant theological differences between the *Unfinished Literal Commentary* and *The Literal Meaning*—namely, how he related the doctrine of the Trinity to an understanding of the image of God. In the *Unfinished Literal Commentary*, he had argued that the image of God in humanity was based on human likeness to the Word—the Son of God (Augustine, *Unfinished Literal Commentary on Genesis*, trans. E. Hill (Brooklyn, NY: New City Press, 2002), 16.60. However, after rereading this account as he was composing *The Retractions*, Augustine decided to add a final paragraph to the *Unfinished Literal Commentary*, putting forward a "preferable choice of meaning" (16.61). He explained that the likeness of the image in humanity is to the Trinity itself, rather than to the Word alone. Thus, he harmonized the final paragraph of the *Unfinished Literal Commentary* with *The Literal Meaning* 3.19.29. The subject of the image of God will be addressed in chapter 6.

5. Augustine, *Unfinished Literal Commentary on Genesis* 2.5. Augustine goes on to explain two other types of interpretation that may be used to understand Genesis, the analogical and aetiological: "analogy, when the harmony of the old and new covenants is being demonstrated; aetiology, when causes of the things that have been said and done are presented." The relationship of the various forms of scriptural interpretation and how Augustine employed and understood them are discussed by B. de Margerie, *An Introduction to the History of Exegesis*, vol. 3, *Saint Augustine*, trans. P. de Fontnouvelle (Petersham, UK: Saint Bede's Publications, 1991); K. E. Green-McCreight, *Ad Litteram: How Augustine, Calvin, and Barth Read the "Plain Sense" of Genesis 1–3* (New York: Peter Lang, 1995), 32–94; F. Van Fleteren, "Principles of Augustine's Hermeneutic: An Overview," in *Augustine: Biblical Exegete*, ed. F. Van Fleteren and J. C. Schnaubelt (New

York: Peter Lang, 2001), 1–32; and T. Williams, "Biblical Interpretation," in *The Cambridge Companion to Augustine*, ed. E. Stump and N. Kretzmann (Cambridge: Cambridge University Press, 2001), 59–70.

6. Augustine, *The Literal Meaning of Genesis*, trans. J. H. Taylor (New York: Newman Press, 1982), 1.17.34. This explanation of the literal and allegorical/figurative interpretations of Genesis is discussed with detailed references in E. Hill, introduction to *The Literal Meaning of Genesis*, in *On Genesis*, trans. E. Hill (Brooklyn, NY: New City Press, 2002), 158–61.

7. Van Fleteren, "Principles of Augustine's Hermeneutic," 8.

8. Thus, he considers at length how God might create corporeal light and darkness at Augustine, *Literal Meaning* 1.9.15–1.12.24 and 2.8.16–19.

9. Augustine, *Literal Meaning* 1.11.23, and 4.28.45–4.30.47.

10. Of course, this also allows him to account for the creation of angels, with which the Genesis text does not deal.

11. *The Literal Meaning* 4.28.45–4.30.47. See Green-McCreight, *Ad Litteram*, 44–48.

12. Hill, introduction, 159–60.

13. See his comments in Augustine, *Retractions* 2.50.

14. Augustine, *Literal Meaning* 5.1.1.

15. Augustine, *Literal Meaning* 5.1.1–5.3.6.

16. Thus, Augustine writes in *Literal Meaning* 5.1.1: "But now the sacred writer says [in 2:4], *This is the book of creation of heaven and earth when day was made*, thus making it quite clear, I believe, that here he does not speak of heaven and earth in the sense in which he used these words in the beginning before mentioning the creation of day, *when darkness was over the abyss*. Now [in 2:4ff.] he is speaking of the creation of heaven and earth when day was made, that is, when all parts of the world had been made distinct and all classes of things had already been formed, and thus the whole of creation, fittingly arranged, presented the appearance of what we call the universe."

17. E.g., Augustine, *Literal Meaning* 5.11.27: "[T]here are two moments of creation: one in the original creation when God made all creatures before resting on the seventh day, and the other in the administration of creatures by which he works even now." "Governance" is another way to translate God's *administratio* of creatures.

18. Augustine uses the verb *condere*, meaning "to found," "to form," "to fashion," throughout *The Literal Meaning*. For example, see 5.20.41: "It is thus that God unfolds the generations which he laid up in creation when first he founded it." In 5.12.14, he shows that he does not use just one term to describe the founding of creation, but rather a variety of similar terms: "Among those beings which were formed from formlessness and are clearly said to be created, or made, or established, the first made was day."

19. See Augustine, *Literal Meaning* 4.11.21–4.12.23.

20. See Augustine, *Literal Meaning* 5.11.27.

21. The invisible and formless void from which the creatures are converted into their spiritual and physical forms does not occupy a significant amount of Augustine's discussion in *The Literal Meaning*, see 1.14.28–1.15.30. It receives

some attention in *Concerning the Nature of the Good*, where he identifies it with the Platonic *hyle*. See A. A. Moon's translation, *The "De Natura Boni" of Saint Augustine* (Washington, DC: Catholic University of America Press, 1955). Rather than treat it in our discussion of how Augustine interprets Genesis 1 in *The Literal Meaning*, we will discuss the *hyle* in chapter 5 in relation to its supposed passive quality in God's controlling "hands."

22. On the creation of time, see Augustine, *Literal Meaning* 1.2.4–6, 5.5.12 and 5.17.35. On creation from nothing in Augustine's thought, see T. Van Bavel, "The Creator and the Integrity of Creation in the Fathers of the Church, Especially in Saint Augustine," *Augustinian Studies* 21 (1990): 4–7; and W. A. Christian, "The Creation of the World," in *A Companion to the Study of St. Augustine*, ed. R. W. Battenhouse (New York: Oxford University Press, 1955), 332–36. We noted above, briefly, that he understood the first day to refer to the creation of angels. Augustine describes at length the formation of angels (they are the light of Gen. 1:3–5), who then witness the creation of the eternal reasons and their subsequent unfolding in their physical forms (the sky, earth and other celestial bodies, and the various earthly creatures [Genesis 1:6–2:1]). The angelic knowledge of other creatures, as those creatures exist in the Word, are the angels' "daytime," while their knowledge of those creatures, as they exist in themselves, are the angels' "evening" because the angels turn from their apprehension of creatures in the Word to the existence of those same creatures in bodies (Augustine, *Literal Meaning* 2.8.16–19 and 4.22.39–4.25.42). The creation of the angelic realm is of one part with the establishment of the creation from nothing and the physical universe's conversion from the formless void. The movement of the creation from a divine idea to physical reality, as observed by angels, is discussed by Taylor in Augustine, *Literal Meaning*, 233 n.22.

23. E.g., Augustine, *Literal Meaning* 1.15.29 and 5.5.12.

24. For an indication of how conversion is employed by Augustine to explain several aspects of God's creative activity, see D. J. Hassel, "Conversion-Theory and *Scientia* in the *De Trinitate*," *Recherches Augustiniennes* 2 (1962): 383–401. Hassell sees "three principal moments of conversion" in Augustine's doctrine of creation: (1) "The creature issues from God's creative hand," which corresponds with the establishment of creation; (2) "the creature is impelled to turn back" to the Word, or "is formed out of formlessness," which corresponds with our second stage of the founding work and also to God's governance; and (3) the creature has "growth in perfection" (384–85), which corresponds with God's work in the divine governance. In Hassell's description of the first two moments, all creatures are included, and the divine act of conversion requires no free decision on the part of the creature. The third moment is applicable only to spiritual creatures, because it refers to a conversion of their wills. Both the second and third moments extend through time as part of God's governance of all creatures, though the second moment "begins" in the founding of creation, inasmuch as the forming of creatures from the formless matter requires God's ongoing governance for their existence to continue.

25. E.g., Augustine, *Literal Meaning* 4.33.51–4.35.56 and 6.6.11. For further analysis of the eternal and causal reasons, and their correspondence to the

creation of everything and its subsequent governance, see Taylor, in Augustine, *Literal Meaning*, 252 n. 67; Basil Studer, *The Grace of Christ and the Grace of God in Augustine of Hippo: Christocentrism or Theocentrism?* trans. M. J. O'Connell (Collegeville, MN: Liturgical Press, 1997), 110–12; and D. X. Burt, *Augustine's World: An Introduction to His Speculative Philosophy* (Lanham, MD: University Press of America, 1996), 208–18. On the causal reasons and their compatibility with aspects of modern evolutionary thought, see M. J. McKeough, *The Meaning of the Rationes Seminales in St. Augustine* (Washington, DC: Catholic University of America Press, 1926).

26. Augustine, *Literal Meaning* 5.23.45.

27. Augustine, *Literal Meaning* 4.12.22. Also see Burt, *Augustine's World*, 210–12.

28. In summary, there are two phases of God's work as creator: founding and governance. Founding has two stages: the establishment of the creation from nothing and the conversion of creatures into substantial forms. Governance equals providential care (to be discussed in chapter 5).

29. Augustine, *Literal Meaning* 1.6.12.

30. In *Literal Meaning* 1.21.41, Augustine suggests that a literal interpretation of scripture should correspond as closely as possible to the authorial intention, but also should not depart from the "the firm basis of Catholic belief." In fact, conformity to such religious norms has more weight than authorial intention in the interpretation of scripture. This is not to say that normative religious belief is superior to, or more important than, understanding authorial intention. Rather, Augustine gives priority to interpreting scripture in light of authoritative religious belief because he recognizes that sometimes authorial intention can be notoriously difficult to ascertain, and also that the truth of something (e.g., God's creation) can encompass more than the words of an author on the subject. Thus, Moses may not have spoken the complete truth in writing the creation accounts of Genesis, though he certainly spoke nothing false or in error, says Augustine in *The Confessions*, trans. H. Chadwick (Oxford: Oxford University Press, 1991), 12.23.32–12.32.43. Therefore, one must carefully and humbly investigate other meanings. Where authorial intention is in question, then one ought to attempt to understand the text in ways that do not contradict normative beliefs. In the case of Genesis 1, assuming the authority and truth of scripture (cf. *Confessions* 4.21.38), the story of God's creative works should be interpreted in such a way that the interpretation does not depart from the normative and biblical belief in God the Trinity. In other words, Augustine's belief in the necessity of trinitarian doctrine (itself established through scripture) must bear upon his interpretation of the biblical text.

31. Augustine, *Literal Meaning* 1.6.12.

32. See Studer, *Grace of Christ*, 110.

33. See our discussion of the trinitarian logic in chapter 2.

34. Augustine, *Literal Meaning* 1.6.12.

35. It already has been indicated above that when Augustine names God as the Father in Genesis 1:1, it is in part because he understands the Father as the source that itself has no beginning—both in the inner Trinity and in the

divine work of creation from nothing. In the context of *The Trinity*, however, when Augustine uses the word "beginning" as a name, it usually is in reference to the Father who is the beginning of the Son (e.g., Augustine, *Trinity* 1.9, 2.27, and 6.3).

36. The referencing of John 1 in relation to the opening words of Genesis happens in *The Literal Meaning* 1.2.6. Augustine also relates Genesis 1 to John 1 in the *Lectures or Tractates on the Gospel According to St. John*, in *Augustin: Homilies on the Gospel of John, Homilies on the First Epistle of John, Soliloquies*, trans. J. Gibb and J. Innes, Nicene and Post-Nicene Fathers, 1st ser., ed. P. Schaff, vol. 7 (1888; reprint, Peabody, MA: Hendrickson, 1995), tractates 9.5–6, 26.8, and 43.17.

37. John 1:18.

38. Augustine, *Literal Meaning* 1.2.6.

39. Augustine, *Literal Meaning* 1.6.12.

40. Augustine, *Literal Meaning* 1.6.12.

41. The connection is implicit in Augustine, *Literal Meaning* 1.6.12.

42. Augustine, *Literal Meaning* 1.5.11.

43. Referring to the Holy Spirit, Augustine writes in *Trinity* 15.38, "But if any person in the Trinity is to be distinctively called the will of God, this name like charity fits the Holy Spirit more than the others. What else after all is charity but the will?" We have already discussed the appropriateness of identifying the Holy Spirit with love in the Godhead in the previous chapter. Here Augustine carries the equivalence of love and will to its logical conclusion, because he understands love as the essence of God. In accordance with his understanding of divine simplicity, whereby the divine essence is indivisible, God's will is not different from his love.

44. Augustine, *Literal Meaning* 1.5.10. Cf. *Confessions* 12.12.15 and *Trinity* 3.21.

45. Augustine, *Literal Meaning* 4.15.26, "For whatever comes from God is so dependent upon Him that it owes its existence to Him, but He does not owe His happiness to any creature He has made." In this quotation, Augustine's reference to God's happiness is explained by the context of the quotation, which is concerned with God's rest in Genesis 2:3. If God was dependent upon creation for his rest (he takes rest to be God's happiness with his creative work), then God's happiness would have increased after creating, thus contradicting divine immutability and simplicity.

46. Augustine, *Literal Meaning* 1.14.28. This is not strictly a definition of creation from nothing, which is not the primary subject of discussion in *The Literal Meaning*. Nevertheless, it indicates that Augustine worked with the concept in mind. For a detailed study of Augustine's understanding of creation from nothing, and his early use of it against the Manichaeans, see N. J. Torchia, *"Creatio Ex Nihilo" and the Theology of St. Augustine: The Anti-Manichaean Polemic and Beyond* (New York: Peter Lang, 1999). The theological tradition that Augustine inherited already had developed the notion. On this development in the early church one may consult G. May, *Creatio Ex Nihilo: The Doctrine of "Creation Out of Nothing" in Early Christian Thought*, trans. A. S. Worrall (Edinburgh: T. and T. Clark, 1994).

47. Augustine, *Literal Meaning* 1.6.12.

48. Augustine, *Literal Meaning* 1.9.15.

49. Compare similar statements at Augustine, *Literal Meaning* 1.17.32 and 12.30.58.

50. Augustine, *Literal Meaning* 1.6.12.

51. In Letter 140.2.3, Augustine implies this idea of an order of spiritual and physical creatures when he speaks of the human soul: "The soul is situated, of course, in a certain mid-rank, having beneath it the bodily creature but having above it the creator of itself and of its body." Augustine, *Letters 100–155*, trans. R. Teske, Works of Saint Augustine, pt. 2, vol. 2 (Brooklyn, NY: New City Press, 2003).

52. Augustine, *Literal Meaning* 8.20.39. N. J. Torchia, "The Implications of the Doctrine of *Creatio Ex Nihilo* in St. Augustine's Theology," in *Studia Patristica 33*, ed. E. A. Livingstone (Leuven: Peeters, 1997), 269, lists the following differences between spiritual natures and material natures that appear across Augustine's larger body of writings on creation: the spiritual are mutable in "temporal, cognitive, and moral terms" and the corporeal "are mutable in regard to time and place." The purpose of Augustine's distinction between the spiritual and corporeal in a hierarchy of creation is not to establish the superiority of the spiritual over the physical, but to help him explain how the Father and the Son founded the creation in an orderly fashion, which in Genesis 1:1 is indicated by listing heaven before the earth. Moreover, as one comes to understand the order of creation, one is led to praise the creator. We will see in chapter 6 that the exercise of dominion by creatures that are higher in this hierarchy is good only when it leads to the worship and praise of God.

53. Augustine, *Literal Meaning* 1.6.12.

54. Augustine, *Literal Meaning* 1.5.11.

55. Augustine, *Literal Meaning* 1.18.36.

56. Augustine, *Literal Meaning* 1.18.36.

57. Augustine, *Literal Meaning* 1.18.36.

58. Augustine, *Literal Meaning* 1.18.36.

59. For Augustine, when creatures develop the capacity for love through the brooding work of the Holy Spirit, they are said to have found their rest in God (*Confessions* 13.4.5). In *The Confessions*, he develops this idea of the stirring/brooding love of the Holy Spirit in reference to Isaiah 11:2, where the Holy Spirit is said to rest on people. Rather than meaning that the Holy Spirit is dependent on people, resting in Isaiah's context signifies making people rest on God (by causing them to have wisdom, knowledge, and fear of God). Augustine uses the same idea of how people are stirred to love God in *Literal Meaning* 1.18.36. Their capacity to love God is stirred up by the brooding activity of the Holy Spirit in whom they find their rest.

60. Augustine, *Literal Meaning* 1.18.36.

61. Augustine, *Literal Meaning* 1.4.9. This also means the Son does nothing without the Father whose eternal Word he is.

62. Some creatures, though, have not yet appeared, because they remain as causal reasons until their appearance. So all creatures now exist either in their

individual, substantial forms, or at least potentially as causal reasons that will appear at their appointed time. God no longer creates new creatures.

63. Augustine, *Literal Meaning* 5.1.1–5.3.6.

64. Augustine, *Literal Meaning* 1.15.29.

65. Augustine, *Literal Meaning* 1.6.12.

66. Augustine describes the creation of unformed matter—the void of Genesis 1:2—and the form given to creatures as simultaneous. In *Confessions* 13.33.48, he writes of creatures: "They are made of nothing by you, not from you, not from some matter not of your making or previously existing, but from matter created by you together with its form—that is, simultaneously. For you gave form to its formlessness with no interval of time between. The matter of heaven and earth is one thing, the beauty of heaven and earth is another. You made the matter from absolutely nothing, but the beauty of the world from formless matter—and both simultaneously so that the form followed the matter without any pause or delay." From the establishment of creation out of nothing, to the creation of the formless matter, to the conversion of the forms of various kinds of creatures from that matter, there is no temporal sequence, but just a causal sequence.

67. Augustine, *Literal Meaning* 1.4.9.

68. Augustine, *Literal Meaning* 1.4.9. The importance of the concept of conversion is dealt with in Vannier, *"Creatio," "Conversio," "Formatio," chez S. Augustin.* Also see J. Oroz Reta, "The Role of Divine Attraction in Conversion according to Saint Augustine," in *From Augustine to Eriugena: Essays on Neoplatonism and Christianity in Honour of J. O'Meara*, ed. F. X. Martin and J. A. Richmond (Washington, DC: Catholic University of America Press, 1991), 155–67. Reta discusses Augustine's understanding of conversion as God's mysterious power to attract creatures to turn to him through the work of his incarnate Son. While his analysis focuses on the redemptive conversion of the human being from sin, much of his discussion fits well in the context of *Literal Meaning* 1.4.9, where the divine attraction of God's Word calls creatures into existence from the formless matter, and keeps them from succumbing to their tendency toward nonexistence. Not only does Augustine use the term "conversion" to explain redemption and creation, but also his description of the meaning of conversion in creation is similar to his description of conversion in redemption. Hassell, "Conversion Theory and Scientia," also draws out this parallel usage. Torchia points out the parallel functions of conversion in redemption from sin and conversion in divine creation, noting that Augustine's use of the term "conversion" to describe the formation of species into their various kinds from the formless matter "places his theory of creation squarely in a moral context" (*Creatio Ex Nihilo*, 107). By "moral context," Torchia means Augustine's conception of God as the summum bonum who attracts the creature toward his goodness. The creation reflects the divine goodness by existing as God's good work.

69. Augustine, *Literal Meaning* 1.4.9.

70. In this section we are focusing on the role of the Trinity in the conversion of the creature from the formless void. In the next chapter we will take up the idea of the creature's conversion again, in terms of the governance of God. God's governance maintains creatures in their perfections.

71. This has been alluded to in our discussion of *Literal Meaning* 1.18.36.

72. Torchia, *Creatio Ex Nihilo*, 107.

73. Augustine, *Literal Meaning* 1.6.12.

74. In Augustine, *Literal Meaning* 2.6.12, the equality of the Father and Son is noted: "But it ill becomes the Trinity that the Son should be, as it were, under orders in performing his work. . . . By what words would the Father order the Son to perform a work, since the Son is the original Word of the Father by which all things have been made?" Augustine is pointing out the equality of the Father and Son by noting that the Son is the Word of God, rather than under God's command. We noted in chapter 3 that Augustine also discussed the difference between conceiving of the Son as the command of God and conceiving him as being under the command of God in *Answer to Maximus the Arian* 2.14.9.

75. Augustine, *Literal Meaning* 2.6.13.

76. Augustine, *Literal Meaning* 1.4.9.

77. Augustine, *Literal Meaning* 1.4.9. This quotation is from Hill's translation of *The Literal Meaning of Genesis* (in *On Genesis* [Brooklyn, NY: New City Press, 2002]), which on this point is clearer than Taylor's.

78. Augustine, *Literal Meaning* 1.4.9. The creature's imitation of the Word, who unchangingly adheres to the Father, is similar to Augustine's description of the human being's redemption from sin, which he understands as its spirit being "made one" (i.e., when the person's spirit is perfected according to its form), just as Christ clings to the Father in the unity (oneness) of substance. In *The Literal Meaning*, the language used by Augustine is that of the creature being perfected, while in redemption he refers to the Christian's spirit being made one. Both happen when the creature/Christian clings to the Son in imitation of the Son's clinging to the Father. See our discussion in chapter 2 of how the Christian's spirit is made one by clinging to Christ in Augustine, *Trinity* 6.9. One finds the form of life for the creature, whether in creation or in redemption, in the relationship of Father and Son who adhere (cling) to each other.

79. Augustine, *Literal Meaning* 1.6.12.

80. Augustine, *Literal Meaning* 1.7.13.

81. Augustine, *Literal Meaning* 1.6.12.

82. See Augustine, *Literal Meaning* 4.3.7. A thorough discussion of this is given in W. J. Roche, "Measure, Number, and Weight in Saint Augustine," *New Scholasticism* 15 (1941): 350–76. It will be discussed in more detail in the next chapter.

83. Augustine, *Concerning the Nature of the Good* 1–3 in *The "De Natura Boni" of Saint Augustine* (Washington, DC: Catholic University of America Press, 1955). A discussion of the divine nature, including Augustine's understanding of the summum bonum, is in Scott MacDonald, "The Divine Nature," in *The Cambridge Companion to Augustine*, ed. E. Stump and N. Kretzmann (Cambridge: Cambridge University Press, 2001), 71–90. Also see Norman Kretzmann, "A General Problem of Creation: Why Would God Create Anything at All?" in *Being and Goodness: The Concept of the Good in Metaphysics and Philosophical Theology*, ed. S. MacDonald (Ithaca, NY: Cornell University Press, 1991), 202–28.

84. Augustine, *Literal Meaning* 4.3.7. Only the Son and the Holy Spirit are said to embody the fullness of God's goodness completely in themselves, since they are of the same divine substance. See chapter 2–3 for our discussion of this idea in *The Trinity*.

85. Augustine, *Literal Meaning* 1.7.13.

86. Augustine, *Literal Meaning* 1.7.13.

87. Augustine, *Literal Meaning* 1.6.12.

88. Augustine, *Literal Meaning* 1.6.12, 1.8.14.

89. Augustine, *Literal Meaning* 2.8.19.

90. Augustine, *Literal Meaning* 1.8.14.

91. E.g., Augustine, *Literal Meaning* 1.7.13–1.8.14. The freedom of God's creative activity is taken up in R. Cousineau, "Creation and Freedom, An Augustinian Problem: '*Quia voluit*'? and/or '*Quia bonus*'?" *Recherches Augustiniennes* 2 (1962): 253–71.

92. Augustine, *Confessions* 13.31.46. James J. O'Donnell, *Augustine: Confessions* (Oxford: Clarendon Press, 1992), 3:410, notes that this is an allegorical interpretation of Genesis 1:31, and not to be taken literally except in an eschatological sense. The allegorical point is that the Holy Spirit is the sight of God, and God's sight is the basis for how creatures can truly see the creation to be from God. As God's Spirit provides a creature with that sight, within the work of redemption, they see it for what it is. However, Augustine's discussion of this passage in the *Confessions* also parallels his discussion in *The Literal Meaning* of how God sees that the creation is good through the divine goodness.

93. J. Burnaby relates the delight of creatures in their creator's good creation to what he calls "love at worship," whereby the dynamism of the creator-creation relationship that the Holy Spirit works between God and creatures issues in the loving worship of God. This worship is not because of God's requirement of worship, but because of the abundance of love that God produces in his creatures—a love originating from his overflowing bounty, which causes creatures to reciprocate that love to God in worship of his goodness by which they are. See Burnaby, *Amor Dei: A Study of the Religion of St. Augustine*, rev. ed. (Norwich, UK: Canterbury Press, 1991), 168.

94. Augustine, *Trinity* 4.29.

95. See our discussion in chapters 2–3.

96. If God's being changed, it would mean that his being was different from what it was, and therefore that God was not perfect. See Augustine, *Trinity* 5.3.

97. See our discussion in chapter 3 of Augustine, *Trinity* 6.7–9.

98. Augustine, *Trinity* 6.7–9.

99. E.g., Augustine, *Literal Meaning* 1.5.11, "But what the Son speaks, the Father speaks, because in the speech of the Father, the Word, who is the Son, is uttered according to God's eternal way—if we can use the term 'way' in describing God's utterance of His eternal Word."

100. E.g., Augustine, *Literal Meaning* 1.8.14, "Moreover, when the works thus begun had been formed and perfected, *God saw that it was good.* For he found His works pleasing, in keeping with the benevolence by which He was pleased to

create them." The benevolence is the love of the Holy Spirit by which creatures exist and in which creatures abide, as we discussed above.

101. Augustine, *Literal Meaning* 1.18.36.

Chapter Five

1. Augustine, *Literal Meaning of Genesis*, trans. J. H. Taylor, 2 vols. (New York: Newman Press, 1982), 2.8.19; cf. 1.5.10–11.

2. The appearance of new creatures and species occurs as the causal reasons unfold at their appropriate times, like a seed germinating unseen in the ground and then sprouting at the appropriate time under God's governance. Thus, no new creating is done after God rests from the founding work (Augustine, *Literal Meaning* 5.23.45).

3. See Augustine, *Literal Meaning* 4.11.21–4.12.23, also 5.23.46.

4. See Augustine, *Literal Meaning* 4.18.34: "For the perfection of each thing according to the limits of its nature is established in a state of rest . . . in Him to whom it owes its being, in whom the universe itself exists." Augustine's reference to a creature's being in God is based on Paul's understanding of being as existing in God (Acts 17:28). The limits of a creaturely nature are its measure, number, and weight, which will be discussed below.

5. Augustine, *Literal Meaning* 5.20.40–41.

6. Augustine, *Literal Meaning* 8.9.17.

7. Augustine, *Literal Meaning* 8.9.17.

8. Augustine, *Literal Meaning* 8.23.44. Augustine also points out that God, who has created everything and has declared it good, when punishing an evil will according to his justice never does so "to the extent of destroying the dignity of its nature."

9. Augustine, *Literal Meaning* 8.24.45.

10. Augustine, *Literal Meaning* 4.12.23.

11. Augustine, *Literal Meaning* 4.12.23. This is a reference to John 5:26.

12. Augustine, *Literal Meaning* 4.12.23, 8.20.39.

13. Augustine, *Literal Meaning* 5.20.40–5.22.43. Also see C. J. O'Toole, *The Philosophy of Creation in the Writings of St. Augustine* (Washington, DC: Catholic University of America Press, 1944), 95–96.

14. David V. Meconi, "St. Augustine's Early Theory of Participation," *Augustinian Studies* 27 (1996): 81–98. He cites seven authors who have written on participation, from 1926 to the present. He overlooks M. Smallbrugge, "La notion de la participation chez Augustin: Quelques observations sur le rapport christianisme-platonisme," in *Collectanea Augustiniana: Mélanges T. J. Van Bavel*, ed. B. Bruning, J. van Houtem, M. Lamberigts (Leuven: Peeters, 1990), 333–47. Smallbrugge's article is concerned chiefly with the manner in which Augustine used the Platonic understanding of participation in his theology. He focuses on how Augustine reversed the Neoplatonic conception of an inferior creation ascending the hierarchy of being to participate in the superior One by emphasizing God's descent through the Incarnation in order to lift up humanity to God.

15. Meconi, "St. Augustine's Early Theory of Participation," 87.

16. See M. Annice, "Historical Sketch of the Theory of Participation," *New Scholasticism* 26 (1952): 49–79.

17. Ibid., 65.

18. Augustine, *Literal Meaning* 1.5.10.

19. Augustine, *Literal Meaning* 1.5.10.

20. Augustine, *Literal Meaning*, 1.6.12.

21. Augustine, *Literal Meaning*, 1.8.14.

22. Meconi, "St. Augustine's Early Theory of Participation," 87.

23. Augustine, *Literal Meaning* 1.17.32.

24. Also see Annice, "Historical Sketch of the Theory of Participation," 61.

25. Augustine, *Unfinished Literal Commentary on Genesis*, in *On Genesis*, trans. E. Hill (Brooklyn, NY: New City Press, 2002), 16.57. Vernon J. Bourke, *Augustine's View of Reality* (Villanova, PA: Villanova Press, 1964), 119–20, notes a similar discussion by Augustine in question 23 in *Eighty-three Different Questions*, trans. D. L. Mosher, Fathers of the Church 70 (Washington, DC: Catholic University of America Press, 1982), 49. There Augustine writes that chastity is a perfection in two ways: "First, the chaste thing produces chastity so that it is chaste by that chastity which it produces and for which it is the generative principle and cause of existence; and second, when by participation in chastity everything is chaste which can at some time not be chaste."

26. Augustine, *Trinity*, trans. E. Hill (Brooklyn, NY: New City Press, 1991), 7.2.

27. Augustine, *Unfinished Literal Commentary on Genesis* 16.57.

28. Annice, "Historical Sketch of the Theory of Participation," 61. See also Augustine, *Confessions*, trans. H. Chadwick (Oxford: Oxford University Press, 1991), 13.8.9, where Augustine describes the absence of God's wisdom and Holy Spirit as the darkness that occurred when angels and human souls fell from their participation in God. Only as rational creatures have the divine presence as their illumination do they stand before God. Otherwise they are in an abyss of darkness. Epistemological participation is God's illuminating presence in rational creatures' lives.

29. Meconi, "St. Augustine's Early Theory of Participation," 85. He is summarizing G. Bonner, "Augustine's Conception of Deification," *Journal of Theological Studies*, n.s., 37 (1986): 369–86.

30. Meconi, "St. Augustine's Early Theory of Participation," 85.

31. Bourke, *Augustine's View of Reality*, 121. Meconi, "St. Augustine's Early Theory of Participation," highlights the roots of participation theory in Plato, and some possible Platonic sources for Augustine (e.g., 86, 91–92). Bourke notes another source for Augustine's understanding of participation in Paul's description of human redemption by participation in the body of Christ (Bourke, *Augustine's View of Reality*, 117–18).

32. Bourke, *Augustine's View of Reality*, 120.

33. See the discussion in chapter 4 of Augustine's description of the Word's conversion of creatures from the formless matter in Augustine, *Literal Meaning* 1.4.9, and the Holy Spirit's brooding over the creation in *Literal Meaning* 1.7.13–1.8.14, 1.18.36.

34. See Augustine, *Literal Meaning* 4.1.1, where Augustine is speculating on the meaning of day and night in Genesis 1. He goes on in the next several chapters to discuss the perfection of the number six and how all creatures are perfected in their existence according to measure, number, and weight, which we will discuss in the next section. Also see *Literal Meaning* 4.9.16 (cf. 4.16.28), where Augustine writes about God's Holy Spirit, who, by pouring out charity into human hearts (Romans 5:5), is thereby the source of human "desire and yearning" to find its rest in God. We shall take up the concept of rest as participation in God in the next chapter. Finally, in *Literal Meaning* 4.18.31–34, Augustine describes creaturely existences as perfected in their orientation toward the creator, according to an "appetite of their weight," by which God draws them to seek their rest in him, which echoes the idea of the Word who calls back creatures to himself (Augustine, *Literal Meaning* 1.4.9), so that they might maintain their forms. "Conversion," "perfecting," and "calling back" describe the attraction of creatures toward God, who is the basis for their existence. In the providential government of creation, creatures are therefore rightly described as continually converted by God.

35. D. J. Hassel, "Conversion-Theory and *Scientia* in the *De Trinitate*," *Recherches Augustiniennes* 2 (1962): 383–401, as has already been noted in chapter 4, describes how two of the three "principal moments of conversion" in Augustine's doctrine of creation are discussed in terms of the governing of the creation. Those two moments are when "the creature is impelled to turn back" to the Word, and when the creature has "growth in perfection" (384–85). They extend through time as part of God's governance. The first is also part of the founding of creation, when the creature is formed by the Word.

36. Augustine, *Literal Meaning* 4.12.23.

37. Augustine, *Literal Meaning* 4.12.23. This is a reference to John 5:26.

38. Augustine, *Literal Meaning* 4.12.23 and 8.20.39.

39. Augustine, *Literal Meaning* 5.20.40–5.22.43. Also see O'Toole, *Philosophy of Creation*, 95–96.

40. Augustine, *Literal Meaning* 4.12.23. For further discussion on creaturely movement as dependent on God's governance, see S. J. Grabowski, *The All-Present God: A Study in St. Augustine* (St. Louis, MO: Herder, 1954), 148–55; and O'Toole, *Philosophy of Creation*, 96–98.

41. We shall see below that this is the "measure" of a creature that is set out by God the Father, in Augustine's description of measure, number, and weight.

42. Augustine, *Literal Meaning* 8.20.39.

43. Augustine, *Literal Meaning* 4.12.23.

44. Augustine, *Literal Meaning* 8.23.44.

45. Augustine, *Trinity* 6.7, 6.9–10.

46. Augustine, *Literal Meaning* 1.6.12–1.7.13, describes the overflowing love of God given to creatures in the founding work of creation.

47. Augustine, *Literal Meaning* 8.26.48.

48. Cf. Augustine, *Confessions* 11.13.16, where God's eternity is described as the time-bridging present of a creature's experience of past and future.

49. God is said to be interior to all things, because all things are in God. Augustine takes care not to be misunderstood as claiming that God is actually

"in" creatures. Taylor points to how Augustine qualifies this in *Confessions* 1.2.2: "Accordingly, my God, I would have no being, I would not have any existence, unless you were in me. Or rather, I would have no being if I were not in you 'of whom are all things, through whom are all things, in whom are all things' " (Augustine, *Literal Meaning*, 263–64 n. 116).

50. Augustine, *Literal Meaning* 8.20.39.

51. Augustine, *Literal Meaning* 8.20.39.

52. Augustine, *Trinity* 7.12.

53. Augustine, *Trinity* 7.12. For more detail on Augustine's understanding of image and likeness, see R. A. Markus, " '*Imago*' and '*Similitudo*' in Augustine," *Revue des Études Augustiniennes* 10 (1964): 125–43.

54. Augustine, *Trinity* 7.12.

55. Augustine, *Unfinished Literal Commentary on Genesis* 16.60. We will discuss the image of God more in the next chapter.

56. Augustine, *Unfinished Literal Commentary on Genesis* 16.59.

57. Augustine, *Unfinished Literal Commentary on Genesis* 16.60.

58. Augustine, *Literal Meaning* 4.12.23.

59. Augustine, *Literal Meaning* 8.20.39. It is interesting to note that Sigurd Bergmann, *Creation Set Free: The Spirit as Liberator of Nature*, trans. D. Stott, (Grand Rapids, MI: Eerdmans, 2005), deals also with the importance of motion in the creational theology of Gregory of Nazianzus, relating it specifically to the work of the Holy Spirit. He discusses Gregory's conception of the relationship between God's inner trinitarian movement and the world created to move toward God. I know of no studies that consider the relationship between Gregory and Augustine with regard to these remarkably similar ideas, though it would not be improbable that Augustine might have been dependent on Gregory in this regard. Such a relationship would further undermine contemporary critiques of Augustine that dissociate him from the so-called Eastern church. Lewis Ayres has shown that Augustine's conception of creation overlaps with that of another Cappadocian, Basil of Caesarea, in *Nicaea and Its Legacy: An Approach to Fourth-Century Trinitarian Theology* (Oxford: Oxford University Press, 2004), 314–24. He specifically compares how a trinitarian conception of God is important in each for establishing God's sustaining involvement in the creation.

60. Augustine, *Trinity* 7.12. For more detail on Augustine's understanding of image and likeness, see Markus, " '*Imago*' and '*Similitudo*' in Augustine," 125–43.

61. Augustine, *Trinity* 6.7, 6.9–10.

62. Augustine, *Trinity* 7.12. Imitating the Son is the subject of this passage, while the Holy Spirit's work of transforming a person to the image of God is the subject of *Trinity* 14.23 and 15.14.

63. Augustine, *Trinity* 8.9–12. As Augustine puts it in *On Christian Teaching*, trans. R. P. H. Green, (Oxford: Oxford University Press, 1997), 1.36.40: "So anyone who thinks that he has understood the divine scriptures or any part of them, but cannot by his understanding build up this double love of God and neighbour, has not yet succeeded in understanding them." The centrality of

loving God and one's neighbor to Augustine's theology is taken up in Raymond Canning, *The Unity of Love for God and Neighbour in St. Augustine* (Heverlee-Leuven: Augustinian Historical Institute, 1993).

64. Augustine, *Literal Meaning* 4.3.7. The importance of Wisdom 11:20 for Augustine's discussion of creation is noted by O. du Roy, *L'intelligence de la foi en la Trinité selon saint Augustin* (Paris: Études Augustiennes, 1966), 421–24. This triad, *mensura et numero et pondere*, appears throughout Augustine's writings; see W. J. Roche, "Measure, Number, Weight in Saint Augustine," *New Scholasticism* 15 (1941): 351–53. Roche notes that besides the scriptural citation, there are also philosophical sources that may have informed Augustine's understanding and application of the triad in Stoic and Platonic writings (355, 372–76).

65. Augustine, *Literal Meaning* 4.3.7–4.10. Also cf. 5.22.43, where Augustine uses the human body as an example to justify his contention that God governs the creation through a "rule of measures, every harmony of numbers, every order of weights."

66. Augustine, *Literal Meaning* 4.2.2–4.3.7. See the discussion of this passage in *La Genèse au sens littéral en douze livres (I–VII)*, trans. P. Agaësse and A. Solignac, in *Œuvres de Saint Augustin*, vol. 48, Bibliothèque Augustinienne (Paris: Desclée de Brouwer, 1972), 633–35.

67. Augustine, *Literal Meaning* 4.2.2–4.3.7.

68. In *Literal Meaning* 4.5.11, Augustine points out that the perfection of all created forms is by God's wisdom, "through whom all things have been made."

69. Augustine, *Literal Meaning* 4.3.7.

70. Augustine, *Literal Meaning* 4.2.2–4.3.7, ". . . God perfected His works in six days because six is a perfect number . . . even if these works did not exist, this number would be perfect. . . ." W. G. Most, "The Scriptural Basis of St. Augustine's Arithmology," *Catholic Biblical Quarterly* 13, no. 3 (1951): 284–95, discusses the relationship between divine wisdom's perfecting work and the power of numbers.

71. Augustine, *Literal Meaning* 4.2.2–4.3.7.

72. Augustine, *Concerning the Nature of the Good*, in *The "De Natura Boni" of Saint Augustine*, trans. A. A. Moon (Washington, DC: Catholic University of America Press, 1955), bk. 1.

73. Augustine, *Concerning the Nature of the Good*. In *The City of God*, Augustine relates the declaration of creation's goodness by God to the fact that creation is made from God's goodness. Augustine, *The City of God Against the Pagans*, trans. R. W. Dyson (Cambridge: Cambridge University Press, 1998), 11.24.

74. Augustine, *Concerning the Nature of the Good* 3. According to Roche, "Measure, Number, Weight," 352, *modus*, *species*, and *ordo* are synonymous in meaning with *mensura*, *numero*, and *pondere*; limit is equivalent to measure; form is equivalent to number; and weight is equivalent to order.

75. Augustine, *Concerning the Nature of the Good* 3.

76. In Augustine, *Literal Meaning* 1.1.6.12

77. Augustine, *Literal Meaning* 4.3.7.

78. Augustine, *Literal Meaning* 4.3.7.
79. Augustine, *Literal Meaning* 4.3.8.
80. Augustine, *Literal Meaning* 4.3.7.
81. Augustine, *Literal Meaning* 4.3.7.
82. Carol Harrison, "Measure, Number, and Weight," *Augustinianum* 28 (1988): 594.
83. Ibid., 595.
84. Augustine, *Literal Meaning* 4.4.8.
85. Augustine, *Literal Meaning* 4.4.8.
86. See chapter 2, where we discuss how the Father is conceived as without beginning.
87. Augustine, *Literal Meaning* 4.3.7.
88. Augustine, *Literal Meaning* 1.4.9.
89. Augustine, *Literal Meaning* 4.4.8.
90. Augustine, *Literal Meaning* 4.4.8.
91. Augustine, *Literal Meaning* 1.4.9.
92. Augustine, *Literal Meaning* 4.4.8.
93. Augustine, *Tractates on the Gospel of John*, trans., J. W. Rettig, Fathers of the Church 78 (Washington, DC: Catholic University of America Press, 1982).
94. Augustine, *Tractates* 1.5.2 and 1.8.1.
95. Augustine, *Tractates* 1.9.2–1.11.2.
96. Augustine, *Tractates* 1.13.3.
97. Augustine, *Tractates* 1.15.1.
98. John 1:4.
99. Augustine, *Tractates* 1.17.2.
100. Sin not only disrupts the order of the world, so that it tends toward nothingness (Augustine, *Tractates* 1.12.1), but also distorts people's ability to see how the creation exists in the Word, just as a blind person, standing in the sunlight, is at the same time absent from the light because of lack of eyesight—thus explaining John 1:5, where the darkness is described as not comprehending the light that has come into the world (Augustine, *Tractates* 1.19.1). The relationship between the Incarnation and God's revelation to human beings who can no longer see or hear the divine revelation in its eternal, invisible nature, as Augustine describes it in the *Tractates*, is discussed in Richard P. Hardy, "The Incarnation and Revelation in Augustine's *Tractatus in Iohannis Evangelium*," *Église et Théologie* 3 (1972): 193–220.
101. Augustine, *Tractates* 2.10.1–2.
102. Augustine, *Tractates* 3.5.4.
103. Augustine, *Tractates* 2.8.1–2.
104. Augustine, *Literal Meaning* 4.3.7.
105. Augustine, *Literal Meaning* 2.1.2. Cf. a similar discussion in Augustine, *Expositions of the Psalms 1–32*, trans. M. Boulding, Works of Saint Augustine, pt. 3, vol. 15 (Hyde Park, NY: New City Press, 2000), 29.[2].10.
106. Augustine, *Literal Meaning* 4.4.8.
107. Augustine, *Confessions* 13.9.10.

108. James J. O'Donnell, *Augustine: Confessions* (Oxford: Oxford University Press, 1997), 3:46–52, 356–57; John Burnaby, *Amor Dei: A Study of the Religion of St. Augustine*, rev. ed. (Norwich, UK: Canterbury Press, 1991), 94; and R. Williams, " 'Good for Nothing'? Augustine on Creation," *Augustinian Studies* 25 (1994): 12–14.

109. Augustine, *Literal Meaning* 4.3.7.

110. Roche, "Measure, Number, Weight," 362–68. In the next chapter, we shall discuss more fully the rest that creatures find when they are drawn by the weight of the Holy Spirit.

111. Augustine, *Literal Meaning* 4.4.8.

112. Augustine, *Literal Meaning* 4.4.8.

113. We did so by comparing his discussion of the Holy Spirit in Augustine, *Literal Meaning* 1.18.36 and in Augustine, *Confessions* 13.4.5.

114. See our discussion of "gift" in chapters 2–3, as Augustine uses the term in *The Trinity*, and of "good will" in chapter 4, as he uses the term in *Literal Meaning* 1.6.11.

115. Augustine, *On Genesis: A Refutation of the Manichees* in *On Genesis*, trans. E. Hill (Brooklyn, NY: New City Press, 2002), 1.16.26.

116. Augustine, *On Genesis: A Refutation of the Manichees* 1.16.25. On the place of beauty in Augustine's conception of creation, see Carol Harrison, *Beauty and Revelation in the Thought of Saint Augustine* (Oxford: Clarendon Press, 1992), esp. chap.3.

117. He does suggest that animals could seem to be "against our interests" (i.e., could cause us harm) "because of our sins" (Augustine, *On Genesis: A Refutation of the Manichees* 1.16.26).

118. Augustine, *On Genesis: A Refutation of the Manichees* 1.16.26.

119. See chapters 2–3.

120. See Augustine, *Trinity* 6.8–9, and 7.1–4. See the discussion of the unity and distinction of the divine persons in his doctrine of the Trinity in chapters 2–3 above.

121. Augustine, *The Trinity* 1.7.

122. Colin Gunton, *The One, the Three and the Many: God, Creation, and the Culture of Modernity* (Cambridge: Cambridge University Press, 1993), 54.

123. The claim is in Anne Primavesi, *From Apocalypse to Genesis: Ecology, Feminism and Christianity* (Minneapolis, MN: Fortress Press, 1991), 203; on her pp. 210–21, Augustine is linked by Primavesi to the idea of God imposing a form by dominating passive matter. There he also is considered a key figure in the history of patriarchalism and authoritarianism, which are two of the key factors that make classical theology unhelpful in ecological and liberationist matters, as we saw in the critiques cited in introduction and in Boff's assessment of the history of the doctrine of the Trinity in chapter 1.

124. Augustine, *Concerning the Nature of the Good* 18. See Michael Hanby, *Augustine and Modernity* (London: Routledge, 2003), 85.

125. Augustine, *Concerning the Nature of the Good* 18.

126. Hanby, *Augustine and Modernity*, 85.

127. Ibid., 86.

128. Ibid., 85–86.

129. Ibid., 218, n. 73.

130. Augustine, *Concerning the Nature of the Good* 1–3.

131. Augustine, *Concerning the Nature of the Good* 18.

132. Augustine, *The City of God Against the Pagans*, trans. R. W. Dyson (Cambridge: Cambridge University Press, 1998), 11.24.

133. We saw this in Augustine, *Literal Meaning* 1.18.36.

134. Augustine, *Trinity* 6.7.

135. Augustine, *City of God* 11.24.

136. R. Williams, " 'Good for Nothing'?" 17ff.

137. Ibid., 16.

138. Ibid.

139. Augustine, *Concerning the Nature of the Good* 1–3.

140. Augustine, *Literal Meaning* 5.20.40–41.

141. Augustine, *Literal Meaning* 3.24.37. The whole of the creation is said to be "very good" in reference to Genesis 1:31. Augustine uses the word "order" not only to refer to weight as it is meant in measure, number, and weight, but also more generally to the order of the whole creation. So it is here that the creation as a whole is very good, because of God's ordering. The word "order" is not used equivocally, though, since the order of the whole and the particular order that each creature manifests are intrinsically related. All order, whether the ordering of the whole or the particular order/weight of the individual, is from God and does not contradict the other, but rather confirms that the order of the creation and the order of individual creatures are part of the same divine ordering.

142. Cf. Augustine, *Literal Meaning* 5.20.40–41.

143. Augustine, *Concerning the Nature of the Good* 1–3.

144. R. Williams, " 'Good for Nothing'?" 14. Williams describes how measure, number, and weight relate to God's governance by grouping together measure and number as one activity, and then naming weight as a second. However, despite Williams's distinct formulation, it leads to the same point as we are making, which is that the Trinity governs creatures through their measure, number, and weight, and that the measure, number, and weight of a creature are how it participates in the triune God. Whether measure, number, and weight can be grouped together into one, two, or three activities does not affect the fact that the three are identified with the Trinity and that, all together, they give a creature its unity.

145. Augustine, *Unfinished Literal Commentary on Genesis* 16.59.

146. The opposite of this, moving away or turning from God, would be to revert to the state of unformed matter from which creatures are shaped. This is also a movement away from the goodness of being to the evilness of nonbeing. On the goodness of creation and the Augustinian conception of evil as privation, see Rowan Williams, "Insubstantial Evil," in *Augustine and His Critics: Essays in Honor of Gerald Bonner*, ed. R. Dodaro and G. Lawless (New York: Routledge, 2000), 105–23.

Chapter Six

1. Augustine, *The Literal Meaning of Genesis*, trans. J. H. Taylor, 2 vols., Ancient Christian Writers, nos. 41–42 (New York: Newman Press, 1982), 4.11.21–4.12.23, 5.23.46.

2. Augustine, *Literal Meaning* 4.16.27.

3. Augustine, *Literal Meaning* 1.6.12.

4. Augustine, *Literal Meaning* 4.16.27.

5. See Augustine, *Literal Meaning* 4.18.34.

6. Augustine, *Literal Meaning* 4.18.34.

7. Augustine, *Literal Meaning* 4.18.34.

8. Augustine describes the divine Word's happiness in *Literal Meaning* 1.5.10: "In His case, not only is being the same thing as living, but living is the same thing as living wisely and happily." Thus, divine happiness is not different from divine being, but is found in the Word's being itself, which also is one being with the Father. This parallels the idea of 4.16.27, where God's goodness—namely, the Holy Spirit—is said to be independent of everything outside of himself, because God is eternally self-sufficient.

9. One finds the goodness of God related to divine happiness in Augustine, *Literal Meaning* 4.16.27, where God's rest is at once described as his happiness and as his independence of any extrinsic goodness. God's happiness is his own goodness. Similarly, in the *City of God*, Augustine speaks of God's goodness as his immutable blessedness. Augustine, *The City of God Against the Pagans*, trans. R. W. Dyson (Cambridge: Cambridge University Press, 1998), 12.1.2.

10. Augustine, *Literal Meaning* 4.16.27.

11. Augustine, *Literal Meaning* 4.18.34.

12. Augustine, *Literal Meaning* 2.1.2. See the discussion in chapter 5.

13. Similarly, in *City of God* 12.1.2, Augustine writes, "Although, therefore, they are not the supreme good—for God is a greater good than they are—those mutable things which can cleave to the immutable good, and so be blessed, are nonetheless great goods. And so completely is He their good that, without Him, they are necessarily miserable."

14. This theme was noted in chapter 5. The rest that human beings find by resting in God is through their clinging to Christ. This was discussed in chapters 2–3, as part of Augustine's establishment of the doctrine of the Trinity from the scriptural presentation of human redemption by God.

15. Augustine, *Literal Meaning* 4.18.34.

16. Augustine, *Literal Meaning* 4.18.34.

17. Augustine, *Literal Meaning* 4.18.34.

18. Augustine, *Literal Meaning* 4.18.34.

19. Moral nature is situated in the human will. It will be recalled that creatures without souls do not find rest in God by a free decision of their will. See D. J. Hassel, "Conversion-Theory and *Scientia* in the *De Trinitate*," *Recherches Augstiniennes* 2 (1962): 383–401.

20. Augustine, *Literal Meaning* 4.17.29.

21. Since movement is basic to creaturely being, people would be wrong to think they can rest apart from their works, which are part of the natural movement of people toward rest in God.

22. Augustine, *Literal Meaning* 4.17.29. Cf. Allan-Fitzgerald and John Cavadini, eds., *Augustine through the Ages: An Encyclopedia* (Grand Rapids, MI: Eerdmans, 1999), s.v. "Pride."

23. Augustine, *Literal Meaning* 4.17.29.

24. Augustine, *Literal Meaning* 4.17.29. Also see Augustine, *The Confessions*, trans. H. Chadwick (Oxford: Oxford University Press, 1991), 13.36.51: "After your 'very good' works, which you made while remaining yourself in repose, you 'rested the seventh day' (Genesis 2:2–3). This utterance in your book foretells for us that after our good works which, because they are your gift to us, are very good, we also may rest in you for the Sabbath of eternal life."

25. The end of the quotation from Augustine, *Literal Meaning* 4.17.29, "He bestows rest in Himself upon us after the good works we have done when justified by Him," points not only to how the proper end of human works is in God, but that that end is only properly reached when God justifies "us." While Augustine discusses the rest that God created humanity to find through its works in God, he also understands that that end is dependent on God's redemptive work of justification, because of human sinfulness.

26. For example, see Augustine, *Confessions* 13.37.52: "Your seeing is not in time, your movement is not in time, and your rest is not in time. Yet, your acting causes us to see things in time, time itself, and the repose which is outside time."

27. Augustine, *Literal Meaning* 4.17.29.

28. Deuteronomy 6:5, Leviticus 19:18, Matthew 22:37–39, and Mark 12:29–31. For more detailed background, see Raymond Canning, *The Unity of Love for God and Neighbour in St. Augustine* (Heverlee-Leuven: Augustinian Historical Institute, 1993), esp. 79–115.

29. Especially in Augustine, *On Christian Teaching*, trans. R. P. H. Green (Oxford: Oxford University Press, 1997), 1.3.3–1.7.7, 1.22.20.

30. The terms, though, are not used strictly according to the definitions found in Augustine, *On Christian Teaching*. See O. O'Donovan, *The Problem of Self-Love in Augustine* (New Haven, CT: Yale University Press, 1980), 25–29.

31. Augustine, *On Christian Teaching* 1.4.4.

32. Augustine, *On Christian Teaching* 1.22.20–21.

33. Thus, in *City of God* 11.25, Augustine judges as perverse those who use God for the sake of some temporal good: "those perverse men who wish to enjoy money and use God, not spending money for God's sake, but worshipping God for money's sake." This perversity is the result of a will turned evil and motivated by a disordered love that no longer desires God. See N. J. Torchia, "The Significance of *Ordo* in St. Augustine's Moral Theory," in *Augustine: Presbyter Factus Sum*, ed. J. T. Lienhard, E. C. Miller, and R. J. Teske (New York: Peter Lang, 1993), 268–70.

34. In this regard, see Augustine, *City of God* 11.25.

35. Rist notes that Augustine left room for the application of "use" and "enjoyment" toward one's neighbor, as well as toward God, after writing book 1 of *On Christian Teaching*. See John M. Rist, *Augustine: Ancient Thought Baptized* (Cambridge: Cambridge University Press, 1994), 165–66.

36. Augustine, *On Christian Teaching* 1.4.4. Rist, *Augustine*, 163, as an example of such a misinterpretation of "use," cites A. Nygren, *Agape and Eros: A Study of the Christian Idea of Love*, trans. P. S. Watson (Philadelphia: Westminster Press, 1953).

37. Rist, *Augustine*, 163–64.

38. So, in the course of his explanation of how one uses the world to enjoy God, Augustine appeals to the example of how the Christian loves God through following the way of his incarnate Son, Jesus Christ (Augustine, *On Christian Teaching* 1.34.38). The Incarnation provides the path to the invisible and transcendent God. It is likely that part of the reason Augustine uses this example is that he recognizes that God's bestowal of goodness (being) upon the world makes it capable of moving toward God—the way to God is through God (i.e., the work of Christ and the Holy Spirit) and through the good things he has created (the Incarnation affirms this). See our discussion of how God draws the creation to himself in chapter 5.

39. Augustine, *On Christian Teaching* 1.33.37. "In God" was used by Augustine prior to *On Christian Teaching* as well as afterward (e.g., Augustine, *Trinity* 9.13); see Rist, *Augustine*, 165–66. For instances of Augustine's conception of use "in God," see Oliver O'Donovan, "*Usus* and *Fruitio* in Augustine, *De Doctrina Christiana* I," *Journal of Theological Studies*, n.s., 33 (1982): 361–97.

40. Augustine, *On Christian Teaching* 1.33.37.

41. Augustine, *On Christian Teaching* 1.33.37.

42. Augustine, *On Christian Teaching* 1.4.4.

43. Augustine, *On Christian Teaching* 1.24.25–1.27.28.

44. Augustine, *On Christian Teaching* 1.24.25–1.27.28. A study of Augustine's understanding of human embodiment and its goodness is George Lawless, "Augustine and Human Embodiment," in *Collectanea Augustiniana: Mélanges T. J. Van Bavel*, ed. B. Bruning, J. van Houtem, M. Lamberigts (Leuven: Peeters, 1990), 167–86.

45. In *Literal Meaning* 3.24.37 Augustine writes, "For when creatures remain in the state in which they have been created, possessing the perfection they have received . . . they are good individually, and all in general are very good." The reference to the whole of the creation being "very good" is Genesis 1:31.

46. We noted earlier that Augustine considered all creatures to be made to the likeness of the creator, but that human beings are made to the image. See John E. Sullivan, *The Image of God: The Doctrine of St. Augustine and Its Influence* (Dubuque, IA: Priory Press, 1963), 11–14; and Robert A. Markus, " '*Imago*' and '*Similitudo*' in Augustine," *Revue des Études Augustiniennes* 10 (1964): 125–43.

47. Augustine, *Literal Meaning* 4.17.29.

48. Augustine, *Literal Meaning* 4.17.29.

49. Augustine, *City of God* 19.13.1.

50. Augustine, *City of God* 19.13.1.

51. This is Augustine's text of Genesis 1:26–27, in *Literal Meaning* 3.19.29.

52. Augustine, *Literal Meaning* 3.19.29. Cf. his *Unfinished Literal Commentary on Genesis*, in *On Genesis*, trans. E. Hill (Brooklyn, NY: New City Press, 2002), 16.61, where he explained, in an emendation, that the likeness of the image in humanity is to the Trinity itself, thus revising his earlier interpretation (16.60) that the image of humanity is to the Word alone. See our discussion in chapter 4.

53. Augustine, *Literal Meaning* 3.19.29. Augustine makes this same point in Sermon 52.18, where he begins the explanation of the idea of humankind being made to the image of God as a reference to the Father and the Son, "and also of course in consequence of the Holy Spirit too. . . . So the Father isn't making without the Son, nor the Son without the Father." (Augustine, *Sermons 51–94*, trans. E. Hill, Works of Saint Augustine, pt. 3, vol. 3 (Brooklyn, NY: New City Press, 1990).

54. Augustine, *Literal Meaning* 3.20.30. Cf. Augustine, *Trinity* 7.12 and 14.25.

55. Augustine, *Sermons 20–50*, trans. E. Hill, Works of Saint Augustine, pt. 3, vol. 2 (Brooklyn, NY: New City Press, 1990).

56. Augustine, *Sermons 20–50*, Sermon 43.4.

57. Our discussion about the image of God will be developed using Augustine's comments about the image as they are related to dominion, since our purpose is to develop a fuller understanding of human dominion. It is impossible to do full justice to Augustine's important discussion of the image in the second half of *The Trinity* in this section, and we will only make limited use of it. We will rely on Rowan Williams's essay on how Augustine develops his argument about the image in *The Trinity*, "*Sapientia* and the Trinity: Reflections on the *De Trinitate*," in *Collectanea Augustiniana: Mélanges T. J. Van Bavel*, ed. B. Bruning, J. van Houtem, M. Lamberigts (Leuven: Peeters, 1990).

58. Cf. Augustine, *Trinity* 12.12. It should be pointed out that even though it is the mind that is renewed from the effects of sin, Augustine also believed that bodies would be renewed. They would not be renewed according to the image of the Trinity, but to the image of the Son who became incarnate. Augustine did not denigrate the body.

59. E.g., Augustine, *Trinity* 15.31 and Augustine, *Literal Meaning* 1.8.14.

60. The importance of love for understanding the image of God is confirmed in the place that it occupies as the starting point (bk. 8) and the conclusion (bks. 14–15) of Augustine's search in *The Trinity*. See R. Williams, "*Sapientia* and the Trinity," 322–23.

61. Augustine, *Trinity* 14.23.

62. Sullivan, *Image of God*, 50–51, 54, 62–63.

63. Augustine, *Literal Meaning* 3.20.30.

64. Augustine, *Sermons 20–50*, Sermon 43.4.

65. R. Williams, "*Sapientia* and the Trinity," 321. The trinitarian work of redeeming the image of God in human beings is also described in detail by Sullivan, *Image of God*, chap. 2.

66. Cf. Sullivan, *Image of God*, 17–21. Augustine describes this movement toward God in *Trinity* 12.10: "Now the more it [the mind] reaches out toward what is eternal, the more it is formed thereby to the image of God." The mind can do this only because it has help from God: "But his success depends on divine assistance; it is after all God who declares, *Without me you can do nothing* (John 15:5)." In this quotation, the divine assistance is specifically the mediator Christ, though in the larger argument of *The Trinity* it is the work of all three persons to reach out.

67. See chapter 5, above.

68. See chapter 4, above.

69. R. Williams, "*Sapientia* and the Trinity," 321.

70. Augustine, *Literal Meaning* 3.20.30 and Sermon 43.3 in Augustine *Sermons 20–50*.

71. It will be recalled (see the introduction) that Moltmann depicts Augustine's understanding of dominion and the image of God to be about the rule of power. Moltmann calls it "a pure analogy of domination . . . a patriarchal analogy to God the Father." Jürgen Moltmann, *God in Creation: A New Theology of Creation and the Spirit of God*, trans. M. Kohl (Minneapolis, MN: Fortress Press, 1993), 240. We also noted how Moltmann's argument is repeated by Boff (see chapter 1), though he does not place the blame for such a dominating and patriarchal view of God solely on Augustine, but rather construes the problem of dominating power to be at the root of ancient and classical societies, also distorting the scriptures. Leondardo Boff, *Cry of the Earth, Cry of the Poor*, trans. P. Berryman (Maryknoll, NY: Orbis Books, 1997), 79.

Moltmann reaches the conclusion that Augustine's conception of the image of God is patriarchal and dominating, in part, because of his understanding of Augustine's argument in *Trinity* 12.10. There Augustine is attempting to explain how man and woman might symbolize the functioning of the image of God according to 1 Corinthians 11:7, which states, "[Man] is the image and reflection of God; but woman is the reflection of man." This is to misunderstand what Augustine is trying to accomplish. He does not reject the woman as a bearer of the image of God in her human nature (*Trinity* 12.10), but rather argues (12.9–10) that in 1 Corinthians 11:7 the woman symbolizes a function that is not called the image, while the male symbolizes a function that is called the image. When he turns from his symbolic reading of 1 Corinthians to speak about the image of God as it applies to human nature, he explicitly states that a woman is the image of God just as much as a man, since both equally share the human nature that bears the image. "It [Genesis 1:27] says that what was made to the image of God is the human nature that is realized in each sex, and it does not exclude the female from the image of God that is meant" (Augustine *Trinity* 12.10).

This is not to deny limitations in Augustine's understanding of subordination with regard to gender. His subordination of women to men is cited in *Quaestiones in Heptateuchum*, Corpus Christianorum, Series Latina (Turnhout, Bel.: Brepols, 1953) 1.153: "[T]here is even a natural order among humankind, such that women should be subject to men . . ." [est etiam ordo naturalis in hominibus, ut seruiant feminae uiris . . .], as a result of their "weaker reason" [infirmior ratio]. In this respect, Augustine reflects a negative hierarchical mind-set prevalent in his day. However, at the very least, Augustine can be said to understand woman to participate fully in the image of God with man, which means that woman and man together can be renewed in that image. It is not surprising, then, that the debate as to how to understand Augustine's theological anthropology with regard to the place of women continues. An overview of recent scholarship on this is E. A. Matter, "Christ, God, and Woman in the Thought of St. Augustine," in *Augustine and His Critics: Essays in Honor of Gerald Bonner*, ed. R. Dodora and G. Lawless (New York: Routledge, 2000), 164–75. Also see M. Miles, "The Body and Human Values in Augustine of Hippo," in *Grace, Politics & Desire: Essays on Augustine*, ed. H. A. Meynell (Calgary: University of Calgary Press, 1990), 55–67.

72. Augustine, *Literal Meaning* 9.17.32.

73. See our discussion of Augustine, *Literal Meaning* 1.4.9 and 2.6.12, in chapter 4; and *The Trinity* 7.1–4 in chapter 3.

74. Augustine, *Literal Meaning* 1.6.12. In chapter 1 we cited the critique of God conceived as king over the creation by S. McFague, "A Square in the Quilt," in *Spirit and Nature: Why the Environment Is a Religious Issue, an Interfaith Dialogue*, ed. S. C. Rockefeller and J. C. Elder (Boston: Beacon Press, 1992), 42–58. It is now clear that McFague's critique of traditional images of divine lordship as a kingly rule does not apply to Augustine's portrayal of God's rule over creation. She described the image of kingly rule as anthropocentric and, ultimately, as a disinterested and distant benevolence that is directed toward the affairs of the creation. Augustine's conception of God's governance is of the Trinity holding together the creation through its providential love of all creatures, which depend on God's presence in order to exist.

75. Similarly, in Augustine, *Trinity* 12.18, Augustine explains Paul's conception of Christians as "justified in his [Christ's] blood" (Romans 5:9) in terms of the blood's "potency" (12.15) of justice, which he understands to be closely related to mercy (12.19). Justice and mercy do not appear to be powerful, as power is understood in the world; nevertheless, as he again quotes Paul (1 Corinthians 1:25), "What is weak of God is stronger than men" (*Trinity* 12.18).

76. Augustine, *Sermons 20–50*, Sermon 43.1.

77. Augustine, Sermons 20–50, Sermon 43.6. H. Paul Santmire, *The Travail of Nature: The Ambiguous Ecological Promise of Christian Theology* (Philadelphia: Fortress Press, 1985), 70, notes that it is in fallen humanity that the urge to dominate others is evident. This tendency, often most visible in the powerful and particularly in political leaders, is challenged in this sermon by Augustine's affirmation of an unlikely, humble source for God's revelation of his salvation.

78. Augustine, *Trinity* 8.7.

79. Augustine, *Sermons 20–50*, Sermon 43.3.

80. "Ubi insinuatur rationem debere dominari irrationabilis vitae" (in *Quaestiones in Heptateuchum* 1.153). R. H. Markus, *Saeculum: History and Society in the Theology of St. Augustine* (Cambridge: Cambridge University Press, 1970), 201–2, comments on this passage. It points out that the context is Augustine's explanation of Genesis 46:32, where Joseph is speaking to his brothers, who are shepherds. Augustine argues that being a shepherd is worthy of merit, because it

is a vocation that is directed toward the proper employment of dominion—namely, over cattle, according to Genesis 1:26.

81. Augustine, *City of God* 19.13.1.

82. Augustine, *Literal Meaning* 3.16.25.

83. Augustine, *Literal Meaning* 3.16.25.

84. Augustine, *Acts or Disputation Against Fortunatus* 15, in *Augustin: The Writings Against the Manichaeans, and Against the Donatists*, trans. J. H. Newman, ed. P. Schaff, Nicene and Post-Nicene Fathers, 1st ser., vol. 4 (1887; reprint, Peabody, MA: Hendrickson, 1995), 116.

85. Augustine, *Against Fortunatus* 15. Tareisius Van Bavel, "The Creator and the Integrity of Creation in the Fathers of the Church, Especially in Saint Augustin," *Augustinian Studies* 21 (1990): 17, cites this passage from *Against Fortunatus*, as well as one from *Quaestiones in Heptateuchum* 3.67 that forms part of Augustine's discussion of Leviticus 18:25. There God warns that when humans sin, the earth will vomit its inhabitants out. Augustine notes that humans suffer when they violate God's ordering of creation through their sins.

86. Augustine, *City of God* 12.4.

87. Augustine, *City of God* 12.4.

88. Augustine, *Literal Meaning* 8.23.44.

89. Augustine, *Literal Meaning* 3.16.25. W. Cizewski has shown how Augustine's discussion of animals in the *The Literal Meaning* reveals his compassion for an animal's suffering as it instinctively struggles to survive in the face of death. See "The Meaning and Purpose of Animals according to Augustine's Genesis Commentaries," in *Augustine: Presbyter Factus Sum*, ed. J. T. Lienhard, E. C. Muller, and R. J. Teske (New York: Peter Lang, 1993), 363–73.

90. Augustine, *Literal Meaning* 3.16.25.

91. Also see Augustine, *On Genesis: A Refutation of the Manichees* in *On Genesis*, trans. E. Hill (Brooklyn, NY: New City Press, 2002), 1.16.25: "[A]ll these things are beautiful to their maker and craftsman, who has a use for them all in his management of the whole universe. . . ." Even though the beauty of creatures may elude some people, as Augustine observes above, nevertheless God knows everything's beauty.

92. Augustine, *Expositions of the Psalms 121–150*, trans. M. Boulding, Works of Saint Augustine, pt. 3, vol. 20 (Hyde Park, NY: New City Press, 2004), 144.7. He laments, though, that often it is not the case that the beauty of creation leads humanity to the praise of God.

93. Augustine, *Expositions of the Psalms 121–150*, 144.13–14.

94. That the whole creation is created according to God's delight in its goodness, both in each individual creature and in the whole, is described a few paragraphs later: "When creatures remain in the state in which they have been created, possessing the perfection they have received . . . they are good individually, and all in general are very good" (Augustine, *Literal Meaning* 3.24.37).

95. Sermon 68.5, in Augustine, *Sermons 51–94*, trans. E. Hill (Brooklyn, NY: New City Press, 1991).

96. Sermon 68.6, in Augustine, *Sermons 51–94*.

97. Sermon 68.6, in Augustine, *Sermons 51–94*.

98. *City of God* 19.13.1.

99. In Augustine, *On Christian Teaching* 1.24.25–1.27.28, Augustine notes how the subjection of one's body to one's spirit is for the flourishing of the body, which will exist in perfect harmony with the spirit after the resurrection. Such a subjection of the body to the spirit, "car[ing] for them in an orderly and prudent manner" (1.25.26), is the fulfillment of the "unalterable law of nature" that "we should love ourselves and our bodies" (1.26.27). The subjection of other bodies to human dominion, one would expect, also requires the application of proper care. The work of maintaining the world's natural harmony is a proper care for the bodies that the Trinity has created in its goodness. The translation used here, for its clarity, is *Teaching Christianity* (*De Doctrina Christiana*), trans. E. Hill, Works of Saint Augustine, pt. 1, vol. 11 (Hyde Park, NY: New City Press, 1996).

100. Augustine, *On Christian Teaching* 2.38.57. Again, we are using Hill's translation.

101. Colin Gunton, *The One, the Three and the Many: God, Creation, and the Culture of Modernity* (Cambridge: Cambridge University Press, 1993), 54.

102. Colin Gunton, *The Triune Creator: A Historical and Systematic Study* (Grand Rapids, MI: Eerdmans, 1998), 75–76. In this same section, Gunton suggests that Augustine's affirmation of divine omnipotence is "a sign of weak theological argument because it is abstract and *a priori*" (75).

103. Augustine, *Literal Meaning* 9.17.32.

104. Augustine, *Literal Meaning* 4.18.34.

105. Augustine, *Trinity* 6.7–9.

106. Augustine, *City of God* 19.13.1.

Conclusion

1. Augustine, *The Literal Meaning of Genesis*, trans. J. H. Taylor (New York: Newman Press, 1982), 3.14.22–23.

2. Sermon 68.6, in Augustine, *Sermons 51–94*, trans. E. Hill (Brooklyn, NY: New City Press, 1991).

3. E.g., the implication of Augustine, *Literal Meaning* 5.18.36.

4. Augustine, *Literal Meaning* 1.7.13.

5. Augustine, *The Trinity*, trans. E. Hill (Brooklyn, NY: New City Press, 1991), 6.6–7.

6. E.g., Letter 140.2.3, Augustine, *Letters 100–155*, trans. R. J. Teske (Brooklyn, NY: New City Press, 2003).

7. Augustine, *Literal Meaning* 8.20.39.

8. Augustine, *Literal Meaning* 3.16.25.

9. Sermon 43, in Augustine, *Sermons 20–50*, trans. E. Hill (Brooklyn, NY: New City Press, 1990).

10. Gunton provides such a catalogue of problems, as we saw in chapter 1.

11. Jürgen Moltmann takes a similar view in *God in Creation: A New Theology of Creation and the Spirit of God*, trans. M. Kohl (Minneapolis, MN: Fortress Press, 1993), 236–40.

12. Regarding the resurrection, Augustine writes, "The flesh will then be spiritual, and subject to the spirit; but it will still be flesh and not spirit. . . ." Augustine, *City of God Against the Pagans*, trans. R. W. Dyson (Cambridge: Cambridge University Press, 1998), 22.21. What will disappear is the corruptible nature of the flesh, and not the flesh itself.

13. Thus, we see the centrality of the redemption worked through the missions of the Son and the Holy Spirit in Augustine's theology, contra Colin Gunton's claims.

14. Sermon 68, in Augustine *Sermons 51–94*. The failure to see God's greatness through his good creation is precisely why there is need for God's redemption.

15. Augustine, *Literal Meaning* 4.12.23.

16. Augustine, *City of God* 19.13.1.

17. This example is based on comments from Augustine, *Expositions of the Psalms 33–50*, trans. M. Boulding, Works of Saint Augustine, pt. 3, vol. 16 (Hyde Park, NY: New City Press, 2000), 35.7.

18. Augustine, *Trinity* 9.13.

19. Augustine, *City of God* 19.13.1.

20. Augustine, *Unfinished Literal Commentary on Genesis*, in *On Genesis*, trans. E. Hill (Brooklyn, NY: New City Press, 2002), 16.59.

21. This comes through in Augustine, *City of God* 19.13–14.

Bibliography

Primary Sources

Corpus Scriptorum Ecclesiasticorum Latinorum (Vienna: Tempsky, 1865–).

25, pt. 1	*Contra Fortunatum*
25, pt. 2	*De Natura Boni*
28, pt. 1	*De Genesi ad Litteram, Imperfectus Liber*
	De Genesi ad Litteram, Libri Duodecim
34, pt. 2	*Epistulae*
44	*Epistulae*
57	*Epistulae*
91	*De Genesi contra Manichaeos*
92	*Contra sermonem Arianorum*

Corpus Christianorum. Series Latina. (Turnhout, Belgium: Brepols, 1953–).

27	*Confessiones*
32	*De Doctrina Christiana*
33	*Quaestiones in Heptateuchum*
36	*In Johannis Evangelium Tractatus*
40	*Enarrationes in Psalmos*
41	*Sermones*
44A	*De Diversis Quaestionibus Octoginta Tribus*
46	*De Haeresibus*
47–48	*De Civitate Dei*
50–50A	*De Trinitate*
57	*Retractiones*

Patrologiae Cursus Completus. Series Latina. (Paris: Migne, 1844–64).

38	*Sermones*
42	*Conlatio cum Maximino Arrianorum Episcopo*
44	*Contra Maximinum Arrianum*

Translations of Works by Augustine

Acts or Disputation Against Fortunatus. In *Augustin: The Writings Against the Manichaeans, and Against the Donatists*, translated by J. H. Newman. In Nicene and Post-Nicene Fathers, 1st ser., vol. 4, ed. P. Schaff. 1887. Reprint, Peabody, MA: Hendrickson, 1995.

Answer to Maximus the Arian. In *Arianism and Other Heresies*, translated by R. J. Teske. The Works of Saint Augustine, pt. 1, vol. 18. Brooklyn, NY: New City Press, 1995.

Answer to the Arian Sermon. In *Arianism and Other Heresies*. Translated by R. J. Teske. The Works of Saint Augustine, pt. 1, vol. 18. Brooklyn, NY: New City Press, 1995.

The City of God Against the Pagans. Translated by R. W. Dyson. Cambridge: Cambridge University Press, 1998.

Concerning the Nature of the Good. In *The "De Natura Boni" of Saint Augustine*, translated by A. A. Moon. Washington: Catholic University of America Press, 1955.

The Confessions. Translated by H. Chadwick. Oxford: Oxford University Press, 1991.

Debate with Maximus the Arian. In *Arianism and Other Heresies*, translated by R. J. Teske. Works of Saint Augustine, pt. 1, vol. 18. Brooklyn, NY: New City Press, 1995.

Eighty-three Different Questions. Translated by D. L. Mosher. Fathers of the Church, vol. 70. Washington, DC: Catholic University of America Press, 1982.

Expositions of the Psalms 1–32. Translated by M. Boulding. The Works of Saint Augustine, pt. 3, vol. 15. Hyde Park, NY: New City Press, 2000.

Expositions of the Psalms 33–50. Translated by M. Boulding. The Works of Saint Augustine, pt. 3, vol. 16. Hyde Park, NY: New City Press, 2000.

Expositions of the Psalms 121–150. Translated by M. Boulding. The Works of Saint Augustine, pt. 3, vol. 20. Brooklyn, NY: New City Press, 2004.

Heresies. In *Arianism and Other Heresies*, translated by R. J. Teske. The Works of Saint Augustine, pt. 1, vol. 18. Brooklyn, NY: New City Press, 1995.

La Genèse au sens littéral en douze livres (I–VII). Translated by P. Agaësse and A. Solignac. In *Œuvres de Saint Augustin*, vol 48. Paris: Desclée de Brouwer, 1972.

Lectures or Tractates On the Gospel According to St. John. In *Augustin: Homilies on the Gospel of John, Homilies on the First Epistle of John, Soliloquies*, translated by J. Gibb and J. Innes. Nicene and Post-Nicene Fathers, 1st ser., vol. 7, ed. P. Schaff. 1888. Reprint, Peabody, MA: Hendrickson, 1995.

Letters. Translated by W. Parsons. Vol. 2. Fathers of the Church, vol. 18. Washington, DC: Catholic University of America Press, 1953. Letters 83–130.

Letters. Translated by W. Parsons. Vol. 4. Fathers of the Church, vol. 30. Washington, DC: Catholic University of America Press, 1955. Letters 165–203.

Letters. Translated by W. Parsons. Vol. 5. Fathers of the Church, vol. 32. Washington, DC: Catholic University of America Press, 1956. Letters 204–70.

Letters 100–155. Translated by R. J. Teske. The Works of Saint Augustine, pt. 2, vol. 2. Brooklyn, NY: New City Press, 2003.

The Literal Meaning of Genesis. Translated by J. H. Taylor. 2 vols. Ancient Christian Writers, nos. 41–42. New York: Newman Press, 1982.

The Literal Meaning of Genesis. In *On Genesis*. Translated by E. Hill. The Works of Saint Augustine, pt. 1, vol. 13. Brooklyn, NY: New City Press, 2002.

On Christian Teaching. Translated by R. P. H. Green. Oxford: Oxford University Press, 1997.

On Genesis: A Refutation of the Manichees. In *On Genesis*, translated by E. Hill. The Works of Saint Augustine, part I, vol. 13. Brooklyn, NY: New City Press, 2002.

The Retractions. Translated by M. I. Bogan. Fathers of the Church, vol. 60. Washington, DC: Catholic University of America Press, 1968.

Sermons 20–50. Translated by E. Hill. The Works of Saint Augustine, pt. 3, vol. 2. Brooklyn, NY: New City Press, 1990.

Sermons 51–94. Translated by E. Hill. The Works of Saint Augustine, pt. 3, vol. 3. Brooklyn, NY: New City Press, 1991.

Teaching Christianity (*De Doctrina Christiana*). Translated by E. Hill. The Works of Saint Augustine, pt. 1, vol. 11. Brooklyn, NY: New City Press, 1996.

Tractates on the Gospel of John. Translated by J. W. Rettig. Fathers of the Church, vol. 78. Washington, DC: Catholic University of America Press, 1982.

The Trinity. Translated by E. Hill. The Works of Saint Augustine, pt. 1, vol. 5. Brooklyn, NY: New City Press, 1991.

Unfinished Literal Commentary on Genesis. In *On Genesis*, translated by E. Hill. The Works of Saint Augustine, pt. 1, vol. 13. Brooklyn, NY: New City Press, 2002.

Secondary Sources

Annice, M. "Historical Sketch of the Theory of Participation." *New Scholasticism* 26 (1952): 49–79.

Ayers, Lewis. "Augustine, Christology, and God as Love: An Introduction to the Homilies on 1 John." In *Nothing Greater, Nothing Better: Theological Essays on the Love of God*, edited by Kevin J. Vanhoozer, 67–93. Grand Rapids, MI: Eerdmans, 2001.

———. "The Fundamental Grammar of Augustine's Trinitarian Theology." In *Augustine and His Critics: Essays in Honor of Gerald Bonner*, edited by R. Dodaro and G. Lawless, 51–76. New York: Routledge, 2000.

———. *Nicaea and Its Legacy: An Approach to Fourth-Century Trinitarian Theology*. Oxford: Oxford University Press, 2004.

———. " 'Remember That You Are Catholic' (Serm. 52.2): Augustine on the Unity of the Triune God." *Journal of Early Christian Studies* 8 (2000): 39–82.

Barnes, Michel R. "The Arians of Book V, and the Genre of *De Trinitate*." *Journal of Theological Studies*, n.s., 44 (1993): 185–95.

———. "Augustine in Contemporary Trinitarian Theology." *Theological Studies* 56 (1995): 237–50.

———. "The Fourth Century as Trinitarian Canon." In *Christian Origins: Theology, Rhetoric, and Community*, edited by L. Ayres and G. Jones, 47–67. New York: Routledge, 1998.

———. "Exegesis and Polemic in Augustine's *De Trinitate* I." *Augustinian Studies* 30 (1999): 43–59.

———. "Rereading Augustine's Theology of the Trinity." In *The Trinity: An International Symposium on the Trinity*, edited by S. T. Davis, D. Kendall, and G. O'Collins, 145–76. Oxford: Oxford University Press, 2002.

Bergmann, Sigurd. *Creation Set Free: The Spirit as Liberator of Nature*. Translated by D. Stott. Grand Rapids, MI: Eerdmans, 2005.

Boff, Leonardo. *Holy Trinity, Perfect Community*. Translated by P. Berryman. Maryknoll, NY: Orbis Books, 2000.

———. *Cry of the Earth, Cry of the Poor*. Translated by P. Berryman. Maryknoll, NY: Orbis Books, 1997.

———. *Trinity and Society*. Translated by P. Burn. Maryknoll, NY: Orbis Books, 1988.

Bonner, Gerald. "Augustine's Conception of Deification." *Journal of Theological Studies*, n.s., 37 (1986): 369–86.

Bourke, Vernon J. *Augustine's View of Reality*. Villanova, PA: Villanova Universioty Press, 1964.

Brown, William P. *The Ethos of the Cosmos: The Genesis of Moral Imagination in the Bible*. Grand Rapids, MI: Eerdmans, 1999.

Brunk, Conrad, and Scott A. Dunham. "Ecosystem Justice in the Canadian Fisheries." In *Just Fish: Ethics and Canadian Marine Fisheries*, edited by H. Coward, R. Ommer, and T. Pitcher, 9–30. St. John's, NF: ISER, 2000.

Burnaby, John. *Amor Dei: A Study of the Religion of St. Augustine*. Rev. ed. Norwich, UK: Canterbury Press, 1991.

Burt, Donald X. *Augustine's World: An Introduction to His Speculative Philosophy*. Lanham, MD: University Press of America, 1996.

Canning, Raymond. *The Unity of Love for God and Neighbour in St. Augustine*. Heverlee-Leuven: Augustinian Historical Institute, 1993.

Christian, William A. "The Creation of the World." In *A Companion to the Study of St. Augustine*, edited by R. W. Battenhouse, 315–42. New York: Oxford University Press, 1955.

Cizewski, Wanda. "The Meaning and Purpose of Animals according to Augustine's Genesis Commentaries." In *Augustine: Presbyter Factus Sum*, edited by J. T. Lienhard, E. C. Muller, and R. J. Teske, 363–73. New York: Peter Lang, 1993.

Cochrane, Charles Norris. *Christianity and Classical Culture: A Study of Thought and Action from Augustus to Augustine*. New York: Oxford University Press, 1957.

Cohen, Jeremy. *Be Fertile and Increase, Fill the Earth and Master It: The Ancient and Medieval Career of a Biblical Text*. Ithaca, NY: Cornell University Press, 1989.

Cousineau, R. "Creation and Freedom, An Augustinian Problem: '*Quia voluit*'? and/or '*Quia bonus*'?" *Recherches Augustiniennes* 2 (1962): 253–71.

Crouse, Robert D. "St. Augustine's *De Trinitate*: Philosophical Method." In *Studia Patristica 16*, edited by E. A. Livingstone, 501–10. Berlin: Akademie-Verlag, 1985.

Daly, Mary. *Beyond God the Father*. Boston: Beacon Press, 1973.

de Margerie, Bertrand. *The Christian Trinity in History*. Translated by E. J. Fortman. *Studies in Historical Theology*, vol. 10. Petersham, UK: St. Bede's, 1982.

———. *An Introduction to the History of Exegesis*. Vol. 3, *Saint Augustine*. Translated by P. de Fontnouvelle. Petersham, UK: Saint Bede's Publications, 1991.

du Roy, Olivier. *L'intelligence de la foi en la Trinité selon saint Augustin*. Paris: Études Augustiennes, 1966.

Fitzgerald, Allan, and John Cavadini, eds. *Augustine through the Ages: An Encyclopedia*. Grand Rapids: Eerdmans, 1999.

Grabowski, Stanislaus J. *The All-Present God: A Study in St. Augustine*. St. Louis, MO: Herder, 1954.

Green-McCreight, K. E. *Ad Litteram: How Augustine, Calvin, and Barth Read the "Plain Sense" of Genesis 1–3*. New York: Peter Lang, 1995.

Gunton, Colin. "Between Allegory and Myth: The Legacy of the Spiritualising of Genesis." In *The Doctrine of Creation*, edited by C. Gunton, 47–62. Edinburgh: T. and T. Clark, 1997.

———. "The End of Causality? The Reformers and Their Predecessors." In *The Doctrine of Creation*, edited by C. Gunton, 63–82. Edinburgh: T. and T. Clark, 1997.

———. *The One, the Three and the Many: God, Creation, and the Culture of Modernity*. Cambridge: Cambridge University Press, 1993.

———. *The Promise of Trinitarian Theology*. Edinburgh: T. and T. Clark, 1991.

———. *The Triune Creator: A Historical and Systematic Study*. Grand Rapids, MI: Eerdmans, 1998.

Hall, Douglas John. *Imaging God: Dominion as Stewardship*. Grand Rapids, MI: Eerdmans, 1986.

———. *The Steward: A Biblical Symbol Come of Age*. Rev. ed. Grand Rapids. MI: Eerdmans, 1990.

Hanby, Michael. *Augustine and Modernity*. London: Routledge, 2003.

Hanson, R. P. C. *The Search for the Christian Doctrine of God*. Edinburgh: T. and T. Clark, 1988.

Hardy, Richard P. "The Incarnation and Revelation in Augustine's *Tractatus in Iohannis Evangelium*." *Église et Théologie* 3 (1972): 193–220.

Harrison, Carol. *Beauty and Revelation in the Thought of Saint Augustine*. Oxford: Clarendon Press, 1992.

———. "Measure, Number, and Weight." *Augustinianum* 28 (1988): 591–602.

Hassel, D. J. "Conversion-Theory and *Scientia* in the *De Trinitate*." *Recherches Augustiniennes* 2 (1962): 383–401.

Hill, E. Introduction to *The Literal Meaning of Genesis*, by Augustine. In *On Genesis*, translated by E. Hill. The Works of Saint Augustine, pt. 1, vol. 13. Brooklyn, NY: New City Press, 2002.

Jenson, Robert W. *The Triune Identity*. Philadelphia: Fortress Press, 1982.

Kelly, J. N. D. *Early Christian Creeds*. 3rd ed. New York: Longman, 1972.

———. *Early Christian Doctrines*. Rev. ed. San Francisco: HarperSanFrancisco, 1976.

Kretzmann, Norman. "A General Problem of Creation: Why Would God Create Anything at All?" In *Being and Goodness: The Concept of the Good in Meta-*

physics and Philosophical Theology, edited by S. MacDonald, 202–28. Ithaca, NY: Cornell University Press, 1991.

LaCugna, Catherine Mowry. *God for Us: The Trinity and Christian Life*. San Francisco: HarperCollins, 1991.

Lawless, George. "Augustine and Human Embodiment." In *Collectanea Augustiniana: Mélanges T. J. Van Bavel*, edited by B. Bruning, J. van Houtem, M. Lambrigts. Leuven: Peeters, 1990, 167–86.

Lienhard, Joseph T. "Friendship in Paulinus of Nola and Augustine." In *Collectanea Augustiniana: Mélanges T. J. Van Bavel*, edited by B. Bruning, J. van Houtem, M. Lambrigts. Leuven: Peeters, 1990.

———. " 'The Glue Itself Is Charity': Ps. 62:9 in Augustine's Thought." In *Augustine: Presbyter Factus Sum*, edited by E. C. Muller, R. J. Teske, and J. T. Lienhard, 375–84. New York: Peter Lang, 1993.

Likens, G. E. *The Ecosystem Approach: Its Use and Abuse*, edited by O. Kinne. Oldendorf/Luhe, Germany: Ecology Institute, 1992. Quoted in The Ecological Society of America, "The Scientific Basis for Ecosystem Management," September 15, 1997, http://www.epa.gov/ecocommunity/tools/ecosysmn.pdf.

MacDonald, Scott. "The Divine Nature." In *The Cambridge Companion to Augustine*, edoted by E. Stump and N. Kretzmann, 71–90. Cambridge: Cambridge University Press, 2001.

Markus, Robert A. " '*Imago*' and '*Similitudo*' in Augustine." *Revue des Etudes Augustiniennes* 10 (1964): 125–43.

———. *Saeculum: History and Society in the Theology of St. Augustine*. Cambridge: Cambridge University Press, 1970.

Marsh, Thomas. *The Triune God*. Mystic, CT: Twenty-third Publications, 1994.

Martland, T. R. "A Study of Cappadocian and Augustinian Trinitarian Methodology." *Anglican Theological Review* 47 (1965): 252–63.

Matter, E. Ann. "Christ, God, and Woman in the Thought of St. Augustine." In *Augustine and His Critics: Essays in Honor of Gerald Bonner*, edited by R. Dodaro and G. Lawless, 164–75. New York: Routledge, 2000.

May, Gerhard. *Creatio Ex Nihilo: The Doctrine of "Creation Out of Nothing" in Early Christian Thought*. Translated by A. S. Worrall. Edinburgh: T. and T. Clark, 1994.

McFague, Sallie. "A Square in the Quilt." In *Spirit and Nature: Why the Environment Is a Religious Issue, an Interfaith Dialogue*, edited by S. C. Rockefeller and J. C. Elder, 42–58. Boston: Beacon Press, 1992.

McKeough, M. J. *The Meaning of the Rationes Seminales in St. Augustine*. Washington, DC: Catholic University of America Press, 1926.

Meconi, David V. "St. Augustine's Early Theory of Participation." *Augustinian Studies* 27 (1996): 81–98.

Middleton, J. Richard. *The Liberating Image: The Imago Dei in Genesis 1*. Grand Rapids, MI: Brazos, 2005.

Milbank, John. "Sacred Triads: Augustine and the Indo-European Soul." *Modern Theology* 13 (1997): 451–74.

Miles, Margaret. "The Body and Human Values in Augustine of Hippo." In *Grace, Politics & Desire: Essays on Augustine*, edited by H. A. Meynell, 55–67. Calgary: University of Calgary Press, 1990.

Moltmann, Jürgen. *God in Creation: A New Theology of Creation and the Spirit of God*. Translated by M. Kohl. Minneapolis, MN: Fortress Press, 1993.

———. "The Inviting Unity of the Triune God." Translated by R. Nowell. *Concilium* 17 (1985): 50–58.

———. *The Trinity and the Kingdom*. Translated by M. Kohl. San Francisco: Harper and Row, 1981.

Most, William G. "The Scriptural Basis of St Augustine's Arithmology." *Catholic Biblical Quarterly* 13 (1951): 284–95.

Muller, Earl. "The Dynamic of Augustine's *De Trinitate*: A Response to a Recent Characterization." *Augustinian Studies* 26 (1995): 65–91.

Nash, James. *Loving Nature: Ecological Integrity and Christian Responsibility*. Nashville, TN: Abingdon, 1991.

Nash, Roderick. *The Rights of Nature: A History of Environmental Ethics*. Madison: University of Wisconsin Press, 1989.

Nygren, Anders. *Agape and Eros: A Study of the Christian Idea of Love*. Translated by P. S. Watson. Philadelphia: Westminster Press, 1953.

O'Donnell, James J. *Augustine: Confessions*. 3 vols. Oxford: Clarendon Press, 1992.

O'Donovan, Oliver. *The Problem of Self-Love in Augustine*. New Haven, CT: Yale University Press, 1980.

———. "*Usus* and *Fruitio* in Augustine, *De Doctrina Christiana* I." *Journal of Theological Studies*, n.s., 33 (1982): 361–97.

Oroz Reta, José. "The Role of Divine Attraction in Conversion according to Saint Augustine." In *From Augustine to Eriugena: Essays On Neoplatonism and Christianity in Honour of J. O'Meara*, edited by F. X. Martin and J. A. Richmond, 155–67. Washington, DC: Catholic University of America Press, 1991.

O'Toole, Christopher J. *The Philosophy of Creation in the Writings of St. Augustine*. Washington, DC: Catholic University of America Press, 1944.

Otto, Randall E. "The Use and Abuse of Perichoresis in Recent Theology." *Scottish Journal of Theology* 54 (2001): 366–84.

Pannenberg, Wolfhart. *Systematic Theology*. Translated by G. Bromiley. 3 vols. Grand Rapids, MI: Eerdmans, 1991–98.

Pelikan, Jaroslav. "*Canonica Regula*: The Trinitarian Hermeneutics of Augustine." In vols. 12/13 of *Proceedings of the PMR Conference at Villanova University*, 17–29. Villanova, PA: Augustinian Historical Institute, 1987–1988.

———. *The Christian Tradition: A History of the Development of Doctrine*. Vol. 1, *The Emergence of the Catholic Tradition (100–600)*. Chicago: University of Chicago Press, 1971.

Poque, Suzanne. *Le langage symbolique dans la prédication d'Augustin d'Hippone*. 2 vols. Paris: Etudes Augustiniennes, 1984.

Primavesi, Anne. *From Apocalypse to Genesis: Ecology, Feminism and Christianity*. Minneapolis: Fortress Press, 1991.

———. "Ecology and Christian Hierarchy." In *Sacred Custodians of the Earth: Women, Spirituality, and the Environment?* edited by A. Low and S. Tremayne, 121–39. New York: Berghahn Books, 2001.

Rahner, Karl. *The Trinity*. Translated by J. Donceel. Wellwood, UK: Burns and Oates, 1970.

Rist, John M. *Augustine: Ancient Thought Baptized*. Cambridge: Cambridge University Press, 1994.

Roach, Catherine M. "Stewards of the Sea: A Model for Justice?" In *Just Fish: Ethics and Canadian Marine Fisheries*, edited by H. Coward, R. Ommer, and T. Pitcher, 67–82. St. John's, NF: ISER, 2000.

Roche, W. J. "Measure, Number, and Weight in Saint Augustine." *New Scholasticism* 15 (1941): 350–76.

Ruether, Rosemary Radford, *Gaia & God: An Ecofeminist Theology of Earth Healing*. San Francisco: HarperSanFrancisco, 1992.

———. *New Woman/New Earth: Sexist Ideologies and Human Liberation*. New York: Seabury Press, 1975.

———. *Sexism and God-Talk: Towards a Feminist Theology*. Boston: Beacon Press, 1983.

Santmire, H. Paul. *The Travail of Nature: The Ambiguous Ecological Promise of Christian Theology*. Philadelphia: Fortress Press, 1985.

Simkins, Ronald A. *Creator and Creation: Nature in the Worldview of Ancient Israel*. Peabody, MA: Hendrickson, 1994.

Smallbrugge, M. "La Notion de la participation chez Augustin: Quelques observations sur le rapport christianisme-platonisme." In *Collectanea Augustiniana: Mélanges T. J. Van Bavel*, ed. B. Bruning, J. van Houtem, M. Lambrigts. Leuven: Peeters, 1990, 333–47.

Studer, Basil. "*Deus, Pater et Dominus* bei Augustinus von Hippo." In *Christian Faith and Greek Philosophy in Late Antiquity: Essays in Tribute to George Christopher Stead*, edited by L. Wickham and C. P. Bammel, 190–212. Leiden: Brill, 1993.

———. *The Grace of Christ and the Grace of God in Augustine of Hippo: Christocentrism or Theocentrism?* Translated by M. J. O'Connell. Collegeville, MN: Liturgical Press, 1997.

———. "History and Faith in Augustine's *De Trinitate*." *Augustinian Studies* 28 (1997): 7–50.

———. *Trinity and Incarnation*. Translated by M. Westerhoff. Edited by A. Louth. Collegeville, MN: Michael Glazier, 1993.

Sullivan, John E. *The Image of God: The Doctrine of St. Augustine and Its Influence*. Dubuque, IA: Priory Press, 1963.

Teske, R.J. Introduction to *Arianism and Other Heresies*, by Augustine. Translated by R. J. Teske. The Works of Saint Augustine, pt. 1, vol. 18. Brooklyn, NY: New City Press, 1995.

Torchia, N. Joseph. *'Creatio Ex Nihilo' and the Theology of St. Augustine: The Anti-Manichaean Polemic and Beyond*. New York: Peter Lang, 1999.

———. "The Implications of the Doctrine of *Creatio Ex Nihilo* in St. Augustine's Theology." In *Studia Patristica 33*, edited by E. A. Livingstone, 266–73. Leuven: Peeters, 1997.

———. "The Significance of *Ordo* in St. Augustine's Moral Theory." In *Augustine: Presbyter Factus Sum*, edited by J. T. Lienhard, E. C. Muller, and R. J. Teske, 263–78. New York: Peter Lang, 1993.

Torrance, T. F. *The Christian Doctrine of God: One Being, Three Persons*. Edinburgh: T. and T. Clark, 1996.

Van Bavel, Tarsicius. "The Creator and the Integrity of Creation in the Fathers of the Church, Especially in Saint Augustine." *Augustinian Studies* 21 (1990): 1–32.

Van Fleteren, Frederick. "Principles of Augustine's Hermeneutic: An Overview." In *Augustine: Biblical Exegete*, edited by F. Van Fleteren and J. C. Schnaubelt, 1–32. New York: Peter Lang, 2001.

Vannier, Marie-Anne. *"Creatio," "Conversio," "Formatio," chez S. Augustin*. Paradosis 31. Fribourg: Éditions universitaires, 1991.

Welker, Michael. *Creation and Reality*. Translated by J. F. Hoffmeyer. Minneapolis, MN: Fortress Press, 1999.

White, Lynn. "The Historical Roots of Our Ecologic Crisis." *Science* 155 (1967): 1203–7.

Widdicombe, Peter. *The Fatherhood of God from Origen to Athanasius*. Rev. ed. Oxford: Clarendon Press, 2000.

Williams, Rowan. " 'Good for Nothing'? Augustine on Creation." *Augustinian Studies* 25 (1994): 9–24.

———. "Insubstantial Evil." In *Augustine and His Critics: Essays in Honor of Gerald Bonner*, edited by R. Dodaro and G. Lawless, 105–23. New York: Routledge, 2000.

———. "*Sapientia* and the Trinity: Reflections on the *De Trinitate*." In *Collectanea Augustiniana: Mélanges T. J. Van Bavel*, edited by B. Bruning, J. van Houtem, M. Lambrigts. Leuven: Peeters, 1990.

Williams, Thomas. "Biblical Interpretation." In *The Cambridge Companion to Augustine*, edited by E. Stump and N. Kretzmann, 59–70. Cambridge: Cambridge University Press, 2001.

Zizioulas, John. *Being as Communion: Studies in Personhood and the Church*. Crestwood, NY: St. Vladimir's Seminary Press, 1985.

Name Index

Subject Index

Scripture Index

Made in the USA
Lexington, KY
23 February 2016